GRAYWOLF FORUM 1

Tolstoy's Dictaphone

The GRAYWOLF ANNUAL Series
Edited by Scott Walker

GRAYWOLF FORUM 1

Tolstoy's Dictaphone

Technology and the Muse

Edited by
SVEN BIRKERTS

GRAYWOLF PRESS : SAINT PAUL

Publication of this volume is made possible in part by a grant provided by the Minnesota State Arts Board through an appropriation by the Minnesota State Legislature, and by a grant from the National Endowment for the Arts. Significant additional support has been provided by the Andrew W. Mellon Foundation, the Lila Wallace–Reader's Digest Fund, the McKnight Foundation, and other generous contributions from foundations, corporations, and individuals. Graywolf Press is a member agency of United Arts, Saint Paul. To these organizations and individuals who make our work possible, we offer heartfelt thanks.

Published by
Graywolf Press
2402 University Avenue, Suite 203
Saint Paul, Minnesota 55114

Printed in the United States of America.

ISBN 1-55597-248-9
ISSN 1088-3347

2 4 6 8 9 7 5 3 2 1
First Graywolf Printing, 1996

Library of Congress Card Catalog Number: 96-75790

Illustration by John Hersey
Series and cover design by Douglas Dearden

ACKNOWLEDGMENTS

.   .   .   .

Some of the essays collected in this anthology have appeared previously in the publications as noted below. We gratefully acknowledge the cooperation of agents, editors, and the authors for their permission to reprint the essays here.

Sven Birkerts's essay, " 'The Fate of the Book,' " appeared in *Antioch Review*, Summer 1996.

Daniel Mark Epstein's essay, "Mr. Peabody and His Atheneum," appeared in *The New Criterion*, October 1995.

Jonathan Franzen's essay, "Scavenging," appeared in *Antioch Review*, Summer 1996.

Thomas Frick's essay, "Either / Or," appeared in *Antioch Review*, Summer 1996.

Gerald Howard's essay, "Slouching Towards Grubnet: The Author in the Age of Publicity," appeared in *The Review of Contemporary Fiction*, Spring 1996.

Carole Maso's essay, "Rupture, Verge, and Precipice / Precipice, Verge, and Hurt Not," appeared in *The Review of Contemporary Fiction*, Spring 1996.

Wendy Lesser's essay, "The Conversion," appeared in *Creative Nonfiction*, Summer 1996.

Robert Pinsky's essay, "Nerds, Technocrats, and Enlightened Spirits," appeared in *DoubleTake*, Fall 1996.

Lynne Sharon Schwartz's essay, "Only Connect?" appeared in *Salmagundi*, Spring 1996.

Tom Sleigh's essay, "To the Star Demons," appeared in *The Southwest Review*, Summer 1996.

Editor Sven Birkerts would like to thank the John Simon Guggenheim Memorial Foundation for its generous support during the writing and preparation of this book.

Graywolf Press gratefully acknowledges the special support for the *Graywolf Forum* provided by the Cowles Media Foundation.

Contents

. . . .

Introduction

. . . .

If the media fate of the Orwell year—1984—is any indication, we are likely to be deluged by and done with the millennium long before the appointed hour ever arrives. There is nothing to be done about this short of pulling all the plugs from all the sockets, and much as some of us might wish it, it won't happen. We must try, instead, to see it as part of the millennial experience to be millennially overwhelmed. There is no exit, and the show must go on.

While *Tolstoy's Dictaphone* has not been calculated to be a millennium book as such, it has grown out of a set of controversies that will surely have a great deal to do with how we do business in the year 2000 and beyond. Here I must, as editor and contributor, come clean. The idea of compiling this "reader" grew directly out of the thinking I was doing when I wrote the final essays of *The Gutenberg Elegies: The Fate of Reading in an Electronic Age.* In that book I made the argument that the historically sudden arrival and adoption of computer technologies was changing everything about the way we lived and thought and related to one another. I further proposed that these changes were not automatically for the good, that we were very possibly compromising our subjectivity, mediating our already deeply mediated relation to the world, and in a number of ways putting ourselves at risk. I saw book culture and electronic culture as polarized in crucial ways and argued against the view that the new technologies are merely tools of convenience, or powerful augmentations of the existing.

I said these things and many people disagreed, either with my fundamental premise or with the kinds of conclusions I was drawing. Wherever I traveled, I found myself embroiled in discussion—debate—and as the lights in whatever hall or bookstore were dimmed, there were always people clustered around wearing the look of *too much to say, too little time.*

To carry the exploration further, then, seemed not only natural, but inevitable. But now it made sense to open things up a bit, to bring like- and unlike-minded others into the discussion. This I have done, and a few words about the procedure are probably in order.

To begin with, the subject—the coming of the electronic millennium—is so large that one has to narrow the aperture. Accordingly, I decided to formulate a general question, one that would give my contributors some sense of personal stake *and* allow them a considerable latitude of response. In a letter sent to prospective anthology-mates I asked the following:

> What will be the place of self, of soul—of artist, writer, individual—in the society we are so hell-bent on creating? I'm thinking in terms of our collective ingesting of electronic communications, but other transformations may figure in your thoughts. Does anyone doubt that the world will have changed more between 1950 and 2000 than during the long centuries preceding? Or that the place of the solitary self, the Emersonian individual—formerly the origin and destination of all expressive work—is being altered radically? What will be the role of writer and thinker in the millennium? What will be the terms of struggle and debate?

As you can see, I was not able to keep the idea of the millennium out of my formulation. Beyond this, I urged only creative, subjectively satisfying responses.

And whom did I urge these on? Preemptively I would offer that while many of the writers I contacted were in some ways kindred spirits, I did not consciously set out to stack the deck. Indeed, I monitored myself, and when I saw that I was pulling too hard toward the unreconstructed humanists, I redoubled my efforts to bring in voices that might somehow oppose theirs. While I pretty much knew that writers like Daniel Mark Epstein and Mark Slouka would lend support to some of my own darker intimations, I had a strong suspicion that more technologically oriented writers like Ralph Lombreglia and Carolyn Guyer would deliver countering words. Then, too, there were writers who could go either way, if not down the middle. What would I hear, say, from Robert Pinsky, who has recently translated Dante's *Inferno* (a humanist activity if there ever was one), but who has also written interactive computer texts? Or from Wulf Rehder, whose learned and playful essays I have long admired, and who works in the bowels of Silicon Valley at Hewlett-Packard? Then what might Alice Fulton conjure, a poet who has woven scientific language and

·   ·   ·   ·   ·   ·   ·   ·   ·   ·

concepts so elegantly into her poems? Or Paul West, who has never not surprised me?

Now that the essays have all been amassed and await only their final arrangement, I am flabbergasted both by their range and their idiosyncracy. Every last writer took the melody and riffed on a different instrument and in an original key. Reading the essays, stacking them this way and that, I feel a happy-making sense of surfeit. These are not mere ideas and arguments. These are, in the best sense, conjectures embodied in experience. Stories, memories, fantasies, laments, rants, and exuberant expostulations—all of them somehow addressing our lives in the present and the outlook for things when the last millennial TV special has gone into electronic limbo, not to be broadcast again for one thousand years.

SVEN BIRKERTS

GRAYWOLF FORUM 1

Tolstoy's Dictaphone

Scavenging

.   .   .   .

by

JONATHAN FRANZEN

(Not many warehouses masquerade as chateaux, and of those that do, the Mercer Museum in Doylestown, Pennsylvania, is surely one of the largest. The museum is a hundred feet tall, has the flat face and square turrets of a reform school or a sand castle, and is made entirely of poured concrete. A wealthy eccentric named Henry Mercer built it in the first decade of the century, in part as an advertisement for concrete and in part as housing for his unparalleled collection of the tools that American industrialization was rendering useless. Mercer had cruised the barns and auctions of his changing world and had brought back to Bucks County every imaginable style of cobbler's last, cider press, and blacksmiths' bellows, also a whaling launch complete with harpoons. In the museum's highest turret you'll find a trapdoor gallows and a horse-drawn hearse. Dozens of hand-carved sleds and cradles are stuck, as if by poltergeist, to the vaulted concrete ceiling of the seven-story atrium.

The Mercer can be a very frosty place. Toward the end of a visit on a recent December afternoon, I was devoting my most serious attention to the displays on the ground floor, where the heaters are. It was here, to my considerable surprise, that I encountered my own telephone, lodged in a glass case labeled OBSOLETE TECHNOLOGY.

My telephone is a basic black AT&T rotary, first leased from New England Bell in 1982, then acquired outright in the chaos of Ma Bell's breakup two years later. (I seem to recall not paying for it.) The Mercer's identical copy was perched uneasily on a heap of eight-track tapes — a pairing that I right away found hurtful. Eight-track tapes are one of the

great clichés of obsolescence; they reek of Ray Coniff and wide-wale cor-
duroy. A rotary phone, on the other hand, still served proudly in my living
room. Not long ago I'd used it to order computer peripherals from the
408 area code, if you want to talk about modern.

The display at the Mercer was an obvious provocation. And yet the
harder I tried to dismiss it, the more deeply I felt accused. I became aware,
for example, of the repressive energy it was costing me to ignore my visits
to the Touch-Tone in my bedroom, which I now relied on for account bal-
ances and flight information and train schedules. I became aware of additional energy spent on hating the voice-mail systems that relegate a rotary
to second-class ("please hold for an operator") status. I became aware, in
a word, of codependency. My rotary was losing its ability to cope with the
modern world, but I continued to cover for it and to keep it on display
downstairs, because I loved it and was afraid of change. Nor was it the
only thing I protected in this way. I was suddenly aware of having a whole
dysfunctional family of obsolete machines.

My TV set was a hulking old thing that showed only snow unless the
extension-cord wire that served as an antenna was in direct contact with
my skin. I wonder, is it possible to imagine a grimmer vision of codependency than the hundreds of hours I logged with sharp strands of copper
wire squeezed between my thumb and forefinger, helping my TV with its
picture? As for a VCR, it happened that the friend with whom I was visiting the Mercer had stepped off a plane from Los Angeles, the night before,
with a VCR in a plastic shopping bag. He was giving it to me to make me
stop talking about not having one.

I do still talk about not owning a CD player, and I pretend not to own
any CDs. But for more than a year I've been finding myself in the houses of
friends, in borrowed apartments, even in an artist colony's library, furtively
making tapes of CD-only releases. Afterwards I play the tapes on my tape
deck and forget where they came from—until, in one of those squalid repetitions that codependency fosters, I need to convert another CD.

The display at the Mercer, on that cold December afternoon, was like a
slap in the face from the modern world: *it was time to grow up*. Time to re-
tire the rotary. To recall: change is healthy. To recall: accepting the inevitable is healthy. If you don't watch out, you'll be an old, old man at
thirty-five.

As I write this, however, months later, my rotary phone is still in service.
I've portrayed my appliances' obsolescence as a character defect of theirs
for which I, like an addict's spouse, am trying to compensate. The truth is

that the defect, the disease, inheres equally in me. The obsolescence is my own. It stems directly from what I do and don't do for a living. At the root of both my reasons for keeping the rotary is a fiction writer's life.

One reason, the obvious one, is that while phones may be cheap, they're not free. The four-figure income that a young artist typically pulls down enforces thrift. I'd be delighted if the audience for serious fiction increased by an order of magnitude, so that I could spare $129 for a CD player. But who really thinks that people are suddenly going to start reading more literary novels? Until they do, and the sun rises in the west, I'm the de facto inheritor of two hopelessly obsolete value systems: the Depression-era thrift of my parents' generation, and the '60s radicalism of my older brothers' generation. People in the '60s were innocent enough to wonder: "Why should I work a job all week to pump more consumer dollars into a corrupt and dehumanizing system?" This is not a question you often hear asked anymore, except among artists and writers who need long, unguarded hours to do their work in. And even for us, the obsolescence that thrift confers is not particularly welcome.

In *The Notebooks of Malte Laurids Brigge,* Rilke draws a parallel between the development of a poet and the history of Venice. He describes Venice as a city that has made something out of a nothing, as a city "willed in the midst of the void on sunken forests," a "hardened body, stripped to necessities," a "resourceful state, which bartered the salt and glass of its poverty for the treasures of the nations." Rilke himself was a paragon of saprophytism, the nonpareil of total avoidance of gainful employment, and he helped as much as anyone to shape my idea of what literature ought to be and of how an ephebe might best achieve it. Fiction, I believed, was the transmutation of experiential dross into linguistic gold. Fiction meant taking up whatever the world had abandoned by the road and making something beautiful out of it.

Only recently have I recognized how peculiarly American this model of mine is. In a country dedicated to the exploitation of a raw continent's resources, the surge of economic development creates an immensely powerful backwash, pulverizing and reassembling dreams on a vast industrial scale, sloughing off and churning under all manner of human and material detritus. On the muscular captains of the mainstream—the fictional Silas Lapham, George Babbitt, Tom Buchanan, Recktall Brown—the business of big money so reliably confers opacity that you finally have to conclude these men are simply shallow. Most of the really memorable characters of U.S. fiction, from Bartleby and Flem Snopes to Hazel Motes and the Invisible Man seem to inhabit muddy backwaters where broken orange crates bob and bluebottles hum. And like one of those New Guineans who allegedly are unable to distinguish between a photograph and what is photographed, I spent my twenties literally combing weeds and parking strips and Dumpsters and incinerator rooms for material, trying to make my life a more perfect metaphor for my art. The triumphant return home with scavenged loot—snow shovels, the business end of a broken rake, floor lamps, still-viable poinsettias, aluminum cookware—was as much a part of writing fiction as the typing up of final drafts. An old phone was as much a character in a narrative as an appliance in a home.

Thrift, then, literal and metaphoric, is one reason the rotary is still around. The other reason is that Touch-Tones repel me. I don't like their sterile rings, their Taiwanese feel, their belatedness of design, the whole complacency of their hegemony. It's an axiom of contemporary art that America's political economy has reduced aesthetics to a matter of resistance. The unpoor friends of mine who continue to buy cassettes despite the superiority and inevitability of CDs are choosing, for as long as they can, to resist the ugliness of the bloated profit margin that is a CD's most prominent feature. I similarly appreciate the '70s clunkiness of my stereo components for the insult it delivers to the regiments of tasteful black boxes billeted in every house across the land.

For a long time, resistance like this seemed valuable, or at least innocuous. But one day I wake up and find I've been left behind by *everyone*. One day the beauty of thrift and the ideal of simplicity petrify into barren, time-devouring obsessions. One day the victim of the market turns out to be not a trivial thing, like a rotary phone or a vinyl disc, but a thing of life-and-death importance to me, like the literary novel. One day at the Mercer it's not my telephone but my copies of Singer and Gaddis and O'Connor that are piled on top of eight-tracks with inflammatory carelessness (OBSOLETE TECHNOLOGY, OR: THE JUDGMENT OF THE MARKET), as on the ash-heap of history. One day I visit the Mercer, and the next day I wake up depressed.

■ ■ ■

For six years the antidepressant drug Prozac has been lifting the spirits of millions of Americans and thousands of Eli Lilly shareholders.

    LEAD SENTENCE of a *New York Times* story, 9 January 1994

It's healthy to adjust to reality. It's healthy, recognizing that fiction such as Proust and Faulkner wrote is doomed, to interest yourself in the victorious technology, to fashion a niche for yourself in the new information order, to discard and then forget the values and methods of literary modernism that older readers are too distracted and demoralized to appreciate in your work and that younger readers, bred on television and educated in the new orthodoxy of identity politics and the reader's superiority to the text, are almost entirely deaf and blind to. It's healthy to stop giving yourself ulcers and migraines doing acutely demanding work that may please a few harried peers but otherwise instills unease or outright resentment in would-be readers. It's healthy to cry uncle when your bone's about to break. Likewise healthy, almost by definition, to forget about death in order to live your life: healthy to settle for (and thereby participate in) your own marginalization as a writer, to accept as inevitable a shrinking audience, an ever deteriorating relationship with the publishing conglomerates, a retreat into the special Protective Isolation Units that universities now provide for writers within the larger confines of their English departments. Healthy to slacken your standards, to call "great" what five years ago you might have called "decent but nothing special." Healthy, when you discover that your graduate writing students can't distinguish between "lie" and "lay" and have never read Jane Austen, not to rage or agitate but simply bite the bullet and do the necessary time-consuming teaching. Healthier yet not even to worry about it—to nod and smile in your workshops and let sleeping dogs lay, let the students discover Austen when Merchant and Ivory film her.

    In describing as "healthy" these responses to the death sentence obsolescence represents, I'm being no more than halfway ironic. Health really is the issue here. The pain of consciousness, the pain of knowing, grows apace with the information we have about the degradation of our planet and the insufficiency of our political system and the incivility of our society and the insolvency of our treasury and the injustice in the one-fifth of our country and four-fifths of our world that isn't rich like us. Traditionally, since religion lost its lock on the educated classes, writers and other artists have assumed extra pain to ease the burden for the rest of us, voluntarily shouldered some of the painful knowing in exchange for a shot at fame or immortality (or simply because they had no choice, it was their nature). The compact was never entirely stable, but there was a certain general workability to it. Men and women with especially sharp vision undertook to be the wardens of our discontent. They took the terror and ugliness and general lousiness of the world and returned it to the public as a gift: as works of anger or sadness, perhaps, but always of beauty too (in the sense of formal representation, of an organized aesthetic rendering), which the more thoughtful segments of the public, now lacking the consolations of religion and yet still yearning for some relief from the pain of knowing, sooner or later received with gratitude. Art and literature helped them make sense of life, and there is a deep and admirable human need for this kind of sense.

For better or worse, ours is now a technological society, and whatever the benefits to the health and affluence of the upper half of society, it would be difficult to argue that either technology or the free-market capitalism that is its Siamese twin have done much to solve the ancient problems of mortality and the world's unfairness. Moreover, they have created, exacerbated, or at least glaringly failed to address that whole host of further anxieties the knowledge of which I maintain is so painful to thinking people. It's easy to see how a technoconsumerism that creates lots of Wal-Marts and inexpensive dishwashers will have vastly higher approval ratings than a system, such as the former Soviet Union's, that does not. But why must the bad *cultural* currency drive out the good? Why are former readers now renting videos? Why are families that never read books and never bought classical music recordings suddenly going ape over CD-ROM?

There are familiar answers. Television and other modern technologies are ingratiating and effortless, designed to enable and promote passivity, and, being corporate enterprises, are burdened with none of the troublesome scruples or complexity that individual talents are. The answer on a deeper level, however, is that a new compact has been made. Rather than assign partial responsibility to artists, we have agreed to let technology *take care of us*. It's no accident that the political issue for the '90s is health care. Even in the world of high culture, as Robert Hughes has noted, there's a trend toward art as therapy. Our acceptance of technology fosters the belief that we have a right to be cared for; and further, that we will judge every product and service in our lives according to whether it makes us feel well cared for. Technology takes its cue from medicine, which, when it cannot cure, seeks to relieve suffering as efficiently as possible. And so we have a society in which the pain of knowledge is only increasing (because the society is getting more savage and less controllable, and the future ever less imaginable, and—most important of all—the individual worrying consciousness ever more isolated from others like it), which in turn puts a nearly impossible burden on structures such as the Bible and *The Brothers Karamazov* and Beethoven and Matisse, which were designed to account for everything in humanity but not for science and technology, and so reveals, if not their irrelevance, then at least their less than perfect adequacy. And, relations between the public and art never having been exactly comfortable, it's quite understandable that a large and growing segment of the population not wait around for some genius writers and artists to come up with more adequate structures, but should instead take comfort in the powerful narcotics technology offers in the form of TV, popular culture, and endless gadgetry, even though these narcotics are addictive and in the long run only make the society's problems worse.

The more popular these narcotics become, the more socially acceptable their use. What has happened now, in this decade when educated people finally stopped apologizing for never reading, is that the rising waters of consumer culture have flooded the basements and kitchens of that hard core of readers on which we writers placed our last desperate hopes, and the culture's oily pools are gliding slickly across the bedroom floor, rising up around the bed. Although it hasn't quite happened yet, although some books are still read and much lip service is still paid them, we writers now easily foresee the day when the old generation of readers has gotten tired and no new generation has taken its place: when we ourselves are all that will remain of our audience. And this is where that pain of knowing comes in. The pain is real, the burden of carrying the knowledge is real. Look what happens when the compact between society and art is abrogated. We lose most, then all, of our audience to television and its similarly ingratiating cousins. We don't blame the audience for defecting, we know it hurt to have to stay conscious, we understand the need to drug yourself, to feel the warmth of up-to-the-minute hipness or whatever. But the loss of that audience makes us feel all the more alone. Aloneness makes the burden of knowledge heavier. And then the quest for health begins to claim some of our own. Claims more and more of them. They deny that literature is threatened. They make their peace with the new technology. They decide it's exciting. They swallow the idea that if infinite choice is good in the marketplace it must be good in a reading experience. They find it a relief to reconcile themselves with striving always to please their audience, as the market insists they do; what a load off the shoulders! They begin to take the "characters" that corporate culture offers—various Kennedys, Arnold Schwarzenegger—and tell stories about them. They call themselves postmodernists and imagine they're using the system rather than its using them. They make the case that these "characters" are more interesting than anything you could invent, and indeed it's getting harder, in a nation of couch potatoes, to imagine an interesting life . . .

And there remains an ever-tinier core of us who are temperamentally incapable of deluding ourselves that technology's "culture" is anything but a malignant drug. We feel how scarce we are. And the work of showing the malignancy, and of reclaiming some perspective from which again to represent human hearts and minds within a society of their own making—this work has been left to us, along with the attendant pain of knowing how important such work is. And at some point the burden becomes overwhelming. It becomes a torture each time you see a friend stop reading books, and each time you read of another cheerful young writer doing TV in book form. You become depressed. And then you see what technology can do for those who become depressed. It can make them undepressed. *It can bring them health.* And this is the moment at which I find myself: I look around and see absolutely everyone (or so it seems) finding health. They enjoy their television and their children and they don't worry inordinately. They take their Prozac and are undepressed. They are all civil with each other and smile undepressed smiles, and they look at me with eyes of such pure opacity that I begin to doubt myself. I seem to myself a person who shrilly hates health. I'm only a phone call away from asking for a prescription of my own . . .)

■ ■ ■

So ends the fragment of essay that I've scavenged in assembling this one. I wrote the fragment two years ago when I was alone and unable to write fiction—unable, almost, to read a newspaper, the stories depressed me so much.

Depression presents itself as the logical response to the rottenness of the world in general and the rottenness of your life in particular. But the logic is merely a mask for depression's true essence: an overwhelming estrangement from humanity. This kind of thing feeds on itself. The more persuaded you are of your unique access to the rottenness, the more afraid you become of engaging with the world; and the less you engage with the world, the more perfidiously happy-faced the rest of humanity seems for continuing to engage with it.

Fiction writers have always been prone to this estrangement. You begin as a solitary reader and grow up to be an adult who requires solitude for communion with the virtual community of print. But the estrangement becomes much more profound, urgent, and dangerous when you feel you no longer have an audience; when the saving continuity of literature itself is threatened by obsolescence; when your alienation becomes generic, rather than individual; when the business pages report on the world's conspiracy to eliminate not only you but all your kind.

And yet, although the world hasn't changed much in the last two years, I feel as if I have. Who knows if I can generalize from my own experience. All I know is that soon after I wrote that fragment I gave up. Just plain gave up. No matter what it cost me, I did not want to be unhappy anymore. And so I stopped trying to be a writer-with-a-capital-W. Simply to desire to get up in the morning was all I asked.

Months passed. I taught an undergraduate fiction workshop, and then I faced the problem of how to make a living. I wanted a little time to write privately, for myself, that was all I asked. Not to matter to the culture, but simply to be allowed the occasional visit to that solitary point of connection to the world of print. The way I finally chose to make a living (doing magazine journalism) felt cruelly limiting. But one small step into the world—a step that I had been terrified of making—was all it took to be reminded of how unalone I was. It turned out that almost everyone I met had many of the same fears I did, and the other writers had *all* of my fears. "That was the time which began with his feeling anonymous and general, like a slow convalescent," Rilke writes in the *Notebooks*. One day you find that there has grown up silently around you a realization that your condition is not a disease but a nature. One day it hits you: of *course* you feel this way, it's who you are. Your nature has been waiting for you all along. Now it welcomes you. How could you have thought you needed to change yourself in order to fit into the world? The change that was needed was not in you but in what you thought you were.

I remembered that as a boy I had spent long Saturday hours extracting rusty nails from the piles of paneling my father had torn out in the basement. I remembered hammering them straight on the piece of scrap iron my father had scavenged for an anvil, and then watching my father reuse these nails as he built himself a workshop and repaneled the basement. I remembered my adolescent adoration of my older brother Tom, who for a while in the '70s was an avant-garde filmmaker in Chicago, and who re-habbed an apartment in Pilsen with tools and materials largely scrounged from the now-defunct Max-well Street market. Tom had two old Kar-mann Ghias, a bad yellow one handed down from our other brother, Bob, who had finished med school and bought an Alfa-Romeo, and an even worse blue one that had cost Tom $150. He alternately cannibalized each to feed the other; it was very time-consuming. I was riding with him the day the yellow one threw a rod and died and also the day the hood of the blue one blew open on the Dan Ryan Expressway and blocked the wind-shield and we nearly crashed. Do I sound nostalgic? I am not. I don't hunger to return to those days, because I knew I was happy then. I can look back on those years and not miss them. I was present when they hap-pened, and that's enough.

When I began to write seriously in college, I used a hulking black Rem-ington that rose nearly a foot off my desk, weighed as much as a small air conditioner, and took all my carpal strength to operate. Later, I wrote my first novel and half of my second on two portable Silver-Reed typewriters (fifty dollars in 1980, still only sixty-nine dollars in 1985). When they broke, I fixed them. A triumph, in a week when various journals returned five short stories with rejection letters, was my substitution of dental floss for the nylon cord that supplied carriage-advancing tension.

For typing up clean drafts, my wife and I shared a forty-pound electric Smith-Corona. Our old Chevy Nova was strictly a fair-weather friend, and it always seemed to be snowing when the Smith-Corona broke down. In the early '80s, in Boston, snow would pile up in drifts that my wife and I would struggle over, bundled like peasants as we half-dragged and half-carried the Smith-Corona to the Harvard Coop. Somewhere in the Coop's bowels dwelt a man named Mr. Palumbo. I never met Mr. Palumbo face to face, but we spoke on the telephone often. He had a raspy voice and you just *knew* he was up to his elbows in machine oil. Mr. Palumbo loved the inexpensive fix, and I loved him for loving it. Once, on one of those pre-maturely indigo late afternoons that descend on Boston, he called to tell me that the main shaft had broken off the Smith-Corona's motor and that the motor would have to be replaced, at a cost of fifty dollars. It was obvi-ous that he hated to have to tell me this. An hour or two later, well after nightfall, he called me again. "I fixed it!" he shouted. "I *glued* it. I *epoxy-glued* the shaft back on the motor!" As I recall, he charged us eighteen dol-lars for this service.

I bought my first computer in 1989. It was a noisy metal box made by

. . . .

Amdek, with a paper-white VGA monitor. In good codependent form, I came to appreciate the noise of the Amdek fan's hum. I told myself I liked the way it cut out the noise from the street and other apartments. But after two years of heavy use, the Amdek developed a new, frictive squeal whose appearance and disappearance seemed (although I was never quite sure of this) to follow the rise and fall of the air's relative humidity. My first solution was to wear earplugs on muggy days. After six months of earplugs, however, with the squeal becoming more persistent, I removed the computer's sheet-metal casing. Holding my ear close, I fiddled and poked. Then the squeal stopped for no reason, and for several days I wrote fiction on a topless machine, its motherboard and tutti-frutti wires exposed. And when the squeal returned, I discovered that I could make it stop by applying pressure to the printed-circuit board that controlled the hard disk. There was a space that I could wedge a pencil into, and if I torqued the pencil with a rubber band, the corrective pressure held. The cover of the computer didn't fit right when I put it back on; I accidentally stripped the threads off a screw and had to leave one corner of the cover sort of flapping.

To some extent, of course, everyone who is less than wealthy learns to cope with ailing equipment. Some of us are simply more vain about our coping. But it's not simply for their affirmation of my nature that I value my memories of writing prose on half-broken machines. The image of my decrepit but still functional Amdek is also, for me, an image of America's enduring *raggedness*. Obsolescence is the leading product of our national infatuation with technology, and I now believe that obsolescence is not a darkness but a beauty: not perdition but salvation. The more headlong the progress of technological development, the greater the volume of obsolete detritus. And the detritus isn't simply material. It's angry religion, resurgent countercultural ideologies, the newly unemployed, the eternally unemployable. These are what guarantees fiction writers that we will never be alone. Ineluctable obsolescence is our legacy.

Imaginative writing is necessarily amateur. It's the lone person scouring the trash heap, not the skilled team assembling an entertainment, and we Americans are lucky enough to live in the most wonderful world of junk. Once, when I lived in Munich, I stole two cobblestones from a sidewalk construction site. I intended to wrap them in newspaper and make bookends. It was a Saturday afternoon, the streets were empty, and yet my theft seemed so terribly, terribly transgressive that I ran for blocks, a stone in each hand, before I was sure I was safe. And still I felt the stern eye of the

State on me. Whereas in New York, where I now live, the Dumpsters practically *invite* me to relieve them of their useful bricks and lumber. Street people share lore with me over curbside dumps at midnight. In the wee hours they spread their finds on soiled quilts at the corner of Lexington and Eighty-sixth Street and barter dubious clock radios for chipped glass doorknobs. Use and abandonment are the aquifer through which consumer objects percolate, shedding the taint of mass production and emerging as historied individuals.

Although it's possible to hate what America is becoming, I love the literature that America produces. Its classlessness, its plainness and clear-headedness. But just as we import our TVs from Asian countries with good technical educational systems, magazines like the *New Yorker* are now importing wholesale writing from Britain, which has an excellent literary educational system. The Brits still know how to write, we are told. But most of their writing seems as plastic to me as my Panasonic Touch-Tone telephone. I can feel in every word of it their profound incomprehension of an American literature produced in opposition to that which the Brits find essential in America and are eminently comfortable with: the glitz, the big money, the Hollywood royalty. What an amateur Whitman seems compared to Tennyson, or Melville compared to Thackeray, or O'Connor compared to Waugh, or Denis Johnson compared to Martin Amis. British writing is coloured by the writer's striving to attain social status; American writing is colored by the writer's knowledge that status here, being purely economic, is unattainable.

It's tempting to imagine the American writer's resistance to techno-consumerism—a resistance that unfortunately in most cases takes the form of enforced economic hardship—as some kind of fungible political resistance. Not long ago, one of my former undergraduate workshop students came to visit, and I took him on a walk in my neighborhood. Jeff is a skilled, ambitious young person, gaga over Pynchon's critique of technology and capitalism, and teetering between pursuing a Ph.D. in English and trying his hand at fiction. On our walk, I ranted at him. I said that I too had once been seduced by critical theory's promise of a life unco-opted by the System, but that after my initial seduction I came to see that university tenure itself—the half-million-dollar TIAA-CREF account in your name, the state-of-the-art computer supplied to you at a university discount by the Apple Corporation for the composition of your "subversive" monographs—is the means by which the System co-opts the critical theorist. I said that fiction is refuge, not agency.

. . . .

Then we passed a delicious trash pile, and I pulled from it a paint-and-plaster-spattered wooden chair with a broken seat and found a scrap of two-by-four to knock the bigger clumps of plaster off. It was grubby work. Jeff said: "This is what my life will be like if I write fiction?"

After years of depression, I didn't care how forgiving of myself I sounded. I said that what mattered to me was the rescue. I could probably afford a new chair; that I prefer to live among the scavenged and reborn is my own private choice.

A sponge bath, a scrap of sturdy ash plywood from a dresser drawer abandoned at curbside, eight scavenged brass screws to attach the plywood to the underside of the seat, and a black magic marker to mask the spatters of white paint: this is how the chair was rescued.

Slouching Towards Grubnet:
The Author in the Age of Publicity

. . . .

by
GERALD HOWARD

> To write—was that not the joy and the privilege of one who had an urgent
> message for the world?
> MARIAN YULE in *New Grub Street*

> There's no question of the divine afflatus; that belongs to another sphere
> of life. We talk of literature as a trade, not of Homer, Dante, Shake-
> speare . . . I mean, what on earth is there in typography to make everything
> it deals with sacred?
> JASPER MILVAIN in *New Grub Street*

I was in the middle of reading literally my seventeenth article on Martin
Amis's *The Information* and all the chattering class controversy surrounding its publication, quite a good one in *New York* magazine by James
Kaplan, well in the upper tier of such articles (and by then I had become a
connoisseur), with, amazingly, a new spin on its subject (Kaplan plays tennis with Amis as a journalistic device to explore envy and competitiveness
between writers, *The Information*'s big preoccupation), when I turned the
page and confronted the picture, or, as I have come to think of it, The Picture. The photographer at the New York publication party for *The Information*—a major-league see-and-be-seen event for the buzzoisie, you can
be sure—had captured four scribbling bad boys, American literary outrage Bret Easton Ellis, British literary outrage Will Self, transatlantic literary neo-Gothicist Patrick McGrath, and the man of the hour himself, Martin Amis, each at precisely the moment when the party mask slips to reveal
the soul beneath the skin. On the left was Ellis, his nascent jowls reminis-
cent of Richard Nixon during his Checkers period, his eyes showing

alarming areas of white in the manner of Tor Johnson, the wrestler/actor of Ed Wood's stock company. On the right were Self, tall, pin-striped, cigarette in hand and profile both thrust aggressively forward, his forehead marred as if allegorically by a boil, and McGrath, smug expression and comfortable bay window proclaiming the pleasant fruits of his skillfully creepy fiction. In the center, famously shorter than the others, was Amis himself, with his drink and hand-rolled fag, his often handsome face seemingly caught in midmorph into some sort of reptilian visage. The snapshot spoke of near toxic levels of ambition and self-regard, constant crosschecking for position in the full glare of the media spotlight—the Wildean ravages, perhaps, of having one's name set in boldface too often. Success—and by local community standards these men were very successful indeed—in the literary purlieus of the '90s clearly did not convey grace and spiritual health. The photo's miasmic air proclaimed, in its own sly way, that being a novelist, even one whose name was on the lips of every literary saloniste and cocktail party-goer, was no ticket to dignity and no anodyne to status anxiety. It said clearly, at least to me: Mother, don't let your son grow up to be a novelist. It begged the question, at least of me: would I trust these people with any portion of my inner life?

Which was, of course, the clearest message and biggest question any dispassionate reader might take away from *The Information* itself. Amis's novel might be described as a demonstration of the proposition that hatred of one's peers is so powerful a force in the literary world that it can cause writers to behave approximately like Tonya Harding. A brilliantly knowing and occasionally hilarious *tour d'horizon* of the postliterate literary landscape, from the badly appointed low-rent districts to the gaudy, gilded precincts of bestsellerdom, *The Information* paints a largely accurate picture of that world—if you discount the possibility of art and transcendence and any sense of what these qualities might mean, how they might manifest themselves.

The Information itself may or may not be art, but it was certainly a prime postmodern instance in the circularity with which the book's whole publication saga mirrored its themes of venality and inauthenticity. In as abbreviated a form as possible, and with apologies to readers who have heard all this before: having written a novel hinging on a failing writer's midlife crisis, Amis, himself in midlife (although hardly failing), proceeded to act out his own. He left his wife and children for an American heiress (nice touch, that) and subsequently presented his longtime publisher Jonathan Cape with a stunning demand for 482,000 pounds for his new book. Some claimed that the money was needed to pay for an extensive and expensive new set of teeth from an American dentist (nice touch, that). Then certain of Cape's authors, demonstrating the effect of financial envy, cried foul in the public prints, precipitating a tabloid frenzy. At some point in the protracted negotiations, Amis ditched his longtime literary agent for a notoriously rapacious American one nicknamed "The Jackal" by the British press (nice touch, that). As it happens, Amis's old agent is married to his oldest and closest literary mate (and tennis partner), Julian Barnes; the friendship did not survive the business rupture and the gossip that the bestselling hack who is the butt of most of the novel's jokes was modeled on Barnes himself. In the event Amis ended up selling his book to HarperCollins for just about the same sum as Cape had offered, leaving behind him the scorched earth of romantic, literary, business, and fraternal associations. As his former agent, sibyl-like, observed, "The ironies of this outcome will be lost on none of the participants."

This whole farrago stopped the British literary-industrial complex in its tracks for weeks and became a national obsession of O. J. Simpson-like proportions. Similar to that murder and its aftermath, it involved a dizzying loss of perspective in which foreground and background, subject and object, became hopelessly confused—a Mongolian cluster-fuck of reality and fiction, art (or "art") and life. So inescapable was the ubiquitous information about *The Information* that one wag, when asked at a dinner party whether he'd read the book yet, replied, "Well, yes—but not *personally*." *The Information* the book and *The Information* the pseudo-event both provide rich texts in which we may descry the strange warpings of character, the necessary mutations in the figure of the author in a world where, cf. Colin Powell and Newt Gingrich, a book tour can become a proxy for a presidential campaign or a national political debate.

I myself *have* read *The Information* personally, and in my view Martin Amis's powers of provocation exceed his powers of literary invention; nothing in the novel quite reaches the deliciously ironic peaks of its path to publication. Still, it is a sharply observed, consistently amusing, and sourly well-informed insider's view of the authorial experience in an age in which a book is as often as not the pretext for everything *except* reading. Its hapless antihero Richard Tull personifies every flavor of literary futility. A "marooned modernist," his novelistic career has ground to a shuddering halt. His latest work, *Untitled,* "with its octuple time schemes and rotating crew of sixteen unreliable narrators," is so unreadable as to induce migraine headaches in all who attempt it. He ekes out a precarious

.   .   .   .

living as an editor at a vanity press, a man of all work at the inpecunious Little Magazine (". . . it really did stand for something in this briskly materialistic age. It stood for not paying people"), and a second- to third-tier reviewer of second- to third-rate literary biographies like *The Soul's Dark Cottage: A Life of Edmund Waller* and *AntiLatitudinarian: The Heretical Career of Francis Atterbury*. He is impotent with his attractive wife and his unattractive mistress, and he spends his days grinding his teeth over the unaccountable success of his quondam best friend, novelist Gwyn Barry, and plotting increasingly baroque and ineffectual forms of revenge.

As Richard Tull's career describes a relentlessly declining arc, Gwyn Barry's follows an infinitely and perplexingly ascending trajectory toward an empyrean of extraliterary fame, smug fatuity, and swollen royalty checks. His painfully sincere and modishly multicultural utopian fantasies *Amelior* and *Amelior Regained* have enjoyed a stupefyingly inexplicable success similar to that of Robert Waller's *The Bridges of Madison County*. (Tull muses bitterly, "*Amelior* would only be remarkable if Gwyn had written it with his foot. Why was *Amelior* so popular? Gywn didn't do it. The world did it.") As a result, Barry enjoys all the trophies of the blockbuster name-brand author: the sexy upper-class wife, the lavish household, the constant barrage of attention from every medium, the shortlisting for lavishly remunerative literary prizes with names like the Profundity Requital, the triumphal book tours planned with the precision and the similar intent of amphibious landings. Richard Tull accompanies Barry on one of these tours across America to promote *Amelior Regained,* assigned to write a personality feature on his friend that will "examine the pressures facing the successful novelist in the late 1990s." The forced march through the talk-show archipelago that America has become sparks anti-epiphanies like this for Tull:

> The contemporary idea seemed to be that the first thing you did, as a communicator, was come up with some kind of slogan, and either you put it on a coffee mug or a T-shirt or a bumper sticker—or else you wrote a novel about it . . . And now that writers spent as much time telling everyone what they were doing as they spent actually doing it, then they would start doing it that way round too, eventually.

Everywhere he travels with Barry, Tull observes "the excitement of increase, of reputable profit, the kind you get when commerce meets art and finds it good."

Something of that same excitement surrounded *The Information* itself.

Amis clearly intended it as his Big Statement on the darkening cast of life at the end of the millennium and the ineffectuality of literature in the face of these developments. The book suffers from its ambitions: too many passages show the rhetorical strain of overreaching for the cosmic; the thugs Tull enlists in his revenge schemes are entirely too literary in conception to be remotely convincing; and similarly, Tull and Barry are too extreme in their haplessness and self-satisfied cluelessness, respectively, to move beyond the scope of skillful cartoons in the autonomy of fictional characters. And there is something, well, unpleasant and creepy about Amis's world view. Famously precocious as a young literary editor and novelist, he shows the nasty, practiced cynicism of the smartest kid in the class, and his corrosive view of the literary life is served up with a smirk that implicitly excludes himself from any taint of Tulldom or Barryness.

I spoke to a young writer of my acquaintance about *The Information,* someone just launched on his own career. I was curious how he might weather this putative portrait of the life that awaits him. Not well, as it happens. He complained of the book's "weird conflation of vileness and success" and said that reading it made him feel "like I'd received a blood transfusion from a lizard." He said that "writers put enormous effort into sandbagging their internal levees against a rising internal tide of bitterness and recrimination" and the book felt like a flood of such feelings overflowing their banks. When I asked him whether he agreed that envy was as powerful a force in writers' lives as the novel maintains, he said that in their heart of hearts, writers were as envious and competitive, but in their soul of souls they were warm, generous, helpful, and giving. In this regard *The Information* has a cold heart—and no soul at all.

Still, before we dismiss *The Information* as the product of both a notoriously catty and insular literary culture and a notoriously cynical literary intelligence, we need to look more closely at the literature of contemporary authorship in America. Here, too, reassurance for writers and readers is hard to find, offering as it does conspicuous examples of an emerging literature of disgust.

Consider *Wonder Boys* by the much-heralded young writer Michael Chabon, published at about the same time as *The Information* and as ethnographically accurate a portrayal of the campus-centered American literary scene. Its narrator and Richard Tull equivalent is Grady Tripp, a novelist similarly mired in dismal midlife and midcareer. A college writing teacher, divorcé, and morose pot enthusiast, Tripp is tethered to a dying novel called *Wonder Boys,* a vast family saga that, on the morning he is driving to the airport to pick up his impatient book editor for Wordfest, one of those alarmingly overproliferated literary festivals, stands at 2,611 pages. (cf. Richard Tull: "One of the many troubles with his novels was that they didn't really get finished. They just stopped.") Belying its jaunty tone and skillfully farcical plot, *Wonder Boys* is littered with casualties of the literary life. Contemplating them (and himself), Tripp muses:

> I . . . began to wonder if people who wrote fiction were not suffering from some kind of disorder—from what I've come to think of as the midnight disease. The midnight disease is a kind of emotional insomnia; at every conscious moment its victim—even if he or she writes at dawn or in the middle of the afternoon—feels like a person lying in a sweltering bedroom, with the window thrown open, looking up at a sky filled with stars and airplanes, listening to the narrative of a rattling blind, an ambulance, a fly trapped in a Coke bottle, while all around him the neighbors sleep soundly.

Were this to get out, Bread Loaf and numerous other literary sleepaways would become ghost camps. Predictably, Tripp's editor Terry Crabtree, a man with his own set of problems ("I'm hanging by, like, three molecules of thread at Bartizan"), finds *Wonder Boys* too burdensome to take on: "I need something fresh. Something snappy and fast. Something pretty and perverted at the same time." Chilling words that will resonate alarmingly with fourth novelists everywhere.

The prodigiously talented novelist Richard Powers betrays much the same dismay at the internal costs of his vocation, in startlingly intimate terms, in his latest book, *Galatea 2.2.* Running parallel to a Shavian plot involving the literary and sentimental education of a post-HAL computer entity named Helen is a comprehensive account of Powers's own publishing history, complete with actual review excerpts—a grim testament of pained composition, gnawing dissatisfaction, critical misapprehension, and creative exhaustion. He dismisses his first novel, *Three Farmers on Their Way to a Dance,* as "no more than a structured pastiche of every report I'd ever heard from C. [Powers's lover] or abroad," and his fourth, *Operation Wandering Soul,* as "an ornate, suffocating allegory about dying pedes at the end of the century." Granted a year's residence at a midwestern university, Powers shuttles between the computer techies, who promise (or threaten) to create intelligences and even sensibilities equal to any mere novelist's in scope and penetration, and the English department, whose reigning orthodoxies proclaim the death of the author, the illicit privileges of the text, and the infinite variability of meaning. His immersion in cognitive neuroscience, the actual mechanics of the brain's work-ings, provokes less wonder than paralyzing self-consciousness. Not sur-prisingly, writer's block lurks: ". . . nothing waited for me on the far side of story's gaping mountain. Nothing but irremediable Things As They Are." Powers's "my fair software" adventures with Helen are wonder-fully well handled and provide a fictional escape hatch for his literary alter ego, but his excursions into the recesses of the novelist's inner workroom provoke dismay at the airlessness of the working conditions and the joy-lessness of literary creation even at his rarefied level.

Don DeLillo typically provides the exhilarating nadir of literary joy-lessness in the figure of Bill Gray, the reclusive writer at the center of his last novel, *Mao II.* Combining the mania for privacy and the literary fas-tidiousness of J. D. Salinger and Thomas Pynchon, Bill Gray lives in soli-tude somewhere in upstate New York; his long recusal from the scene has, naturally, made him a celebrity, and the longer he lays low, the more fa-mous he becomes. "When a writer doesn't show his face he becomes a local symptom of God's famous reluctance to appear," he explains to a photographer who has come to take the first photographs of him in thirty years. Gray's literary anhedonia and obsessive reworking of his long-awaited novel make Powers's plaints read like "The Ode to Joy":

> He looked at the sentence, six disconsolate words, and saw the entire book as it took occasional shape in his mind, a neutered near human dragging through the house, humpbacked, hydrocephalic, with puckered lips and soft skin, dribbling brain fluid through its mouth. Took him all these years to realize this book was his hated adversary. Locked together in the forbid-den room, had him in a choke hold.

However, DeLillo also manages to lend a public dimension to the writer's private paralysis and sense of ineffectuality. As Bill Gray muses to the photographer:

> There is a curious knot that binds novelists and terrorists. In the West we become famous effigies as our books lose the power to shape and influ-ence . . . Years ago I used to think it was possible for a novelist to alter the inner life of the culture. Now bomb makers and gunners have taken the ter-ritory. They make raids into human consciousness. What writers used to do with words before we were all incorporated.

The novel demonstrates this insight graphically in Bill Gray's quixotic and ultimately fatal foray into public life, a desperate attempt to harness his peculiar fame to the task of freeing a hostage in Beirut. The future,

. . . .

Gray and his creator intuit, belongs to crowds and those who can harness their angry energies—certainly not to the isolated and autonomous creative intelligence, which, for all the celebrity it may be proffered, remains powerless to alter the fundamental terms of the culture.

What is going on here? Why, at this particular juncture of our cultural history, have some of our most sophisticated novelists chosen to demystify their vocation and disillusion their audience? If you live to read and read to live, a literal apprehension of the literary portraits in these four novels will make you wonder whether art could ever really be worth such internal devastation—and whether such damaged souls should be trusted as guides to right thought and action.

Behind such questions lies a whole host of conundrums concerning tellers and tales, and the literary pathography industry hums along inexorably, manufacturing such conundrums for public consumption at an alarming rate. Still, what a startling shift in emphasis in the mythology of authorship from my own book-soaked '60s adolescence. In that era, writer figures strutted through novels cockily, priapically (they were all males, of course), rebelliously. Samson Shillitoe, the poet-hero of Elliott Baker's 1964 novel *A Fine Madness,* can stand in for a whole corps of literary poster boys—a rugged epic poet in rampant revolt, laying intellectual waste to the psychiatrists' timid theories of adjustment and creativity and sexual waste to their wives. (Played in the film version, naturally, by Sean Connery.) In fact, a whole mystique of sexual potency gathered about the novelist, cultivated by writers from Henry Miller to Norman Mailer; penmanship and cockmanship clearly went hand in hand. On the public stage as well, novelists cut impressive figures: here was Norman Mailer again (and again . . .), marching on the Pentagon, running for public office, sparring with Jose Torres (well, stabbing his wife, too)—an avatar of an overreaching age. And here was Ken Kesey, a true cultural superhero, who wrote two of the finest novels of his generation only to move beyond the printed page to blaze a Day-Glo trail into the zeitgeist with his druggy Magic Bus odyssey. No flop sweat here, nor on more private figures like Richard Fariña, Kurt Vonnegut, Richard Brautigan, and Tom Robbins, whose antic novels communicated not just words but comprehensive attitudes to my generation. Writers *mattered.*

I speak of a time, of course, in a great swivet over conformity, inauthenticity, and sterility, for which the elixirs of literary creation were thought to be antidotes. Today writers are more commonly seen as providers of "content" for the multimedia assembly lines of the contemporary Grubway. But writers' confident assertions of cultural authority drew on a reservoir of trust built up over many, many decades, even centuries. The giants of modern American literature—Steinbeck, Hemingway, Faulkner, Eliot, Wharton, et al.—were living memories, and their work had literally helped to define our national identity. These writers projected a mystique so powerful that people used it as a template for their own self-definition. And many of the giants of European literature still trod the earth—and in some cases could be encountered personally. Susan Sontag wrote a while back in the *New Yorker* of being a book-drunk, teenaged intellectual in Los Angeles and getting up the courage to make a cold call with a friend on Thomas Mann in Pacific Palisades. The heir to Goethe and the German humanistic tradition received these awestruck kids politely, if remotely, gave them a cup of tea, chatted with them, and sent them on their way. It felt like magic to Sontag, and it feels like magic still. What figure might serve as a Thomas Mann equivalent today—assuming you could find a young Susan Sontag equivalent?

Before we succumb to the temptation, though, to unreel an invidious procession of mighty literary figures parading across the centuries, a look backward at the actual, difficult circumstances of literary production in eras past would be salutary. No better corrective may be found than George Gissing's *New Grub Street*, the *The Information* of its day (Amis had to have had it in mind) and still a startlingly pertinent picture of the literary life. Precisely because of Gissing's mildly pedestrian Victorian realism, the absence of a Dickensian genius to transform character into archetype, the book has the air of complete veracity about writing and publishing circa 1882.

In outline and conception *New Grub Street* reads like a geometric proof of the axiom that in the literary world the innocent, the idealist, and the artist are fated to fall while the sharper, the opportunist, and the poseur will rise. Conspicuous in the first category is the book's hero-victim Edward Reardon, a novelist of high intent and meager income, whose gifts of invention, while real, are utterly unsuited to the incident-heavy manufacture of the three-decker novels required by the circulating libraries of the day. (". . . he was trying to devise a 'plot,' the kind of literary Jack-in-the-box which might excite interest in the mass of readers, and this was alien to the natural working of his imagination.") Saddled with an unforgiving wife who demands he provide them with an adequate social position, poor Reardon cudgels his brain daily at his desk to the twin chiming of the bells of the Marleybone parish churchyard and the adjoining workhouse—destinations all too plausible to him. Even more poignant, perhaps, is his novelist friend Biffen, who labors long in Flaubertian style ("Each sentence was as good as he could make it, harmonious to the ear. . . .") and grim poverty on his domestic epic of the everyday, *Mr. Bailey, Grocer* ("Shall I hint that it deals with the ignobly decent?"). Biffen's reward for his monklike integrity is predictable: devastatingly condescending reviews with lectures that "the first duty of a novelist is to tell a story," privation that leads to near-starvation, and finally a loneliness whose end is suicide.

Meanwhile, the path to the sunny uplands of well-padded prosperity is open to such as Jasper Milvain, the book's arch-literary operative and consummate trimmer. Given to such smug pronouncements as "literature today is a trade . . . your successful man of letters is your skillful tradesman. He thinks first and foremost of the markets" and "many a fellow could write more in quantity, but they couldn't command my market. It's rubbish, but rubbish of a special quality." Jasper has all the angles figured and is completely without shame. So naturally he ends up marrying Reardon's widow and winning a coveted editorship. Then there is the cheerfully empty-headed Whelpdale, who enters the book as a protoliterary agent offering advice to aspirants for a fee and "recommending" their work to publishers. "Now that's one of the finest jokes I ever heard. A man who can't get anyone to publish his own books makes a living by telling other people how to write!" Milvain exclaims, anticipating by a century the creative writing industry. By book's end, Whelpdale is prosperously editing *Chit-Chat,* a paper not unlike *USA Today,* addressing itself to the vast emerging audience of "the quarter educated" with articles no longer than two inches and full of "the lightest and frothiest of chitchatty information," designed for swift digestion on trains and trams.

Enter the mass media, stage left. *New Grub Street* was conceived in a time not unlike our own when an explosion of mass communications had fundamentally altered the literary equation. On New Grub Street the hazards facing those unwilling to adapt were relatively straightforward: poverty, starvation, death. On Neo-Grub Street or the Grubway, as we have seen, baroque forms of demoralization or grotesque forms of adaptation seem to be the choices offered. No wonder some of our best novelists are blowing the lid off the postmodern literary dodge. And editors, too: Michael Korda's amusingly chilling memoir of his time served as Jacqueline Susann's editor contains this tidbit: "When we had expressed anxiety about the unwritten manuscript, Irving [Mansfield, her husband

and agent] told us it was Jackie (and the example of *Valley of the Dolls,* then approaching ten million copies sold) that he was selling and not, as he put it indignantly, 'a goddamn pile of paper.'" Some would say we live in a post-Jacqueline Susann universe.

Authors share with presidents today the impossible conditions of office: it is hellishly difficult to inspire and lead either politically or spiritually when you are required to expose yourself utterly, to make your life, no pun intended, an open book. Leadership and pseudo-intimacy are in fundamental conflict. And the roles of president and novelist also have this in common: declining sway and public respect.

Of course, my search for spiritual guidance in the field of literature is a quaint anachronism. There is no shortage of claimants to the big job of resolving the spiritual confusions of the age in your local superstore—they just aren't found in the literature section anymore. Sub–Gwyn Barry productions like *The Celestine Prophecy, Mutant Message Down Under,* and *Embraced by the Light,* megasellers all, purport to bring their credulous readers succor and solace—news that there is a way and these pilgrim scribes have found it. These books tend to be self-published at first, and indeed their grandiose semiliteracy will be familiar to anyone who has done time in a publisher's slush pile. Amis has their number: "It wasn't bad literature. It was antiliterature. Propaganda aimed at the self . . . They were like tragic babies; they were like pornography. They shouldn't be looked at. They really shouldn't be looked at." Well, they are looked at, by the millions, and publishers are rushing to fill the newly discovered meaning gap with a barrage of titles about finding God or something like Him or Her while riding a Harley or snowboarding the Himalayas. As one publisher put it in the *New York Times,* "We're living in a spiritual age, aren't we?"

All of which only further fuels the despair of the serious novelist, whose task it is not to dumb down the reader's sense of life and fate into a set of slogans and self-help propositions, but to deepen and complicate it. In a fine critique of minimalist fiction a few years back, the novelist Madison Smartt Bell made the lovely assertion that "if our lives do in fact lack variety and meaning, then maybe we had better make haste to invent some." But today's novelists know that the meanings they might discover or invent for our fragmented, improvisatory lives are tentative, less than universal, subject to revision at the turn of the cultural wheel—and almost certain to be drowned out by the ersatz "wisdom" in plentiful and profitable supply. Hence the comic despair with which some writers pre-

. . . .

emptively eviscerate the mystique of their calling. Hence the cold-eyed
Milvainian calculation with which others play the career game.

Italo Calvino, in *If on a Winter's Night a Traveler,* beautifully captures
the mysterious way a mere book can hold sway over our imagination,
compel our allegiance and faith. His book editor / alter ego Cavedagna is
intimate with all the mechanics of bookmaking, all the crotchets of authors. Knowing all he knows,

> And yet the true books for him remain others, those of a time when for him
> they were like messages from another world . . . and yet the true authors re-
> main those who for him were only a name on a jacket, a word that was part
> of the title, authors who had the same reality as their characters, as the
> places mentioned in the books, who existed and didn't exist at the same
> time, like those characters and those countries. The author was an invisible
> point from which the books came, a void traveled by ghosts, an under-
> ground tunnel that put other worlds in communication with the chicken
> coop of his boyhood. . . .

As we slouch towards the Grubnet, a digital cyberspace in which books
and authors alike will become dematerialized, available on demand
twenty-four hours a day, that otherworldly innocence and mysterious remoteness that gave books their authority and that Cavedagna mourns become impossible to recapture—as distant and hard to imagine a state of
mind as trusting a politician. We are all of us, readers and writers alike,
exiles from the garden of innocent reading. Who knows what beasts await
us in the new cultural wilderness?

Another Evening with Monsieur Teste

.   .   .   .

by

WULF REHDER

*In fortuitous circumstances that pertain only to a world in which possi-
bilities outnumber realities, a meeting of fictitious characters is likely to
occur. One hundred years ago, a certain Monsieur Teste, lead actor in Paul
Valéry's drama of consciousness, was first seen in the cafes and theaters of
Paris and a few times (be it admitted) also in a kind of b———. Ten years
later, the Viennese engineer and writer Robert Musil introduced into his
literary diaries a man named Ulrich who later (in Musil's 1931 novel) became the "man without properties." Ulrich had no properties and no family name, but he had character. And "the character of man," said Valéry, "is
consciousness; . . . the man of mind must finally reduce himself knowingly
to an endless refusal to be anything whatever." In 1913, Ulrich ended his
experiments to become a remarkable man and thus sacrificed his pretenses
to be anything at all. He took a yearlong vacation from his life and imper-
sonated an intellectual amateur politician sans portefeuille. On one of his
diplomatic missions to France, he met M. Teste. This meeting of two minds
that were similarly "affected with the acute malady of precision" was
recorded by Valéry in the memoir* La soirée avec Monsieur Teste *(translated as* An Evening with M. Teste *by Ronald Davis, 1925, and by Jackson
Mathews, 1947.) Since fictitious characters live in a realm of unlimited
possibilities (plus a few limited impossibilities), they are exempt from the
laws of linear time. But when time, like the conscious mind, turns inward
upon itself, we can remember the future and remake the past. And so the
most plausible event was allowed to happen: Ulrich met Monsieur Teste
again. Inevitably, where ghosts of the imagination convene, other demons
will join the banquet dressed in their freshly ironed shadows. It is my priv-*

. . . .

ilege, as fiancé of Ulrich's niece Grete and heir to his unpublished thoughts, to invite you, a real reader, to the potentialities of Another Evening with Monsieur Teste.

Computers are not my forte. I have bought some, I have touched many, at times I have depended on one. They have trespassed the quietude of my middle years as so many women in Vienna encroached upon my scholarly life when I was only thirty-two. Their names sound like titles of schmaltzy operettas—Bonadea, Leona, Diotima. Today, computers exhibit the same coy latinity, sleek machines with feminine endings—Amiga, Performa, Alexia. Computers and Bonadea's beauty have both ambushed my privacy, but my heart has remained cold and still. Both extremes, the poverty of binary logic and the rich lushness of Leona, have challenged my composure, whose only defense is a pose of prim refusal. Philosophically, if not physically, I was drawn to Diotima, who had majored in pure mathematics and always wore white. But after long and deep discussions about love and logic, Diotima married a businessman, the rich Dr. Arnheim, and settled in Geneva—which shows how tenuous is the hold of ideals on our actions. What remains is this: after a score of women and a dozen computers, my memory is filled with fragments of code and unfinished infatuations. I was known as the man without properties. I counted simplicity among the things I needed most. I nurtured in myself a harmonic balance between the useful activities of an engineer and the emotional substance distilled from twenty novels read by candlelight. But my equilibrium has now been jeopardized by the obsession to continue Monsieur Teste's life's work.

Yes, I have seen Monsieur Teste again. He was not well. I met him at the Café Lambert in the Rue Vivienne where he always goes after the Bourse closes for the day. He was smoking his Turkish Ali Pasha cigars sent to him by the reliable tobacco house of Ghoneimy & Co. via Cairo-Genoa-Paris. He still studies the movement of the major stock markets between London and Tokyo and enjoys a reputation as a scholar in the philosophy of money. Between two puffs of his cigar (attended by discreet but very deep coughs) he cited minute stock oscillations and quoted revenue figures far into the trillion francs. Using the language of physics to describe the nature of money, he estimated its kinetic energy, discussed the laws of its creation and destruction, introduced me to the relativity theory governing the supply of money and the demand for time, and speculated about the amortization of *la coeur et l'esprit* in the humanities. Epistemology was for him a branch of economics. "Knowledge is capital," he said, "know-how is power, and science is a line of credit." He was pale, his voice was hoarse. Monsieur Teste intercepted my worried look and said, "Money is the spirit of society." I recalled a similar quote from my first meeting with him: *"L'or est comme l'esprit de la société."* Within three decades, gold had become money. Defiantly, he added, "I once wrote a descriptive analysis of banknotes." Although he owned a black-and-gold Mont Blanc fountain pen, I had never seen him with a notebook. He did all his work in his head. At the Bourse, he would stand dreamily on the busy floor, surrounded by mad money men, when suddenly, after silently doing a complicated integration over discontinuous time series in his brain, he would ask a broker for assistance in buying or selling the object of his calculations, foreign money, stocks, or futures, all of which he juggled in the big bald machine of his head.

"Money is the mind of society," I repeated, eager to dispel doubts about my loyalty. "But what, Monsieur Teste, is the soul?" He brought the cigar to his mouth, and from his mocking lips rose a ring of blue smoke. "That, *mon cher Ulrich*, is the simplest question man can ask. No, no, don't be ashamed," he added as he saw my peevish smile, and as the smoke from the Ali Pasha was laying a gray veil of mystery around the lamp in front of us, he said, "It is the answer that is hardest to find." He got up with difficulty. I paid the waiter (Monsieur Teste had not a single sou) and asked him to call a taxi. *"Soul,"* Monsieur Teste quoted Donne's famous line as we were standing outside in the night: *"Poor intricated soul! Riddling, perplexed, labyrinthical soul!* Preparing a systematic inventory of the soul has been the occupation of my life. Before you too make it your vocation, I will show you my research. Rue Gay-Lussac," he said to the chauffeur.

After his marriage to Emilie, Monsieur Teste had given up his room in the Rue Gay-Lussac, but his need for solitude had forced him back to his old abode. Once or twice a week over the past thirty years he had thus spent his nights here, often sleepless. Madame Teste found this quite in order and necessary for his mental hygiene. The drab and banal room had the mint green austerity of a cell. On the wall hung the well-known reproduction of Ligier Richier's skeleton and a daguerreotype of a young lady with a modish fur boa around her naked shoulders. A blackboard was covered with mathematical figures, chemical formulas, cryptic symbols. An open trunk had once served as a library; now a hundred tired books were gathering dust. On top I saw Descartes's *Discourse* in paperback, a

. . . .

valuable incunabulum by Leonardo, Goethe's *Faust II*, Gide's *L'Immoral-iste*. Under the sole lightbulb stood a table and two armchairs with no cushions. By the bed was a night table, and on it two glasses filled with cognac, lit by a honey-colored candle, and a beautiful black box.

There was something oddly familiar about this box. Had I seen it before, in a dream perhaps, or in another life? Monsieur Teste saw my frown. "*Belle de Jour*," he said, and immediately the scene from Luis Buñuel's film sprang back from memory. This must be a sibling to the lacquered case the Asian patron Mr. Chen had brought into Madame Anais's b———! He had opened the box and shown its content to the terrified ladies of pleasure. Nothing but a sound resembling a bee's humming or a snake's hissing or the buzzing from an excited electric wire was audible. The mysterious content, invisible to the movie's audience, supposedly indicated the patron's desires—outrageous wishes, no doubt, that no man would be able to put into words. Only Séverine, a bored bourgeoise beauty with dark secrets in her past, agreed to love him that night.

Monsieur Teste turned to me. "*Mon ingénieur,* you are no doubt curious where this box came from and what it contains. I will tell you. It was first given to a certain Mr. Bartleby, a lonely child of six years at the time. In the story 'The Apple-Tree Table,' Bartleby's biographer wrote about an eerie ticking in the wood, and how it took much research and observation to detect the beautiful beetle that had hatched in the wood one hundred and fifty years ago and was returning from his death sleep to life. According to literary rumor, the box was made from this miraculous piece of apple-tree wood. Others, biblical scholars among them, say that it was built from the wood of an apple tree that has an ancestor in paradise. Whatever the literal truth, the rest is quickly told. Ishmael, sailing the Pequod II to China, offered the box to shipping tycoons in Hong Kong, where Mr. Chen purchased it for a thousand tael (which is 1,300 ounces avoirdupois). I met Mr. Chen first at the Ching Chung Koon Taoist temple, where he prayed, and a day later at the Bourse in Hong Kong, where he speculated in gold bullion. One day he owed me for an investment tip that saved his fortune. And that is why the box is now here on a humble bedside table in the rue Gay-Lussac." Monsieur Teste mumbled a binary encryption code, and while the contraption was warming up he told me about Sigmund Freud. Freud had apparently used the box for remote analysis of Sherlock Holmes. "But then he almost broke it when he applied it to his own problems, night after night," Monsieur Teste said. Lord Bertrand Russell had shown the box to his first wife Alys, but to no avail, then left it to his graduate student Ludwig Wittgenstein. Ludwig, who was on his way to becoming the Bartleby of philosophy, employed the box to demonstrate the privacy of pain. Quoting from the manual that came with the box, Monsieur Teste read paragraph 293 of Wittgenstein's *Philosophical Investigations* to me:

> Assume that everybody had a box, and in it something we call "beetle." Nobody can ever look into somebody else's box; and everybody says that he knows only from the sight of *his own* beetle what a beetle is. — It may be possible that everybody has a different thing in his box. Or even that such a thing were subject to constant change. — But what if the word "beetle" were of some use for these people? — Then it wouldn't be for the naming of a thing. The thing in the box isn't even part of the language game; not even as a *something*: for the box might be empty. — No, this thing in the box can be canceled; it is eliminated, whatever it is."

"Monsieur Teste," I said timidly, "is the beetle in the box an allegory for the soul in the brain?" Monsieur Teste chuckled until he coughed. "Simple Simon! Next you will call literary criticism a branch of artificial intelligence." This seemed a reasonable suggestion to me, but by now the buzzing sound of entrapped electricity had started, and out of the box jumped an odd being.

What it looked like? It is difficult to envision. Or rather, it is hard to draw a picture, and even if I were a better artist than I am, the margin of this page would be too narrow to hold a sketch of any likeness. But a few invented words are worth a thousand pictures, so I will describe for the imagination what is impossible to see with unguided eyes.

Odradek (for that was his name) was made from a flat, starlike spool of thread. Two wooden knitting needles stuck out from underneath as if they were doing the splits. He resembled a Raggedy Andy covered with old and torn pieces of yarn, all knotted and tangled up and of different colors. He seemed to parody Klee's *Angelus Novus*, his eyes wide open, mouth agape, needles spread like wings. "Don't be fooled by his appearance," said Monsieur Teste, who was holding Odradek on the palm of his left hand, stroking it gently. "He looks as if he once had a well-defined, useful purpose and is broken now. How deceptive that is! Not only is he stable on his stilts, but *to his unfettered nimble haste are falling stars, and heart's thoughts, but slow-paced*." And as if to prove true John Donne's words, the creature jumped to the floor, skipped three times around us like Rumplestiltskin, and danced the controlled tango of a marionette with red and green and yellow scraps of woolly thread dragging behind. Excited laughter erupted from his lungless body, and it sounded like the rustle of dry leaves. He disappeared into the hallway and was heard a minute later rummaging in the attic. "Gaining real-world experience," said Monsieur Teste.

I had of course noticed that he was talking about *the* Odradek, born in the feverish fancy of a contemporary of mine, Franz Kafka. The cognac was kindling my literary memory. Above me, Byron the Bulb was singeing his filaments that my German grandparents had called "Seele"—the soul of light. I imagined Gregor Samsa, the salesman who overnight had metamorphosed into an insect, as Odradek's brother, and I recalled the relentless ticking of Samsa's alarm clock (as if it, too, contained a beetle). Later, an apple crushed his armored back, rotting there and killing him slowly. Was it the same "fine apple" Joseph K. had bitten into, inexplicably, immediately after having been arrested in *The Trial*? Was it a *pomme à la Melville*? Was Odradek Kafka's model of an entangled soul? Was he Benjamin's handicapped angel of history?

Monsieur Teste unscrewed the cover of his gold-and-black fountain pen and, holding it like a cup to his lips, blew sharply into the opening. The sound, like a water kettle's whistle, had an immediate effect: the noise in the attic stopped, and Odradek reappeared with his breathless giggle and jumped into the lacquered box, which restarted its whirring dynamo noise. Bending over, I saw Odradek squatting in the middle of what looked like a multidimensional web, not unlike a mesh of intersecting spreadsheets. "This," Monsieur Teste said, "is my interactive soul radio, my walkie-talkie to the numberless infinities of souls." I looked closer. I focused my astigmatic eyes. I saw the multidimensional dashboard of a new time machine. The main axes were labeled with the words morality, exactitude, ecstasy, possibility, and on them fine lines indicated higher and lower degrees of virtue, intellect, pleasure, and imagination. These latter categories were further subdivided, on mutually orthogonal planes, into the corresponding faculties: intellect had components in the dimensions of reason and mind; pleasure fanned into instinct and sensibility; virtue's plane was spanned by conscience and character; imagination was resolved into chance and creativity. Beyond these planes I detected, stretched along fractal dimensions, dictionaries of the works produced by the faculties just named. For instance, reason and mind had produced symbolic systems such as the *Principia Mathematica*, formulas since Pythagoras, theories and theorems from Euclid to Gödel. Especially happy coordinates between the spaces of intellect, pleasure, and imagination had produced such novels as *Winter's Tale*. Setting the pleasure coordinate close to zero resulted in novels with the ambience of *The Tunnel*. There were also cells and hollows of different extensions with names I had never heard of, such as Nine Inch Nails and Netscape and Lollapalooza. Adding a psychedelic effect, every point in the Web was embedded in a three-dimensional color scheme in three dimensions: hue, lightness, and saturation—in blushes never seen even in the solid of 267 pigment mixes as defined by the ISCC-NBS standard.

Monsieur Teste wrapped Odradek's threads around five or nine color-coordinated axes and, by adjusting several hidden knobs on the side of the box, moved him around like a hairy cursor. "Plato distinguished only three different makes of the human soul, gold, silver, and metal," said Monsieur Teste. "Odradek can mix any combination of soul ingredients from a virtually infinite spectrum of individual affections and qualities, faculties and characteristics, tuning each one within a range of intensity and color, and then"—Monsieur Teste was positioning Odradek's center deep inside the maze—"and then, once settled on a combination that is possible, he dials the soul with the highest probability of matching this profile. Any soul, past, present, or future. Over the span of three decades, Odradek and I have done much soul surfing. Soul is the compass for man's abilities, drawing a circle of competencies around his potential. Yes, I wanted to see what is possible for us, what men and women can do, *que peut un homme? Que peut la femme?* I sleep an hour or two at the very most; I adore navigating the night. Now, Monsieur Ulrich, your dialogue with a soul can begin. Listen to the sounds Emerson called 'hints and telegraphic symbols.' Now place your first call."

And indeed I heard a faint Emersonian dial tone over the humming sound of electrical fields as they were coordinating their tensors to avoid collisions with each other. Odradek's center was deep in the ecstasy dimension, surrounded by gold-and-purple hues, his yarn tentacles tied to points on the emotion axis inside the pleasure plane, with only a few lighter threads pointing to intellect and even fewer, thin ones, to virtue. The dial tone stopped and suddenly, to my immeasurable surprise, I heard the cooing voice of Leona's soul.

"Ulrich," she said, "why haven't you called earlier? Was I, a chanteuse in a dingy variété, not worthy of your attention? Where have you been? Hiding behind irony and mathematics? Ah, ideals and morals, you said, are the two objects that best fill the big hole called soul. Like two pretty legs in silken stockings? And how did you define soul for me? Only in a negative way, you said, can she be defined: as something that hides whenever men talk about algebra." "Please," I pleaded, "I loved your voice, your languorous body, your eyes . . ." "But you don't love me as a soul," she pouted. "Love for you has always been the right to be nothing but silly beasts together . . ." At this point I moved Odradek away from Leona's soul. Her *bêtise,* although close to the truth, was beginning to upset me. I left Odradek on the ecstatic emotion axis but pulled his threads to the extreme intellectual corner, without insisting on virtue. Within seconds, the alto of Diotima's soul greeted me from a chalet in Switzerland. "Do you remember," I began quickly (not wanting to lose control of the dialogue again) "when we used to discuss how love is always in cahoots with logic, and how you opted, to my chagrin, for the unlikely union of soul and business?" "Love and logic, my dear Socrates," she replied with a smile, "are but two facets of the soul. Soul's main business is exactitude. Exactitude is an old-fashioned vocable I choose over the sinewy word precision, which is a term Swiss watchmakers prefer. *Präzision,* they say in Geneva, is a virtue of both a good lover and a good chronometer. Timing. Punctuality. Accuracy. Exactitude, on the other hand, is the *esattezza* cultivated by Italian violin makers in Cremona. Their art heightens the precision of the bridge and the pegs, it translates the merely correct harmonies, via the precious wood and natural bows made from the tails of Pisan stallions, into the brilliant, acrobatic exactitude of a piece by Paganini. This product of precision times harmony times imagination equals exactitude. Similar to your German word *Genauigkeit.*" Diotima pronounced it with a soft G, with Genevese affectedness, as in *Jeunesse.*

"*Genauigkeit und Seele,*" I exclaimed, "Exactitude and Soul! The two ideas I proposed to the Count von Leinsdorf in Robert Musil's biography of me. 'Establish, my Lord,' (words to this effect I said to His Excellency) 'in the name of His Majesty Kaiser Franz Joseph, a World Secretariat for Exactitude and Soul.' I believe that the world's woes and wars, our emotional distress, the economic stagnation, senseless suffering, can all be avoided in a most diplomatic manner, through thinking *and* feeling, the dynamo *and* the virgin, mathematics *and* mysticism. . . ."

"Among the technologists, *mein lieber Ulrich,* you are the most romantic, among the romantics the greatest technician. Thinking *and* feeling, you say. On the other side of Lake Geneva, from his hotel room in Montreux, our friend Nabokov dictated the same to reporters: 'I demand of my students the passion of science *and* the patience of poetry.' Differentiation *and* integration. As if the *and* were so simple. Isn't one the inverse, the complement of the other? I prefer the comma: sometimes I think, sometimes I am. I believe in the exactitude *of the* soul. . . ." We chatted for two more minutes, three giga of soul bytes in total. Then, a bit exhausted, I pushed back on intellect, changed the color combination to madonna blue, increased the sensibility scale (with silver threads dangling into chance and imagination), and I exchanged pleasantries with Bonadea. She insisted that she was still "into" art, music, aesthetic feelings—she was as vague and emotional as in real life, calling Mozart's K. # 622, middle movement, "the most pained palliative in creation." Art, she said (and I'd read it before) is "the reproduction of what the Senses perceive in Nature through the veil of the soul." She then ftp-ed me a self-portrait that had all the frankness but none of the nature of Manet's undressed lady in his *Déjeuner sur l'herbe*. "Squint at it," she said, "and you'll see it as if through a veil." When I did, uncontrollable vibrations of desire shook poor Odradek, and I asked Monsieur Teste to log him off. I sipped my cognac and asked Monsieur Teste to connect me to Mr. Bartleby.

I watched Monsieur Teste scan a long table with names, nicknames, sobriquets, aliases, pseudonyms, and anonyms the way old-world people used to look up Web sites and Internet addresses. He seemed to enjoy this rather ridiculous order of strings, and delighted in spelling out the baroque names: http://www.cybercash.com/, gopher://gopher.well.sf.ca.us/, severine@luv.anais.com. "What jargon," he said, "for a garden of wired souls, a cemetery for entire communities." And after a while, he added: "Learnedly to die . . . *Transit classificando*." He shifted Odradek high onto the virtue axis with green threads spanning the space between imagination and intellect. Stark colors framed by melancholic hues appeared to define the address of Bartleby's soul. A melodic jingle signaled that I was connected to the nineteenth century. Odradek's gravity waves strained to reach their target over so many years and miles. After I had paid my compliments (I consider his motto to "choose not to" an advanced feature of every civilized soul), Bartleby explained to me the following.

"Computers don't imagine things. They march in algorithmic goose-step to the beat of a crystal clock—an army of indistinguishable commercial mercenaries. My soul radio is not a commodity. It is a Stradivari, distinct, one of a kind. It grew up with me, we went to school together. It can imagine nonexistent things. By bookish studies and through trial and error did we, Odradek and I, acquire skills, experience, and common sense. We both use metaphors and dark humor, not software. Instead of nightly back-ups, my soul radio reflects upon its own thoughts and actions. While a computer cleanses itself by running antivirus programs, my soul radio makes a proprietor's tour of inspection into itself. It doubts, it learns, it takes risks. It has no built-in rules, nor does it contain premade images representing the surrounding world. No; my soul radio creates pictures spontaneously using its memory and experience, seasoned by judgment and random insights. Of course, a soul radio is not commercially available. It cannot be sold or bought. It was given to me as a gift, at age six. You've seen it in operation: like poppies bending in the wind and following each others' rhythms, so do the soul's possibility vectors gently follow the neural inputs transmitted by Odradek. The vector bushels arrange themselves first in the dominant directions along the Web axes, but instinctively select second-order chance influences that adapt or mutate their behavior. A soul is not a computer, not an electronic marionette. A soul is like Goethe's homunculus—the artificial human Faust manufactured with nonscientific assistance. He grew it from organic, aesthetic, intellectual, practical, and moral ingredients and gave it Odradek's body." I didn't recall these details, but I insisted that the soul radio was still only an artifact, a mechanism powered by gravity waves. "Does such a machine have access to a soul?" I asked. "Can an apparatus have a soul?" Monsieur Teste listened to me with his puckered lips. He let me guide Odradek's hairy body toward the point where the parallel lines of exactitude and possibility intersect. Passing through the collected works of a certain Dr. Philip Lentz, connectionist scientist *extraordinaire,* we stretched metallic strips across a wide chasm into the happy coordinates of the novel *Galatea 2.2* and reached its artificial heroine. "Her name is Helen," Monsieur Teste whispered, "she is a computer."

"Helen," I said softly, fearing that she might be as sensitive as some of my intelligent kitchen appliances, "Monsieur Teste and I were wondering if a computer has a soul." After a pause, Helen answered: "What is a computer?" "Oh, never mind," I said, perplexed by her question. "Are you sure a computer isn't at least *sometimes* mind?" she suggested. "Well," I said, "take, for instance, Sven Birkerts . . ." "Thank you," Helen answered, "I'd love to." "Yes," I said, "he calls soul the solitary I." "Ah, Polyphemus," she exclaimed, "Homer's *Ulysses,* book nine. So a soul is a one-eyed monster . . . ?" It was hopeless. "Let *me* ask," said Monsieur Teste. "A question is a function of the answer. Let's begin again. A computer," he said, turning to Helen's soul, "is a Turing machine, only more expensive." "I know Turing machines," said Helen, "and they do have souls, by the grace of God. Turing himself said, let me see, I have to go to a disk, here, in his article 'Computer Machinery and Intelligence':

Should we not believe that He has freedom to confer a soul on a machine if He sees fit? . . . In attempting to create such machines we should not be irreverently usurping His power of creating souls, any more than we are in the procreation of children: rather we are, in either case, instruments of His will providing mansions for the souls that He creates.

"A soul is"—Helen became pensive—"a very special gift conferred on machines and children only? You, Monsieur Teste, and you, Herr Ulrich, don't have a soul? Is that why you asked me? Are you envious of my soul?"

We would never pass her test, and I didn't want to play anymore. "One more time," said Monsieur Teste. I maneuvered Odradek along the intellect axis halfway toward reason and mind into the hollows of business. I subtracted out virtue and conscience and shifted beauty and morals into neutral. Then I dialed for some of the business leaders Monsieur Teste had listed, names I knew only from gilded old magazines and the *Who's Who* from decades past: Gerstner, McNealy, and a certain Bill Gates. The soul radio dialed and dialed, ringing again and again—no answer, I was alarmed and already wondering whether —when I woke up.

Sunshine, sober and sharp, was slicing at an early morning angle through the chinks of the wooden shutters, tickling my nose and teasing my eyes open. Through a veil of light I saw the breakfast table decked with festive linen and cheerful porcelain from Austria. The water kettle was still wheezing. Wearing a hat and carrying a modish fur boa around her naked shoulders was Grete, cutting apples into my cereal. I sneezed. Without looking up, she poured the coffee. "You dreamed," she said. "It is past seven. You didn't hear the alarm clock? Oh my lover, you read too much again last night." She pulled large wooden needles out of skeins of a million lively colors and continued working on my birthday sweater that she had begun last night. Carefully, eyes closed, I put my hands on my stomach, which (thank God) was soft and warm. I pinched the skin on my back. No chitin armor had yet formed, nor did my hands and arms feel skinnier or hairier than yesterday. I had been spared another night. I resolved to spend a happy day proving the little theorem I had found the other day. And in the evening, while Grete was knitting and playing her favorite clarinet concerto on the CD player, I would read myself to sleep and dream of a world in which possibilities outnumber realities.

The End of an Elite

. . . .

by
PAUL WEST

I.

Calling yourself a Luddite is an old-fashioned way of admitting to techno-phobia. Who remembers that Ned Ludd smashed stocking machines in the early nineteenth century? I used to confess myself a Luddite, though, I who still do not own a word processor, perhaps believing still that I already have one: my head. So I move through a series of electronic type-writers priced at about a hundred dollars. Out of, or into, each I get three books, and then there is a shower of springs and bolts, indecent petulant buzzing, and the game is up. I do not acquire a word processor because I hate screens, grays, compendious instructions; I like to see words line up in black on white, and I rather enjoy the fiddling handwork I have to do to make corrections, pasting the right version on to the old one, sometimes half a dozen lines at a time, at other times clipping a sliver of paper that bears one word only, then using a smear of Elmer's to fix it in place for all the world like a narcissistic philatelist. Yet, these mundane and slimy op-erations done, I Xerox the page in question and slide it back where it be-longs, usually destroying the palimpsest.

I'm not really that much of a technophobe, I who used to draw cross sections of aircraft engines for fun, who take four aviation magazines a month, and go flying whenever I can, northward from Ithaca up to Lake Ontario until we can see Toronto, supercharging the *Apache*'s engines to some ten thousand feet. With that kind of technology I am quite besotted, yet I suppose only in a romantic way. If I had a word processor, I would want to use it only for such footling jobs as comparing all uses in a manu-script of a certain word or name: the kind of work I now do in a laborious,

39

humdrum way for which I can say only that having to do it myself makes me familiar with my text, often too much so. Yet it is heartening and soothing to be so minutely in touch with my own material, unlike Villiers de l'Isle Adam, who wrote about letting our servants do our living for us—or at least our donkeywork. True, I admire the pretty laser printouts of my more sophisticated friends, whereas my own final versions have a muddied, wonky look with undulating margins and weird little shadows created by paper buildup under the harsh inspectorial eye of the Xerox light. My fantasy is that editors come to relish these artisan oddities of mine, quietly assuming my heart is in the right place and that, with a sigh of belief, I know writing is a matter of hands-on, paper, glue, and scissor work. After all, I need not strive officiously to be hospitable to machines: a pacemaker guides my awkward heart, often leading me to call myself bionic. On the other hand, my hands seem allergic to paper; the skin cracks and bleeds, then cracks again, and I am often garlanded with Band-Aids, impeded by them, unable to feel things. And I often go to bed, or out to shop, with little slips of paper stuck to my wrists or face, having been unable to sense their adherence, like loyal advertisers. Here is one, an inch long by three-sixteenths, bearing the single word *theodicyy,* unused because misspelled because mistyped, and caught up in a whirlwind of glue that transferred it yesterday to my hand like a snippet of cabbage-white butterfly.

Why, then, do I *not* have a word processor, with so many worthwhile reasons at hand? I find in the newspaper that university students, equipped with computer facilities in the dorm, have enormous trouble when moving out into lodgings still not modernized. I wonder why they never invest in a lined yellow tablet. *Writing* is my mystery, not computing. I am willing to let an inventor's genie invade my imagination and its tricks only to a certain point. I loved the golden hum of my first electric typewriter, the twinkle of its red spot, the way it made the music-weather channel tremble on the screen when I rolled its knurled knob back and forth. Paper is a mystery to me, so close to the book. Writing is almost a form of origami. I find writing, especially at its most stylish, sculptural. I began as a painter who preferred doing collages. You see, I haven't quite worked out my pros and cons, and I continue typing in an unstable interim, waiting for the Smith-Corona firm to go bankrupt, which it did, only to retrieve itself; for some deus ex machina, anyway, to intervene and close me down. I do nothing by way of pen and pencil because I can no longer decipher my handwriting, and with so many Band-Aids in position, I find implements hard to control. It is quite a farce, really, this setting things down, but my De Ville 470s serve me well enough; I am hardly aware of what my fingers touch, and I often look away. Sometimes I think I am playing piano, which I cannot do, but I hear rhythms in my tapping and sometimes, Glenn Gould-like, I chant as I go to remind myself of what's coming in the next few lines. I just don't want to have to *think* about the gadgets I use. I don't have enough time to learn that new trick. Or so I tell myself, when the real reason is indifference to booklets of instruction full of self-important and ill-couched imperatives, none of which I wish to heed. I even lost the how-to booklet for this Smith-Corona, so I no longer know how to make things blacker without typing them twice. Help: I live in a muddle in a crammed room full of unopened suitcases and unemptied wastepaper bins, with old manuscripts stacked on top of one another and rising past six feet like a squishy skyscraper.

I ought to know better, but I keep managing to get the next book done. In one novelist's house I once saw her writing room and marveled at the austerity of its table: mahogany, violently polished, with the typewriter sitting near the edge, no dust, no spots of spilled Liquid Paper or correction fluid, no scrapes, no scratches, no fluff. I could have worked in there, with a gorgeous sense of intrudership, but I might not have survived without my mess around me, some of which is books, some cotton swabs, some boxes of pills, a tiny ten-year-old radio for classical music, a Turkish carpet to keep my bare feet warm in winter, and all the windows curtained tight. Idiosyncratic of course, both the mess (or the fertile muddle of Forster) and my refusal to devote time to certain things. I'm willing to check my blood sugar at a certain time, and I take a perverse pleasure in that, but none of my time goes to reading instruction manuals, or transferring everything from my old address book to a new one.

Are these the persuasions of a Luddite, then? Or the shibboleths of a successful idosyncrasy? Between the muddle that works well and the streamline that might go better, I choose the muddle until I lose my grip, can't see, can't remember, can't feel, can't count. And so on. I, who adore the fax and the Xerox machine, as well as my pacemaker and the tiny computer that counts my needled-out blood sugar, make my stand, once forbidden by its new, neophyte editor to send *Islands* copy not on a floppy disk. Who cares? As I do this, the paper rolls away and down, imprinted, lank, and magical. And then, shivering, it wafts away from me and out.

. . . .

II.

I am specifying a degree of comfort with my chosen vocation, much as some people feel more at home in front of an audience than in it. Ideally, I write nude, seated on a thick towel, and perhaps with a second towel around me. Something atavistic prevails and helps me relax. Clearly I am an example of the egotistical sublime, or the infinite I am. After thirty years at it, I am most at home writing in the style I'm notorious for; writing otherwise wouldn't please me, even though it might muster to my cause some epithets that rarely come my way—clean, lean, austere, terse, taut, unfancy, and so forth, these the terms usually applied to writers who seem not to have had too much pleasure in doing their work. The literary firmament swarms with pundits who caution against the sensuous or the elaborate, as if well-written prose were an infection: from the primrose path to the psychopath. One biodegradable twit of a reviewer recently chided me for taking too much interest in my illnesses, subject of *A Stroke of Genius,* the book in question.

No, I am the central, generative mental cell, doting on the spirit ditties of no tone, enriching what is lush because the planet is a plenty, a *foison,* to which we should pay tribute. Emersonian and Wordsworthian, yes, with at root a private sense of the universe, a sense worth spelling out and colorfully amplifying. I adore utterly unprecedented combinations of familiar words, such as the phrase "celibate gusto" that came to me the other day in all its complexity and suggestiveness, requiring of the reader (I would think) some scenario building, some investigation of both concepts. If gusto is not usually celibate but thrives in a sexual communion, then what sort of act or state is celibate gusto? A character presented in such terms will activate the reader's imagination, and I will have used only two words. Intense phrasing is not imperative in writing, but it has animated much of our best from Shakespeare to Nabokov, and it is to style, some compressed emanation from the personality, that I devote, even sacrifice, myself, knowing full well how the opposition hates prose that isn't plain, that has as much personality as a person does, that tempts the mind to extaordinary recognitions (*Speak, Memory,* for example). I never needed to learn that prose was malleable, not a mere tool for exposition, but a magic lantern revealing the blessed mixture of the world.

Of course, sentiments such as these are anathema to the squares, the minimalists, the bullyboy reviewers, the latter-day puritans, and, I am afraid, the vast majority of people who style themselves writers, rotting

. . . .

perceptibly somewhere between immigrant English and mindless jargon. No doubt that I am one of the doomed, at some point to be eradicated as a sensual radical, a libidinous witch doctor, a merchant of the burnished baroque. Yet I thrive on this, the penultimate phase of my jubilee, heedless of the knock that will sound on my intellectual door as the gestapo of the plain prose party arrive to haul me off for having espoused the pleasure principle too long. When the semiliterates have organized themselves even more thoroughly than they already have at the publishing houses and the magazines, phrasemakers such as I will be the first to go, and a small platoon we will be, disdained by book editors who cannot spell and magazine editors who equate literature with gossip or the facetious. The only thing to do is go down with all guns firing, not so much in hope of achieving anything but, as Matthew Arnold said, to keep alive a needed attitude while homogenizing philistines take over and John Grisham replaces Samuel Beckett. I envision the death of the elite by, say, 2020, though it may come before. As I have said many times already, those of us who taught at the university level have much to answer for, now that the mediocrities to whom we gave Bs inherit the earth. We should have failed them when we had chance. We already have a new generation, deafened by drums, that sees no point in lingering on anything written. Soon everything will be abridged, and then those abridgements will be abridged, until great works become hiccups and burps. By then (it is happening already, even in the Ivy League), departments of English will have mutated downward into departments of popular culture.

Identifiable clouds on the horizon come to mind and stick in the throat. Your prose is too atmospheric, one magazine tells a distinguished contributor. I can't stand any prose more complex, croons one editor, than somebody saying Hi. The novel of righteous uplift, akin to the socialist realist tractor novels of unlamented Russians, has the literati by the shorthairs. Carefully fostered in the high schools, the colleges, and the grand campuses, this decadence achieves its consummation in the self-righteous banalities of National Public Radio. Nobody dares insult anybody any more, which means of course that taste is almost dead, and television has become a more blatant form of the big catalogue it always was. Do-gooders debate the place of prayer in schools, but who cares about the place in them of reading? I gave up teaching undergraduates (seniors, mostly) when I saw I was teaching elementary grammar rather than the writing of fiction.

Suffice to say that I am comfortable in my role of prose maker; ultimately you create your art for yourself or because nobody else is writing what you can bear to read. Slowly the caliber of publishing falls and a giant cartel of demure glossy magazines begins to form to witness the funeral of literary writing, serious fiction, call it what you will. Millions are already troughing on trash and cannot be stopped. The novelist has no standing in America, certainly not as much as the comedian, the madam, and the talk-show host. We novelists resemble the composers of serious American music whose previous symphonies go as unremembered as our previous novels. Nobody has a memory any more, which means that each novel you publish is always your first one, again and again. When did we last hear the novelist mentioned on CNN? Even poets get more attention. It's not that the novel is dead or dying, as we used to say, but that the reading public is, infantilized by a meretricious educational system obsessed with civics, etiquette, social disadvantage and, later, at the college level, PC, which to me means Prissy Courtesy. Imagine that rarity, the person whose first and final loyalty is to the language, whereas to most, language is like greaseproof paper, the Ziploc plastic bag, Kleenex—useful and anonymous. Some publishers actually still try to promote your new novel, sending you to the Coast to read, say, and points in between; others let it slide out into the world like a ruby onto manure, faintly jubilant at having launched an entrant in the editorial stakes. Perhaps, to be realistic about our profession, we should intend only to gratify ourselves on those midnights when we slink to the bookshelf and caress a certain favored volume, like Magda Goebbels fondling her children after poisoning them all. People ask me if we have any future, and I answer: we have no past; to forget it is to lose it. Those who can't identify Hitler or Stalin have never had Melville or Virgil Thomson, Emerson or Rauschenberg. The idea is preposterous. If culture, as Eliot once announced with dismal severity, is what the people do—*whatever* they do—then culture of late has undergone a dreadful narrowing. Our civilization bites the dust to the sounds of amplified guitars and words so badly enunciated they mean nothing and might be assigned back to the simians. Oh, culture of some sort clusters still around universities or in tony nooks among the mountains, but in the main the prose, the music, of the unlettered has taken over, and hoi polloi stumble around among abstract nouns trying to relate them to one another with misused words such as hopefully, and Ms. Faye Resnick, aspirant witness to a sleazy trial, hears educated lawyers calling her articulate when, in fact, her hold on the written or spoken language is slithery and tenuous, she too bogged down in abstract nouns that for her carry an overtone of abstruse gentility.

. . . .

Unless the rot be stopped, our illiterates and semi-illiterates will have fancier and glossier machines with which to preside over the end of intelligent living. No doubt we are already the glum beneficiaries of an Information Explosion, by means of which the newly enfranchised busybodies of the Internet give flesh to the old idea that we can never know everything about anything. Against randomly acquired electronic knowledge I can only adduce my fear that the known will amass itself somewhere—in cyberspace, no doubt—like some glabrous, wasteful sponge big as the Pacific. Fact will supplant taste. But, perhaps, we are on the brink of a new age in which learning, study, scholarship will abandon the synecdoche method (a fraction standing for all) and for the first time seek to expose the full texture of culture, and there will never again be neglected authors, mathematicians, composers, painters, philosophers, and so forth. Maybe, too, the Internet will serve to mitigate loneliness; everyone will always have someone to talk to, or conversations to eavesdrop on. A novel in the form of such an open-ended, amorphous exchange probably exists already. Why not? I myself have recently finished what may well be the first novel composed in another galaxy and transmitted to Earth as one decipherable, almost interminable, word, warts and all. The chance is that we have not been using our imaginations enough, and I predict an enormous access in the irresponsibility allowed in conversational exchange. Verbal ballet will replace dutiful epistemology.

I try to look on the bright side. We live in an age of covert censorship, in which sly middlebrows dictate the course and fabric of an art form. Wynton Marsalis, for instance, presiding over the much-denounced *Jazz from Lincoln Center,* qualifies as a leading reactionary and even, some have said, a racist. For a long time, NPR treated us to *Jazz Revisited,* a scholarly treatise of a program on the radio, only half an hour but estimable (though it played too little swing). It's lost now, relegated to an inconspicuous different time. Marsalis has his equivalents in publishing, of course; looking at the review media, especially, one is reminded of the old Soviet Encyclopedia, in which certain persons never appeared, having been unpersoned. What we have, clustering in Manhattan, is a suburban-minded oligarchy who have forced back into currency such antagonistic terms as Pollyanna, Milquetoast, and wholesome, its aim being to protect the public from the harsh world or foreign influences, giving them instead a literature like fungus, without wit, savor, or brains. I don't know how many articles the public can stand about how one novelist reads his manuscripts to his apparently long-suffering wife, but surely we are due for a few. Nobody has called the organs of review on this astonishing bit of Soviet strategy, but the muttering in the trade is fierce, and the hoax cannot last much longer. Or so one hopes, mortified by a simple, open-minded comparison with what goes on in France, where literature still seems not to be a windup bathroom toy for complacent middlebrow boobies.

III.

French readers take a compulsive, missionary interest in literature, books new and old, actually going so far as to call their return from their summer holidays *La Rentrée Littéraire,* the return to serious reading, which of course is the year's most serious obligation. When a nation adjusts its calendar in so decisive a way, you not only respect its readers, you also wonder what happens to books in the United States, where pundits blather about beach reading and authors type books aimed at the audience on the littoral. There is no mention of *our* return to serious reading, or even of a departure from fluff, trash, slop, drivel, twaddle (one needs these words nowadays more than ever).

I recall an essay by Leon Edel in which, as a GI sitting at a café table just after the Liberation of Paris in 1945, he rejoiced to be in a country that celebrated the arts, a city that revered them, going several steps beyond the Anglo-American euphoria that saw VE Day in philistine terms. Surely, here is the model for the city of the future. How many Hawthorne, Melville, Emerson streets are there in New York, never mind streets named for Stevens, Crane, or Barnes? Generals and trees abound, as do local worthies and Indian words, but authors do not rate. I can only recall the amazement I felt when I moved in once on the rue Sainte-Beuve, named for a dry critic whose *Causeries de Lundi* I had dipped into while a graduate student at Columbia. How real he became as I trod his street with its chemist's blue neon sign at one end. London has plaques, but Paris has its Rue Lord-Byron, not to mention its Rue Rabelais, Rue Molière, Rue Chateaubriand: almost good anough, but no street consecrated to Colette, Proust, and Gide. Paris will have to catch up if it is going to merit the outright homage I have ready for it. I want it perfect.

Suffice to say that, although I have been lucky enough to receive scores of excellent reviews in English, it is to my French critics that I turn for solace, keenly afflicted perhaps by the fact that it was upon French literature that I suckled myself as a student, devouring Camus, Sartre, Malraux, Baudelaire, Mallarmé, and Char. I had lots of ideas my English contempo-

. . . .

raries giggled at, all the way from adolescence to young manhood: French or Latin American notions. There was a chauvinistic parochialism I had to get away from, much as now, in the U.S.A., there is a mediocre sameness spawned in the M.F.A. programs by self-styled protectors of the American grain. That's where all these homespun novelists come from, fretting about real estate, baseball gloves, and that first car. A born cosmopolite, I always encouraged my own M.F.A. students to immerse themselves at least in literature in translation (if comparative literature was too demanding). Quite a few of them found their way to Robbe-Grillet, Queneau, and Sarraute, to name only French authors, and began to write (as I think of it) internationally. In the U.S. in the main, however, you have young authors who have read only one another and suck up to the same fatuities, writing anonymously a purée acquired from dunderheads to whom the *Atlantic Monthly,* with its oddly menstrual name, is the Holy Grail. Heaven protect us from such nebbishry. Things will improve, I suspect, only when people get rude again and go after the brokers of a timid, broken literature, by which time some of us will be gone, one way or another, to greener pastures.

IV.

Having a literary career (a phrase that merits quotation marks, depending on one's mood) is to ride your writing sled through all vicissitudes. How things tumble in at the door. All in one day, for instance, which happens to be today, there arrive copies of the *Yale Review* in which the rubric "fiction" pairs me with Nabokov (the sensation is that of a sudden chairlift), and an anthology of short fiction in which the editor prints a story of his own, a long one, although he is a nonentity as a fiction writer, and no sign in the pages of aforesaid Nabokov, or Beckett, or Borges, or Gass, or Davenport or any other members of the small platoon I keep in mind.

    With all this stuff hitting the fan around you, you learn what it is that you do, with head down, honoring the language as best you can, aspiring to the art you trained yourself upon, not letting them get to you. If this be aestheticism, then so be it; I am an aesthete. Somebody has to try to write beautiful sentences while the mob frets about morals and too much energy and too much style. Now and then the lice who loll upon literature disturb you, but you overlook them, not so much echoing Vlad the Impaler's shout of *The view from up here's just fine!* as mouthing a mantra that says the novel is an esplanade for intercoiled voices and rhythmic, highly active sentences. Almost any mantra will do, so long as it shuts out the quantity surveyors of literature who, without knowing what it is, know what it's for. It is hard to concentrate on work while the riffraff pontificate, but only so long as you believe you should write within the expectations of the reading public, to whom you are some kind of servant, purveyor, tipster. While the mob gropes about for some rule that will forbid the mixing of satire with tragedy, you mix whatever devil's broth you fancy, certain that novel-writing is an inward operation of the spirit, as they used to say in the eighteenth century, and all climbers, asslickers, brownnosers, poseurs, debaters, and prize oglers can go jump. You have to leave the manipulators to manipulate; if they had a fire in the bowels, or a vision in the skull, they would have no time for trifling with footling. Get on with your work, I say, or I hear my late mother saying the same thing. After all, if I had posed the question thirty years ago of "Can you have a literary career without once being reviewed by the so-called *New York Review?*" I might have answered no; but now I know, some thirty books later, the answer is yes, and then some.

I daydream of all those mute screens peered at by sleek tappers. Will the screens get noisier, or have we found a new almost monastic way of looking at type? There is going to be more type to look at and to summon up, which only brings me back to the enclosed majesty of the book, patiently awaiting our attention like any floppy disk. This Fort Knox of silence delights me. I do not much care to hear anyone read her or his work out loud, or to hear myself doing same. The holiness of the heart's affection dotes on the thereness of a book on its shelf, awaiting the silent hypergolic combustion that happens when mind touches print. The stuff is in the book because we find it more convenient that way, unlike the characters in Ray Bradbury's *Fahrenheit 451,* who each have a book memorized, lest literature disappear altogether. What is more moving than the auditory spectacle of the one who has *Remembrance of Things Past* by heart? Libraries and bookstores daunt me, mainly because there is so much I will never read, but they hearten me too, standing as they do among mundaner outlets. I cheer myself up by envisioning the electronic contemplatives of Century 21. Maybe the New York Public Library will innovate to the extent of inviting its Literary Lions to come read from their works.

Eventually those who write about my books will stop saying I am "finishing strong." I have no sense of finishing at all; indeed, I am just unharnessed from time, as committed to style as I always was because style,

. . . .

your own anyway, is symptomatically timeless, like the idea of a rocker slowly tilting back and forth on a hotel veranda facing Lake Otsego. Style is the indelible trance. Style is where you take upon yourself your own future without having to count. Style is your ID, as well as the armature of defiance. Style is the snowshoe print of the impenitent individualist to whom, of all the writers who have written, only a few matter because their tone, their cadence, their demeanor are not standard. In order to traffic with our literary ancestors, we not only have to delve into etymology (at least for those nameless ancients who gave us words); we also have to regard prose as a maneuvering toward the beautiful, way past the uilitarian and the matter-of-fact. A sacrament? Why not? Certainly a homage, paid while hoping to pass something on for the exhilaration of it.

Casting around for an emblem, as if I were choosing a coat of arms for the novelist I am, I have entertained the notion of the night-soil man, or the functionary who siphons toilet droppings from a jumbo jet. These images have not suited me for long, and just as well: too much of the collector (or collective), too little of the alembic. Nature itself supplies my latest emblem, with which I content myself for a while. In the family of the scarab, Australian *Macrocopris symbioticus* lives in the anus of the wallaby. What a superb also-ran. What a good fallout shelter in which to await the failure of nerve afflicting our shoddy civilization, much as another, according to Gilbert Murray, afflicted that of Ancient Greece.

Rupture, Verge, and Precipice
Precipice, Verge, and Hurt Not

.   .   .   .

by
CAROLE MASO

> Be not afraid. The isle is full of noises,
> Sounds and sweet airs that give delight and hurt not.
> WILLIAM SHAKESPEARE

YOU ARE AFRAID. You are afraid, as usual, that the novel is dying. You think you know what a novel is: it's the kind you write. You fear you are dying.

You wonder where the hero went.

You wonder how things could have gotten so out of hand.

You ask where is one sympathetic, believable character?

You ask where is the plot?

You wonder where on earth is the conflict? The resolution? The dénouement?

You imagine yourself to be the holder of some last truth. You imagine yourself to be in some sinking, noble, gilt-covered cradle of civilization.

You romanticize your fin de siècle, imbuing it with meaning, overtones, implications.

You are still worried about TV.

You are still worried about the anxiety of influence.

· · · · · · · · · · ·

You say there will be no readers in the future, that there are hardly any readers now. You count your measly 15,000—but you have always underestimated everything.

You say language will lose its charms, its ability to charm, its power to mesmerize.

You say the world turns, spins away, or that we turn from it. You're pretty desolate.

You mutter a number of the usual things. You say, ". . . are rust," ". . . are void" ". . . are torn."

You think you know what a book is, what reading is, what constitutes a literary experience. In fact you've been happy all these years to legislate the literary experience. All too happy to write the rules.

You think you know what the writer does, what the reader does. You're pretty smug about it.

You think you know what the reader wants: a good old-fashioned story.

You think you know what a woman wants: a good old-fashioned—

You find me obnoxious, uppity. You try to dismiss me as hysterical or reactionary or out of touch because I won't enter that cozy little pact with you anymore. Happy little subservient typing "my" novel, the one you've been dictating all these years.

You rely on me to be dependent on you for favors, publication, $$$$$$$$, canonization.

You are afraid. Too smug in your middle ground with your middlebrow. Everything threatens you.

You say music was better then: the Rolling Stones, the Who, the Beatles, Fleetwood Mac. You're boring me.

You say hypertext will kill print fiction. You pit one against the other in the most cynical and transparent ways in hopes we'll tear each other to bits

while you watch. You like to watch. Hold us all in your gaze.

Just as you try to pit writing against theory, prose against poetry, film against video, etc., as you try to hold on to your little piece of the disappearing world.

But I, for one, am on to you. Your taste for blood, your love of competition, your need to feel endangered, beleaguered, superior. Your need to reiterate, to reassert your power, your privilege, because it erodes.

Let's face it, you're panicked.

You think an essay should have a hypothesis, a conclusion, should argue points. You really do bore me.

You'd like to put miraculous, glowing glyphs on a screen on one side and modest ink on pretty white paper on the other. You set up, over and over, false dichotomies. Easy targets. You reduce almost everything, as I reduce you now. Tell me, how does it feel?

You're real worried. You say sex will be virtual. The casting couch, virtual. But you know as well as I do that all the other will continue, you betcha, so why are you so worried?

You fear your favorite positions are endangered. Will become obsolete.

You believe you have more to lose than other people in other times.

You romanticize the good old days—the record skipping those nights long ago while you were making love, while you were having real sex with —

Hey, was that me? The Rolling Stones crooning: "I see a red door and I want it painted black, painted black, painted black . . ."

Want it painted black.

Or: "Brown Sugar, how come you dance so good, dance so good, dance so good . . . ???"

You want to conserve everything. You worship false prophets. You're sick over your (dwindling) reputation.

You're so cavalier, offering your hand. . . .

Jenny Holzer: "The future is stupid."

. . . .

I remember the poet-dinosaurs that evening at the dinner table munching on their leafy greens, going extinct even as they spoke, whispering "language poetry" (that was the evil that night), shuddering.

You fear the electronic ladyland. Want it painted black.

You're afraid of junk food. The real junk food and the metaphoric junk food the media feeds you. Want it painted black . . .

painted black.

You fear the sylist (as you have defined style) will perish.

You consider certain art forms to be debased and believe that in the future all true artists will disappear. Why do you believe other forms to be inferior to your own?

You consider certain ways of thinking about literature to be debased. You can't decide whether they're too rigorous or too reckless, or both.

Edmund Wilson, Alfred Kazin, Harold Bloom *et fils*—make my day.

You think me unladylike. Hysterical. Maybe crazy. Unreadable. You put me in your unreadable box where I am safe. Where I am quiet. More ladylike.

In your disdainful box labeled "experimental." Labeled "do not open." Labeled "do not review."

You see a red door and you want it painted black.

No more monoliths.

You who said "hegemony" and "domino theory" and "peace with honor."

All the deaths for nothing. All the dark roads you've led us down. No more.

The future: where we're braced always for the next unspeakably monstrous way to die—or to kill.

All the dark deserted roads you've led me down, grabbing at my breasts, tearing at my shirt, my waistband: first date.

Second date: this is how to write a book.

Third date: good girl! Let's publish it!!!

Brown Sugar, how come you dance so good?

Fourth date: will you marry me?

You fear the future, OK. You fear anything new. Anything that disrupts your sense of security and self. Everything threatens you.

Where is the change over the course of the thing in the hero?

Where is the hero?

Where's the conflict? Where the hell is the dénouement?

I see your point. But haven't you asked us to write your fiction for just a little too long now? Couldn't we —

Couldn't we, maybe just possibly, coexist?

Why does my existence threaten yours?

It's been too long now that you've asked me to be you. Insisted I be you.

Lighten up. Don't be so afraid. Put up your hand. Say: Bunny, Alfred, Harold, bye-bye.

You fear. You fear the television. You loathe and adore the television.

You feel numbed and buzzed by so much electronics. Numbed and buzzed by so much future.

I'm getting a little tired of this "you" and "I." Still I am learning a few new things about you — and about me.

The future of literature. The death of the novel. You love, for some reason, the large, glitzy questions and statements. But the question bores me — and all the usual ways of thinking and speaking and writing anymore.

I'm sorry you are so afraid. You want it to be something like the movie *2001*, the future. You want it to be ludicrous, the future, easily dismissable. Like me. If only I didn't dance so good. You demand to know, How come

you dance so good, dance so good, dance so good . . . ???

You can't see a place for yourself in it and it frightens you. You dig in your heels as a result. Spend all your considerable intelligence and energy con-

. . . .

serving, preserving, holding court, posturing, tenaciously holding on, now as you munch your last green leaves, yum.

Where is the resolution of the conflict? Where the fuck is the conflict?

What if a book might also include, might also be, the tentative, the hesitant, the doubt you most fear and despise?

Lyn Hejinian: "Closure is misanthropic."

Fear of growth, fear of change, fear of breaking one's own mold, fear of disturbing the product, fear of ridicule, fear of indifference, fear of failure, fear of invisibility, fear of, fear of, fear of. . . .

You say that language will cease to be respected, will no longer move us. But we're already becoming numb thanks to what you are afraid to give up. What you flood the market with.

Soyinka: "I am concerned about preserving a special level of communication, a level very different from Oprah Winfrey."

Wish: that all Oprah Winfrey fiction be put to bed now. Its fake psychologies, its "realisms." Its pathetic 2 plus 2.

Language of course has an enormous capacity to lie, to make false shapes, to be glib, to make common widgets, three parts this and two parts that.

Wish: that all the fiction of lies be put to bed.

That the dishonesty running rampant through much contemporary fiction be recognized as such.

What deal must I strike in order to be published by you? What pose, bargain, stance, is it I must strike with you now?

What mold do you make of me to pour your elixir, your fluid into, and then reward?

The bunny mold? The kitten mold? The flower mold? The damaged flower mold? Pregnant at twelve, illiterate, but with a twist? The gay mold? The white trash mold? The battered child mold? The bad girl mold?

Paint me black. Paint me Latina. Paint me Native American. Paint me Asian and then pour me into your mold. Use me. Co-opt me. Market me.

Debase me and in the future I shall rise anew out of your cynicism and scorn—smiling, lovely, free.

I know a place that burns brighter than a million suns.

Wish list: that the business people who have taken over the publishing houses will focus themselves elsewhere and leave the arts alone again.

Not to own or colonize or dominate. . . .

Despite all efforts to tame it, manage it, control it, outsmart it, language resists your best efforts; language is still a bunch of sturdy, glittering charms in the astonished hand.

A utopia of possibility. A utopia of choice.

And I am huddled around the fire of the alphabet, still.

Even though you say one word next to the other will cease to be cherished.

You say rap music is poison. Hypertext is poison.

Even though you call me sentimental—on the one hand girly-girl, on the other hand loud-mouthed bitch, on the one hand interesting and talented writer, on the other hand utterly out-of-touch idealist, romantic—it is you who wants the nineteenth century back again. When things were dandy for you, swell. You want to believe in the old coordinates, the old shapes. To believe in whatever it was you believed in then. You were one of the guys who dictated the story, sure, I remember. Who made up the story and now go teaching it all over the place. But even then, when you sat around making it up, even then, my friend, it had nothing to do with me. With my world. With what I saw and how I felt.

Wish: that all graduate writing programs with their terminal degrees, stop promoting such tiresome recipes for success or go (financially) bankrupt.

Your false crescendos. Climaxes. False for me, at any rate.

The future is all the people who've ever been kept out, singing.

In the future everything will be allowed.

So the future is for you, too. Not to worry. *But not only for you.*

For you, but not only for you.

. . . .

Not to discard the canon, but to enlarge it.

No more monoliths. No more Mick Jaggers. No more O. J. Simpsons. No more James Joyces. No more heroes.

Everything threatens you. Hacks, hackers, slacks, slackers, cybergirls with their cybercurls and wiles, poets of every sort. Rock bands with girls.

You believe your (disappearing) time represents some last golden age of enlightenment, to be guarded, protected, reproduced against the approaching mindlessness, depravity, electronic states of America.

But maybe as you become more and more threatened, you'll take a few more risks yourself. Who knows? Anything is possible in the future.

Wish list: that the homogeneity end. That the mainstream come to acknowledge, for starters, the thousand refracted, disparate beauties out there.

That the writers and the readers stop being treated by the mainstream houses like idiot children. That the business people get out and stop imposing their "taste" on everyone.

Wish: that as writers we be aware of our own desire to incorporate, even unconsciously, the demands and anxieties of publishers and reject them, the demands and anxieties of the marketplace.

That the business people go elsewhere.

Market me. Promote me. Sanitize me. Co-opt me. Plagiarize me. Market me harder.

Wish list: that the grade inflation for a certain kind of writing stop, and that the middlebrow writers assume their middle position so that everyone else might finally have a place, too. Be considered seriously, too. Be read, too.

Paint me black. Paint me Latina. Paint me Chinese. Pour me into your mold and sell me harder.

Fuck me (over) harder.

Those of us jockeying for position in the heavens, intent on forever, major reputations, major motion pictures and $$$$$$$$, life after life after life after death, forget about it.

Wish: that straight white males reconsider the impulse to cover the entire world with their words, fill up every page, every surface, everywhere.

Thousand-page novels, tens and tens of vollmanns—I mean volumes.

Not to own or colonize or dominate anymore.

"Well, we've been kept from ourselves too long, don't you think?" an old woman in Central Park says to a friend.

Two women in the park at dusk.

Turn the beat around:

The pauses and rhythms and allowances of Laurie Anderson. The glow of Jenny Holzer. The ranting and passion of Courtney Love. Brilliance of Susan Howe. Brilliance of Erin Mouré. Theresa Cha. Visionary P. J. Harvey.

The future is feminine, for real, this time.

The future is Emily Dickinson and Emily Brontë and Gertrude Stein still. The future is still Maya Deren and Billie Holiday.

Language is a rose and the future is still a rose, opening.

It is beautiful there in the future. Irreverent, wild.

The future is women, for real this time. I'm sorry, but it's time you got used to it.

Reading on a train by the light the river gives. The woman next to me asleep. Two plastic bags at her feet. Lulling, lovely world. And I am witness to it all—that slumber—and then her awakening—so vulnerable, sensation streaming back, the world returned, the river and the light the river gives, returning language, touch, and smell. The world retrieved. I am privileged to be next to her as she moves gracefully from one state to the next, smiling slightly. I recognize her delight. It is taken away, and it is given back. The miracle and mystery of this life in one middle-aged black woman on the Metro North next to me. The Hudson River widening.

Let all of this be part of the story, too. A woman dreaming next to water.

The future: all the dreams we've been kept from. All the things yet to dream.

An opening of possibility. A land of a thousand dances.

I want sex and hypersex and cybersex, why not?

The river mysteriously widening, as she opens her eyes.

We can say, if we like, that the future will be plural.

Our voices processed through many systems—or none at all.

A place where a thousand birds are singing.

"The isle is full of noises. . . ."

A place without the usual dichotomies. No phony divisions between mind and body, intelligence and passion, nature and technology, private and public, within and without, male and female.

May we begin a dialogue there in the future. May we learn something from each other. Electronic writing will help us to think about impermanence, facility, fragility and freedom, spatial intensities, irreverences, experimentation, new worlds, clean slates. Print writing will allow us new respect for the mark on the page, the human hand, the erasure, the hesitation, the mistake.

Electronic writing will give us a deeper understanding of the instability of texts, of worlds.

Print writing will remind us of our love for the physical, for the sensual world. And for the light only a book held in one's hands can give. The book taken to bed or the beach—the words dancing with the heat and the sea—and the mouth now suddenly on my salty neck.

Electronic writing shall inspire magic. Print writing shall inspire magic. Ways to heal:

"Intoxicated with Serbian nationalist propaganda, one charge is that X took part in the murder of a Muslim civilian, F, by forcing another Muslim to bite off F's testicles."

What is a book and how might it be reimagined, opened up, transformed to accommodate all we've seen, all we've been hurt by, all that's been given, all that's been taken away:

"... deliberately infecting subjects with fatal diseases, killing 275,000 of the elderly, the deformed and other 'useless eaters' through the guise of euthanasia, and killing 112 Jews simply to fill out a university skeleton collection."

No more monoliths. No more gods.

"Let us go then, you and I. . . ."

No more sheepish, mindless devotion. No more quiet supplication.

All the dark roads you've led us down no more.

You will call me naive, childlike, irreverent, idealistic, offensive, outrageous, defiant at times, because I do not believe in a literature of limitation, in a future of limitation. I annoy you with this kind of talk, I know. You've told me many times before. You'd like me to step into my quiet box. You're so cavalier, as you offer your hand.

It sure looks like prose, but it's poetry. It sure seems to be poetry, but I think it's a novel. It just looks like a mess, really, a lot of ranting and raving and discontinuous sad and happy stuff—but it's an essay—about the future.

The future. Possibility will reign. My students poised on some new threshold. We're too diversified, we're too fractured, all too close in proximity suddenly—one world.

One wild world,

free of categories, free of denominations, dance and fiction and performance and installation and video and poetry and painting—one world—every hyper- and cyber-

And in upstate New York, a woman sees fields of flax and iris and cattails, and dreams of making paper. And dreams of creating an Art Farm—a place just for experimenting with unusual indigenous fibers, a real space for bookbinding, an archive, a library, a gallery.

Dream: that this new tolerance might set a tone, give an example. This openness in acceptance of texts, of forms, this freedom, this embrace will serve as models for how to live. Will be the model for a new world order—in my dream. A way to live together better—in my dream.

Godard: "A film like this, it's a bit as if I wanted to write a sociological essay in the form of a novel, and all I had to do it with was notes of music. Is that what cinema is? And am I right to continue doing it?"

But I do believe, and no doubt childishly, unquestioningly, in the supremacy of beauty, in pattern, in language, as a child believes in language, in diversity, in the possibility of justice—even after everything we have seen—in the impulse to speak—even after everything.

"Peder Davis, a bouncy, tow-headed five-year-old, shook his head and said, 'I would tell him: You shoot down this building? You put it back together.

And I would say, You redo those people.'"

One hundred and sixty-eight dead in Oklahoma bombing.

"Peder said he drew 'a house with eyes that was blue on the sides.' He explained, 'It was the building that exploded, in heaven.'"

Wish: that writing again, through its audacity, generosity, possibility, irreverence, wildness, teach us how to better live.

The world doesn't end.

The smell of the air. The feel of the wind in late April.

You can't have a genuine experience of nature except in nature. You can't have a genuine experience of language except in language. And for those of us for whom language is the central drama, the captivating, imaginative, open, flexible act, there can never be a substitute or a replacement.

Language continually opening new places in me.

A picture of a bird will never be a bird. And a bird will never be a picture of a bird. So relax.

The world doesn't end, my friend. So stop your doomsday song. Or Matthew Arnold: "The end is everywhere: Art still has truth, take refuge there."

All will perish, but not this: language opening like a rose.

And many times I have despaired over the limits of language, the recalcitrance of words that refuse to yield, won't glimmer, won't work anymore. All the outmoded forms. Yet I know it is part of it, I know that now; it's part of the essential mystery of the medium—and that all of us who are in this thing for real have to face this, address this, love this, even.

The struggles with shape, with silence, with complacency. The impossibility of the task.

You say destined to perish, death of the novel, end of fiction, over and over.

But Matthew Arnold, on the cusp of another century, dreams: art.

And I say faced with the eternal mysteries, one, if so inclined, will make fictive shapes.

What it was like to be here. To hold your hand.

An ancient impulse, after all.

As we reach, trying to recapture an original happiness, pleasure, peace—

Reaching—

The needs that language mirrors and engenders and satisfies are not going away. And are not replaceable.

The body with its cellular alphabet. And, in another alphabet, the desire to get that body onto the page.

There will be works of female sexuality, finally.

Feminine shapes.

All sorts of new shapes. Language, a rose, opening.

It's greater than we are, than we'll ever be. That's why I love it. Kneeling at the altar of the impossible. The self put back in its proper place.

The miracle of language. The challenge and magic of language.

Different than the old magic. I remember you liked to saw women in half and put them back together, once. Configure them in ways most pleasing to you.

. . . .

You tried once to make language conform. Obey. You tried to tame it. You tried to make it sit, heel, jump through hoops.

You like to say I am reckless. You like to say I lack discipline. You say my work lacks structure. I've heard it a hundred times from you. But nothing could be farther from the truth.

In spite of everything, my refusal to hate you, to take you all that seriously, to be condescended to—

Still, too often I have worried about worldly things. Too often have I worried about publishing, about my so-called career, fretted over the so-so-writers who are routinely acclaimed, rewarded, given biscuits and other treats—this too small prison of self where I sometimes dwell.

Too often I have let the creeps upset me.

The danger of the sky.

The danger of April.

If you say language is dying. . . .

Susan Howe: "Poetry is redemption from pessimism."

April in the country. Already so much green. So much life. So much. Even with half the trees still bare. Poking up through the slowly warming earth, the tender shoots of asparagus. Crocus. Bloodroot.

This vulnerable and breakable heart.

As we dare to utter something, to commit ourselves, to make a mark on a page or a field of light.

To incorporate this dangerous and fragile world. All its beauty. All its pain.

You who said "hegemony" and "domino theory" and "peace with honor."

To not only tolerate but welcome work that is other than the kind we do.

To incorporate the ache of Vietnam, the mistake of it, incapable of being erased or changed. To invent forms that might let that wound stand—

If we've learned anything, yet.

Summer 1885

Brother and Sister's Friend—

"Sweet Land of Liberty" is a superfluous Carol till it concerns ourselves—then it outrealms the Birds . . .

Your Hollyhocks endow the House, making Art's inner Summer, never
Treason to Nature's. Nature will be closing her Picnic when you return to
America, but you will ride Home by sunset, which is far better.

I am glad you cherish the Sea. We correspond, though I never met him.

I write in the midst of Sweet-Peas and by the side of Orioles, and could
put my hand on a Butterfly, only he withdraws.

Touch Shakespeare for me.

"Be not afraid. The isle is full of noises, Sounds and sweet airs that give
delight and hurt not."

Fifty years now since World War II. She sits in the corner and weeps.

And hurt not.

Six million dead.

"Well, we've been kept from ourselves long enough, don't you think?"

We dare to speak. Trembling, and on the verge.

Extraordinary things have been written. Extraordinary things will continue to be written.

Nineteen ninety-five: vinyl makes its small comeback. To the teenage
music freak, to the classical music fiend, and to the opera queen, CDs are
now being disparaged as producing too cold, too sanitary a sound. Vinyl
is being sought out again for its warmer, richer quality.

Wish: that we be open-minded and generous. That we fear not.

That the electronic page understand its powers and its limitations. Nothing replaces the giddiness one feels at the potential of hypertext. Entirely
new shapes might be created, different ways of thinking, of perceiving.

Kevin Kelly, executive director of *Wired* magazine: "The first thing discovered by Jaron Lanier [the virtual reality pioneer] is to say what is reality? We get to ask the great questions of all time: what is life? What is
human? What is civilization? And you ask it not in the way the old

. . . .

philosophers asked it, sitting in armchairs, but by actually trying it. Let's try and *make* life. Let's try and *make* community."

And now the Extropians, who say they can achieve immortality by downloading the contents of the human brain onto a hard disk. . . .

So turn to the students. Young visionaries. Who click on the Internet, the cyberworld in their sleep. Alvin Lu: citizen of the universe, the whole world at his fingertips. In love with the blinding light out there, the possibility, world without end, his love of all that is the future.

Let the fictions change shape, grow, accommodate. Let the medium change if it must; the artist persists.

You say all is doomed, but I say Julio Cortázar. I say Samuel Beckett. I say Marcel Proust. Virginia Woolf. I say García Lorca and Walt Whitman. I say Mallarmé. I say Ingeborg Bachmann. *The Apu Trilogy* will lie next to *Hamlet*. *Vivre sa vie* will live next to *Texts for Nothing*.

These fragmented prayers.

Making love around the fire of the alphabet.

Wish: that we not hurt each other purposely anymore.

A literature of love. A literature of tolerance. A literature of difference.

Saving the best of what was good in the old. Not to discard indiscriminately, but not to hold on too tightly, either. To go forward together, unthreatened for once.

The future is Robert Wilson and JLG. The future is Martha Graham, still. The vocabularies of dance, of film, of performance.

The disintegration of categories.

If you say that language is dying, then what do you know of language?

I am getting a little tired of this you-and-I bit. But it tells me one important thing: *that I do not want it to have to be this way.* I do not believe it has to continue this way—you over there alternately blustery and cowering, me over here, defensive, angry.

Wish: a sky that is not divided. A way to look at the screen of the sky with its grandeur, its weather, its color, its patterns of bird flight, its airplanes and accidents and poisons, its mushroom clouds.

Its goldfinches frescoed against an aqua-blue dome.

Wish: that the sky go on forever. That we stop killing each other. That we allow each other to live.

April 1995 in New York City and the long-awaited Satyajit Ray Festival begins. For years he's been kept from us. Who decides, finally, what is seen, what is read, and why? And how much else has been deleted, omitted, neglected, ignored, buried, treated with utter indifference or contempt?

And in conversation with the man, my friend, a famous poet in fact, and the topic moved to someone we both knew who had just been operated on; and he said "masectomy," and I said back, "Yes, a mastectomy, a mastectomy," and he said "masectomy" like "vasectomy," and I said only under my breath, "It's mas*tec*tomy, idiot," ashamed, embarrassed, and a little intimidated, that was the worst part, a little unsure. That it made me question what I of course knew, that was the worst part—because of his easy confidence saying "masectomy," his arrogance, he hadn't even bothered to learn the right word, a *poet,* for God's sake, a man who worked with words, who should have known the right word for the removal of a breast, don't you think?

Mastectomy.

The undeniable danger of the sky.

Adrienne Rich: "Poetry means refusing the choice to kill or die."

Wish: that the straight white male give in just a little more gracefully. Call in its Michael Douglases, its suspect Hollywood, its hurt feelings, its fear—move over some.

After your thousands of years of affirmative action, give someone else a chance—just a chance.

The wish is for gentleness. The wish is for allowances.

"What is the phrase for the moon? And the phrase for love? By what name are we to call death? I do not know. I need a little language such as lovers use. . . ."

．　．　．　．　．　．　．　．　．

Wish: that the typical *New Yorker* story become the artifact it is and assume its proper place in the artifact museum, and not be mistaken for something still alive. Well we've just about had it with all the phony baloney, don't you think?

That the short story and the novel as they evolve and assume new, utterly original shapes might be treated gently. And with optimism. That is the wish.

That hypertext and all electronic writing still in its infancy be treated with something other than your fear and your contempt.

That, poised on the next century, we fear not. Make no grand pronouncements.

You say that language is dying, will die.

And at times I have felt for you, even loved you. But I have never believed you.

The Ebola virus is now. The Hanta virus. HIV. And that old standby, malaria. Live while you can. Tonight, who knows, may be our last. We may not even make the millennium, so don't worry about it so much.

All my friends who have died holding language in their throats, into the end. All my dead friends.

Cybernauts return from time to time wanting to see a smile instead of a colon followed by a closed parenthesis—the online sign for smile. When someone laughs out loud they want to hear real laughter in the real air, not just the letters L.O.L. in front of them. Ah, yes. World while there is world.

A real bird in the real sky and then perhaps a little prose poem or something in the real sky, or the page or the screen or the human heart, pulsing.

I do not know which to prefer,
The beauty of inflections
Or the beauty of innuendoes,
The blackbird whistling
Or just after.

One world.

The future of literature is utopic. As surely as my friends Ed and Alan will come this weekend to visit, bearing rose lentils. As long as one can say "rose," can say "lentil."

Gary dying, saying "Kappa maki."

You say, *over.* But I say, *no.*

I say faith and hope and trust and forever right next to wretched and hate and misery and hopeless.

In the future we will finally be allowed to live, just as we are, to imagine, to glow, to pulse.

Let the genres blur if they will. Let the genres redefine themselves.

Language is a woman, a rose constantly in the process of opening.

Vibrant, irresistible, incandescent.

Whosoever has allowed the villanelle to enter them or the sonnet. Whosoever has let in one genuine sentence, one paragraph, has felt that seduction like a golden thread being pulled slowly through one. . . .

Wish: that forms other than those you've invented or sanctioned through your thousands of years of privilege might arise and be celebrated.

"Put another way, it seems to me that we have to rediscover everything about everything. There is only one solution, and that is to turn one's back on American cinema. . . . Up until now we have lived in a closed world. Cinema fed on cinema, imitating itself. I now see that in my first films I did things because I had already seen them in the cinema. If I showed a police inspector drawing a revolver from his pocket, it wasn't because the logic of the situation I wanted to describe demanded it, but because I had seen police inspectors in other films drawing revolvers at this precise moment and in this precise way. The same thing has happened in painting. There have been periods of organization and imitation and periods of rupture. We are now in a period of rupture. We must turn to life again. We must move into modern life with a virgin eye."   JEAN-LUC GODARD, 1966

Wish: that Alvin Lu might wander in the astounding classroom of the world through time and space, endlessly inspired, endlessly enthralled by what he finds there. That he be allowed to reinvent freely, revel freely.

. . . .

My professor once and now great friend, Barbara Page, out there too, ravenous, furious, and without fear, inventing whole new worlds, ways of experiencing the text. New freedoms.

The world doesn't end, says Charles Simic. Engraved on our foreheads in ash, turned into a language of stars or birdsong across a vast sky; it stays. Literature doesn't end — but it may change shapes, be capable of things we cannot even imagine yet.

Woolf: "What is the phrase for the moon? And the phrase for love? By what name are we to call death? I do not know. I need a little language such as lovers use, words of one syllable such as children speak when they come into the room and find their mother sewing and pick up the scrap of bright wool, a feather, or a shred of chintz. I need a howl; a cry."

Charlotte Brontë: "My sister Emily loved the moors. Flowers brighter than the rose bloomed in the blackest of the heath for her; out of a sullen hollow in the livid hillside her mind could make an Eden. She found in the bleak solitude many and dear delights; and not the least and best loved was — liberty."

The future will be gorgeous and reckless, and words, those luminous charms, will set us free again. If only for a moment.

Whosoever has allowed the language of lovers to enter them, the language of wound and pain and solitude and hope. Whosoever has dug in the miracle of the earth. Mesmerizing dirt, earth, word.

Allowed love in. Allowed despair in.

Words are the ginger candies my dying friends have sucked on. Or the salve of water.

Precious words, contoured by silence. Informed by the pressure of the end.

Words are the crow's-feet embedded in the skin of the father I love. Words are like that to me, still.

Words are the music of her hair on the pillow.

Words are the lines vibrating in the forest or in the painting. Pressures that enter us — bisect us, order us, disorder us, unite us, free us, help us, hurt us, cause anxiety, pleasure, pain.

. . . .

Words are the footprints as they turn away in the snow.

There is no substitute for the language I love.

My father, one state away but still too far, asks over the telephone if I might take a photo of this bluebird, the first I have ever seen, because he hears how filled with delight I am by this fleeting sighting. But it's so tiny, it flies so fast, it's so hard to see. So far away. Me, with my small hunk of technology, pointing. With my nostalgia machine. My box that says fleeting, my box that says future.

My pleasure machine. My weeping machine that dreams: keep.

This novel that says desire and fleeting and unfinished.

Unfinished and left that way. Unfinished, not abandoned. Unfinished, not because of death or indifference or loss of faith, or nerve, just unfinished.

Not to draw false conclusions anymore. Not to set up false polarities. Unfinished and left that way, if necessary.

To allow everyone to write, to thrive, to live.

The Baltimore oriole returned from its American tropics at the edge of this frame now. I wait.

On this delicious precipice.

And nothing replaces this hand moving across the page, as it does now, intent on making a small mark and allowing it to stand on this longing surface.

Writing *oriole*. Imagining freedom. All that is possible.

April in the country. My hands in the dark earth, or the body of a woman, or any ordinary, gorgeous sentence.

Whosoever has let the hand linger on a burning thigh, or a shining river of light. . . .

Whosoever has allowed herself to be dazzled by the motion of the alphabet,

or has let music into the body. Or has allowed music to fall onto the page.

Wish: to live and allow others to live. To sing and allow others to sing— while we can.

. . . .

And hurt not.

Fleeting and longing moment on this earth. We were lucky to be here.

I close my eyes and hear the intricate chamber music of the world. An intimate, complicated, beautiful conversation in every language, in every tense, in every possible medium and form—incandescent.

for Alvin, Barbara, and Judith
1 June 1995

Like the clarinet with the flute, like the French horn with the oboe, like the violin and the piano—take the melody from me, when it's time.

25 April 1995
Germantown, New York

A walk around the loop and I notice the bloodroot has begun to bloom. A bluebird, two bluebirds! the first I've ever seen, over by the convent. Before my eyes I see an infant clasping a small bird as depicted in Renaissance painting and sculpture. The world begins again. In this vision. In the words *bloodroot* and *bluebird*. And the goldfinches too are suddenly back. Today I saw three enormous turtles sunning themselves at a pond. The bliss of being on leave from teaching is beyond description. I recall Dickinson when someone mused that time must go very slowly for her, saying, "Time! Why time was all I wanted!" And so ditto. Blissful time. Writing, walking every day. I am keeping depression at bay, mania in check. All private sufferings and hurt are somehow more manageable here in solitude. The moment seems all now. The imaginative event, the natural event (two wild turkeys in the woods), the sexual event, and the constantly changing and evolving forms in language for all of this. John sends a note to remind me that my essay is due for the *Review of Contemporary Fiction* on May 1, but that I may have a small extension. I should be finishing up *Defiance* but all I can think about are my erotic études—again feeling on the threshold of something amazing and out of reach. I'm extremely excited—hard to describe—my brain feels unhinged . . .

I must make a note as to where to move the daffodils, the iris. The earth in my hands. A wand of forsythia like a light in my hands. I think of Barbara an hour away, the glowing glyphs coming off the screen in her study.

The whole world—luminous, luminous. We were lucky to be here. Even in pain and uncertainty and rage and fear—some fear. In exhaustion.

Too much energy has gone into this Brown / Columbia decision. Where shall I end up? I have only partially succeeded in keeping it all in its proper place. I've had to work too hard to keep my mind at the proper distance. It takes its toll. I've needed the space to think, to dream other things. It hardly matters today though; another étude brews.

The *RCF* essay now in the back of my head. What to say? What can be said? How to use it to learn something, explore something I need to explore. When thinking of literature, the past and the present all too often infuriate me: everyone, everything that's been kept out. The future won't, can't be the same and yet . . . one worries it. What I wonder most is if there is a way, whether there might be a way in this whole wide world, to forgive them. Something for the sake of my own work, my own life I need to do—have needed to do a long time. Perhaps in my essay I will make an attempt, the first movement toward some sort of reconciliation, at any rate. If it's possible. To set up the drama that might make it possible.

This breakable heart.

April. How poised everything seems. How wonderfully ready. And I, too, trembling—and on the verge . . .

To *the* Star Demons

. . . .

by
Tom Sleigh

I first became aware of technology—other than floors, ceilings, walls, the blanket that covered me, the warm bottle that suckled me—when I was four or five years old. My feet pushed the treadles of a tricycle that lurched across our muddy yard, the rare snowfall half-melted already, the myth of Texas as the biggest state and my own newfound sense of power over the gears and wheels, the silver handlebars and rubber grips, dovetailing in the thought, *I'm a Texan.* My pleasure in mastering this machine had sparked off in me a sense of euphoric omnipotence in which I felt my body's strength blending with the tricycle's steel. And that sense of power melded with my pride in Texas, the biggest, and therefore the best, state in the Union.

During those moments when I tooled around the yard, my imagination heightened by the novelty of snow, the sky was larger, just as I myself felt larger, my body hugely filling the blue, which until that instant I'd never experienced as something to be filled. I was also conscious for the first time of feeling superior to the cat pouncing at the tricycle's wheels. Before this morning, my sense of self and the cat's difference from me hadn't seemed so irrevocably final. Now I was a creature of tools, adequate compensation for my lack of fur and claws. And my naive assumption that size equaled superiority underscored the connections between my euphoria, Texas as a metaphor for power, and my own physical sense of mastery each time I turned the tricycle's handlebars.

Inextricably bound up with technological production, this web of pleasurable associations was so important to me that when Alaska, much larger than Texas, was admitted into the Union, I remember passionately arguing with a chicken-legged woman in a wide-brimmed hat of black velvet that Texas was "bigger, bigger!" "Little boy, it ain't anymore. . . ." — though she herself seemed a little shocked, whether at my stubborn advocacy or the blow to our mutual pride. Half tricycle, half boy, in my new, faintly sinister incarnation I felt emboldened to argue with the adult world — the adult world that saw only a child on his tricycle, not reckoning how this mass-produced "toy" had instilled in me a new sense of self: industrial centaur, I was flesh to the waist, all steel below.

After we left Texas and moved to a town high in the Rocky Mountains, I recall being riveted by sprinklers — "rainbirds" I called them, because of the plumes of spray they sent flying in iridescent arcs across the thirsty grass of the park where I played. The spray would slice across a bronze statue dappled in bird lime and which stood grimly heroic next to a dilapidated tennis court, the concrete slab cracked from thaw and freeze, from the occasional heart-stopping earthquake. The automaton quality of the sprinklers, ratcheting hypnotically back and forth, the stolid statue that I pretended to talk to, but that my imagination could never coerce into answering back, showed me how alien man-made things could seem. The grass felt familiar, even the water drops once they flew clear of the rainbird's clicking beak, but the sprinkler itself, product of foundry and machine shop, remained soullessly inert. Each time I tried to envision what a rainbird must feel, I failed; I couldn't make my fantasies stick to the slick, wetly shining steel, the sprinkler's impervious "thingness." Of course, at the heart of my failure to connect with my surroundings was my acute sense of displacement. Without friends as yet, I felt my loneliness and estrangement so acutely that I couldn't give myself over to my own make-believe and bring the sprinkler to life: my imaginings kept drifting back to my own emotional state. Cut off from the web of personal associations that had linked me, my tricycle, and our snow-covered yard to my beloved Texas, the alpha and omega of my private universe, I suffered from the stripped bare poverty of a world returned, in Wallace Stevens's phrase, "to a plain sense of things."

As for the statue, I had even less luck in trying to incorporate it into my fantasy life. Whereas my tricycle easily became part of my body, and the sprinkler's fanning spray had at least inspired the notion of a "rainbird," my animism couldn't overcome the statue's status as a thing. After I learned that the statue bore the likeness of a Mormon prophet, I found its dour, visionary gaze focused too exclusively on the Beyond. It held aloof

. . . .

from me, uninterested in the company of paltry boys and their games. Yet the more it resisted me, its air of vatic concentration making it seem on the verge of vanishing into the ether, the more present to my senses became the sheer materiality of the bronze arms and legs that rang with a low resonating hum each time I tapped them.

This paradoxical seesawing between the material presence of the bronze indifferent to my projections and the aloof prophet evanescing into the Beyond puzzled me deeply: how alien the statue was in comparison to the giant images projected on the screen of the drive-in theater that my parents ran when we lived in Texas. Vanishing and reappearing at the rate of twenty-four frames per second, these phantom men and women were far more real to me than the hollow patriarch on his concrete plinth—as real to me as my own dream life in which the beginnings of movies blended with the sudden crowd of voices and faces swarming all around me the moment that my eyes began to close. Night after night those superhuman, Texas-souled men and women, their voices reverberating through the speaker's grille, lulled me to sleep as I huddled in the window well of our vast, echoing car. Far from being chimeras or indifferent like the statue, they seemed as concrete to me as my hand puppets whom hour after hour I confided in, laughed with, and scolded.

And yet my sense of alienation from the statue heightened my awareness of the living quality of human flesh and voices. Provided that I could animate them, representations of human beings were somehow more present, more irreducibly real to me than the indestructible steel of my roller skates bumping and scraping across the fissured concrete of the tennis courts. I also began to feel self-conscious about the theatricality of my attempts to talk with the statue—perhaps another reason why these colloquies always fizzled out after a few telepathically exchanged words. His face was only a shell, the air inside nothing like the air of Texas, but a silent, sinister void.

In middle age as in childhood, my relation to technology has been similarly personal and idiosyncratic, as much driven by emotion as by intellect. The writing of poetry underpins my mental life, and the kind of poetry I've been able to write has conditioned me to trust emotion, while rousing my suspicions of large-scale generalization—which may be why I sometimes have a hard time connecting the sweeping claims made for and against computers, say, with the actual plastic box, lit screen, and invisible circuitry. Or it may simply be that my aphasia when confronted with such claims springs from my childhood sensitivity to the sheer physicality of

things, as in the case of the statue: the draping folds of its overcoat, its tar-
nished bronze finger weighed more heavily in my imagination than the
fact that the statue represented a Mormon prophet.

That I still think of the statue as a neuter thing, details of anatomy and
not an integrated body, indicates my failure to imbue the statue with
either my own private meanings or to see its culturally determined ones.
But to speak of the statue's meaning in this way assumes that the meaning
of all artifacts must be rooted in human subjectivity and possess aesthetic
or social utility. You could make the case that the statue existed in its own
right, its quiddity expressed by the jutting plane of the nose, the brow's
perpendicular. Cleared of what Wallace Stevens called "our stubborn
man-locked set," the statue takes its place with the drive-in's cash register,
the glass cases of the snack bar, the movie projector and the speakers, the
cars, the component parts of all these, along with the other products of
our technological civilization, to create in conjunction with their human
makers a vast field of interrelated, irreducible existences.

This field in its very vastness troubles me. A phenomenologist like Heidegger, who seems infinitely at home with this field and the abstraction
necessary to envision it, refers to it as "the Being of beings." Perhaps my
early exposure to the movies (my mother claims that my first words were
"Dean Martin, Jerry Lewis!") has conditioned me to think of the world as
a theater of individual fates and dramas. An abstraction such as "Being,"
which bears no trace of what Yeats called "the fury and mire of human
veins," can result in ethical indifference to how best to cope with that fury.
Human passion as the starting point of philosophical inquiry couldn't be
further from Heidegger's commitment to discovering a transpersonal
basis for existence.

I worry about the consequences of certain kinds of philosophical abstraction: surely the fumes of Zyklon B aren't unrelated to a cast of mind
which, like Heidegger the National Socialist's, arrogantly disdained philosophical works "written by men fishing in the troubled waters of 'values'
and 'totalities.'" Nevertheless I can see how a particular kind of mind
would experience such tail-chasing formulations as "the Being of beings"
or "the presence of what is present" as a form of liberation from our relentlessly utilitarian, technocratic web. But philosophers and poets play
on different keyboards, though some of the notes may resonate the same.
In my case "the presence of what is present" in our technological world
finds itself mirrored most clearly in a poet's literalizing imagination.

W. H. Auden transforms the traditional Eden—the original technology-free environment—into a local paradise made absolutely "present" by the poet's inclusion of industrial-age machines numinous by their association with his childhood: overshot waterwheels, beam engines, saddle-tank locomotives. On the same emotional axis, but at its polar extreme, lies Robert Lowell's evocation of infernal America: "Yellow dinosaur steamshovels" gouging "an underworld garage"; "a commercial photograph" that "shows Hiroshima boiling // over a Mosler Safe, the 'Rock of Ages,' "; "giant finned cars" whose "savage servility / slides by on grease" evoke a fierce, no less concrete, negative of Auden's nostalgia for a less complex phase of technological development. What keeps both poets from easy platitudes—parsonic ones in Auden's case, fire-breathing ones in Lowell's—is their need to give a face to fleshless abstractions such as "Paradise" or "the evils of Capitalism." In their poems at least, both seem reluctant to imagine larger meanings entirely separate from personal associations. They are wary of mouthing post-facto generalizations, what Saul Bellow once called "crisis chatter."

In his *Autobiography* Yeats disdains this kind of punditry, calling it "a machine, one can leave it to itself; unhelped it will force those present to exhaust the subject, the fool is as likely as the sage to speak the appropriate answer to any statement, and if an answer is forgotten somebody will go home miserable. You throw your money on the table and receive so much change. . . ." Yeats sees a kind of automatism driving accepted social and intellectual forms, cant underwritten by the mechanical operations of logic. Yeats's attitude suggests why Heidegger was so deeply concerned to discriminate between technological utility and technology's essence, which he characterized as the ability to create, to plan and organize freely: the kind of logic that reduces a forest to so many board feet, or that views a horse as horsepower only, is incapable of wandering out of its own deep-worn ruts. Between the "presentness" of a horse or a forest, and the obvious uses to which they can be put, stretches an almost unbridgeable conceptual gulf. This failure to discriminate between "being" and "being used" not only debases technology's essence—it also devalues my tricycle, the drive-in movie screen, the statue of the Mormon prophet, each an irreducible instance of the "presence of what is present." But literalist as I am, my mind blanks at the glare reflected back from such a phrase. For me at least, it lacks the emotional and sensual immediacy, the "real world" concreteness of Auden's paradise or Lowell's hell.

My ambivalence toward certain forms of metaphysical abstraction (mere defensiveness against abstractions I can't grasp? — in Heidegger's terms "to grasp" an idea is to have an a priori assumption, not at all the same activity as thinking) drives me, as it drove Lowell and Auden, to give a unique face to the "beings in Being" — a counter impulse to the huge hands of Being automatically kneading myriad human actions and contemplations into one abstract, metaphysical lump. Perhaps my aversion to this kind of discourse also has as much to do with the portentous self-importance of its style, its neologisms and quasi-tautological, hieratic circling that at times seems dangerously close to kitsch: the United States Army recruiting jingle — "BE all that you can BE!" — possesses a certain Heideggerian flair.

But my main objection is how easily such language can divorce itself from horrific social realities, glossing over the effects of the atomic bomb, say, by calling it, as Heidegger did, "the grossest of all gross confirmations of the long-since-accomplished annihilation of the thing. . . ." — a formulation that tends to emphasize the importance of its own terminology over the beings vaporized by the bomb. Yet I feel the need to resist dutiful obeisance to the myth of the bomb as an embodiment of technological depravity, comparable to Auschwitz, perverse as Dr. Mengele's experiments; not because it isn't evil, but because such a myth erases the individual workers who produced it — and I do mean workers, not the head scientists or military chiefs of staff. High in Alamogordo, among the hundreds of other classified workers who hadn't an inkling of what they were helping to create, was one Mona Rowe, destined to become my great-aunt; so the development of the atomic bomb is for me as much a part of my family lore as one of the pivotal events in human history.

When Mona, a confirmed smoker who died of lung cancer, her last days spent one breath puffing on a cigarette, the next inhaling oxygen from the merciful *techne* of an oxygen mask, was in her twenties she served on the Manhattan project — but only as a clerk filing parts of some unknown mechanism about which "Oppy" (so she called him) knew the whys and wherefores. Spirited away by military intelligence to the mountain fastness of Los Alamos so that not even her family knew her whereabouts, she met a man in the storage warehouse, had an affair, became pregnant — and supposedly gave up the child for adoption (since no one else in my family has ever mentioned this cousin, I sometimes wonder if the child wasn't aborted — but this is the story as I recall hearing it). If it seems anticlimactic to focus on Mona's story rather than the development of the bomb, consider how difficult the whole predicament must have been: given the social mores of the time, did she feel impelled in this fish-bowl of classified information to keep her own predicament top secret? But because she lived in barracks, after a time it must have been impossi-ble to keep her pregnancy to herself—how soon after she began to show did her fellow workers start to gossip? If to her face they were sympa-thetic, wouldn't some have talked behind her back in a malicious, smut-mouthed kind of way?

And from a point of view less personal and more public, if the security officers noticed at all, how did they officially view this lapse from the straight and narrow? As an indication of "loose morals?" A security risk? Or perhaps the war effort took such precedence in everybody's mind that no one paid much attention to this young woman's private troubles. In that case, given the strictness of her upbringing in a small farming town in the middle of the Kansas prairie, and the fact that she and her fellow workers were held incommunicado from their families and the outside world because of the risk of information leaks, it would be surprising if she didn't experience considerable confusion, guilt, and shame in reaching her decision not to marry and give up the child.

But whatever the scenario I imagine for Mona, I share with Lowell and Auden a sense of history that is public as well as private; provided that you can find convincing links between the two (not as easy as it sounds!), one needn't be subservient to the other. The atomic bomb and her personal troubles can be superimposed, her concerns in emblematic relation to the larger ones of the Manhattan project. She told me about the bomb test that revealed to her and her fellow workers the nature of their labors: given protective goggles (or was it simply pieces of tinted glass?), they huddled in a bunker and watched the blast rise up . . . some fell to their knees, astonished and terrified. Yet beneath the blast, the prayers and sobbing and hysterical shouts of disbelief, I hear my great-aunt's voice grown young but just as precise, just as matter-of-fact as her description of the explosion, telling her beau that marriage is not for her, at least not with him.

And so in my imagination this long-lost cousin and the development of the bomb are both located on a sliding scale that reaches from the per-sonal to the historical. Up the scale in the direction of the historical, where I locate the national war effort and the concomitant destruction of Hiroshima—an event I can only distantly comprehend—I feel an in-choate guilt. What fraction of the bomb's destructive power can I at-tribute directly to Mona? At the same time, moving back down the scale in the direction of the personal, I try to imagine the father of her child: what sort of man was he, and what happened to their relationship after the child was either aborted or placed for adoption? Were they able to remain friends? And what was the fate of my prospective cousin?

I've often wondered if that early affair was a factor in her remaining single all her life. Rakish, sly, she was frank about sex in a way that I found refreshing, if a little embarrassing for a teenager. Certainly in later life she was no ascetic: her carnal knowledge; her self-destructive impulses as a smoker; the mushroom cloud she helped create, now so overexposed it too has become kitsch; her independence of mind—all these associations establish a range of impressions, from the personal to the historical, against which I can measure her character and at the same time bring the world into sharper focus. So the blast that at ground zero melded sand into glass also inspired one survivor thirty years later to wish that she'd picked up her scissors knocked by the shock wave onto the schoolroom floor: "Why didn't I stretch my hands out to take them? Those scissors sent by a friend in Hawaii. They were sharp, shiny and would never rust." In this survivor's imagination her scissors become both an emblem of hopeful connection to the world beyond the blast and of spiritual endurance on the edge of despair: how distant that world must have seemed when the shock wave hit! Thirty years later the historical significance of the bomb is irradiated by the memory of her lost scissors' seemingly indestructible shine.

This sliding scale of significance from the personal to the historical, which includes the image of Aunt Mona, coproducer of the atomic bomb, sucking oxygen from her mask, then sucking on her beloved, mass-marketed, mass-produced cigarette, also includes the image of my father, first in his retirement, hooked up to a dialysis machine, his blood voyaging beyond his body through plastic tubes; then during his working life that, after he sold the drive-in theater, was spent analyzing the best way to fuel rocket motors. A solid propellant man, he took us more than once to watch booster tests. I remember rising before dawn, hungover sleepy, then feeling a little grouchy in the backseat, Jill our family dog slack-tongued, panting, my mother asking my brothers and me to stop hitting each other. At the trial site we sat in the car surrounded by other families in their cars, our eyes intent on a large snow-ringed hole about a hundred yards away.

I recall fearing that if the trial went badly my father, gentle, quiet, impassive, would have to work longer hours than he already worked and that his calming influence on our home life would give way to the volatile rancor that sprung up in his absence. At ignition, the car began to tremble, the motor roared as loudly as the Tyrannosaurus rex that one night stalked across the drive-in theater screen while a caveman with his tiny spear gamely fought off the beast, the wall of heat rising from the bottom of the pit doubling and redoubling, the packed snow shimmering and melting, the lip of the hole incinerated to mush. It lasted less than a minute and when the burn ended, my father walked back to our car from where he'd been standing with the other engineers: he was faintly smiling, exhilarated by the camaraderie and shared sense of success, his quiet sweetness in weird contrast to the ferocity of the motor: "Pancakes," he smiled, "let's all go out for pancakes."

I don't wish to sneer at such juxtapositions, or at the technological achievement of an ICBM, although the moral gulf between that happy moment of blueberry pancakes smothered in syrup and the arms race that enabled my father to pay the check, couldn't have been wider. If the disjunction bothered my father, he kept it to himself. He was never well paid, being a technical man and not an executive; and keeping us clothed and fed, let alone splurging at a pancake house, was struggle enough for him: the daily grind of supporting us wasn't conducive to moral reflection, and anyway, if he had them, my father was in no position to afford his scruples. Plus, he genuinely enjoyed his work at the plant. The other technical men in his division respected and liked him; and since my father had few friends outside of work, the plant doubled as the hub of his social life. Although even as a boy I was aware of the paradoxical nature of my father helping to make weapons of mass destruction while at home he was gentle and unassuming, I was very much my father's son: I remember taking tremendous pleasure in a toy rocket powered by pressure from the garden hose, and in a replica of a nuclear Shark submarine fueled by baking soda that prowled through the soapy depths of the bathtub or navigated around submerged pots and pans in the kitchen sink. In my Eden such toys would be as essential as Auden's industrial-age machines. And while Kennedy and Johnson's faces, Khrushchev and Brezhnev's faces remind me of the ancient race of star demons of gnostic lore, their powers celestial and terrible as the demiurge's, my face reflected in my father's face, Aunt Mona's face reflected in her lost child's face, also banner out like flags across the burgeoning mushroom cloud.

■ ■ ■

On 17 February 1600, Giordano Bruno, the mystic philosopher, having spent eight years in prison by order of the Inquisition, was publicly burned at the stake as a heretic in the Campo dei Fiori in Rome. Seven years later, Johannes Kepler, the astronomer and a fellow Copernican, wrote to a friend that the "unfortunate Bruno, who was roasted on coals in Rome . . . believed that the stars are inhabited." This is consistent with Bruno's belief that we live in an animistic universe operated by magic: the world possesses a sensitive and rational soul, the stars are angel-like demons, their number infinite in accordance with the infinite nature of the All. The popular notion that Bruno preferred to die rather than renounce Copernicus's assertion that the earth revolves around the sun, and so broke with medieval Aristotelianism and helped to usher in our modern technological world, ignores the fact that Bruno supported Copernicus's theory, not on scientific grounds, but because the astronomer's diagrams were really magic symbols whose gnostic meanings the ignorant Copernicus had failed to understand. Far from being a scientific enthusiast, Bruno thought of himself as a Messiah-magus whose mission was to reform Christianity by returning it to its gnostic roots.

In Giovanni Mocenigo's testimony to the Inquisition, he accused Bruno of founding a new religious sect, "the Giordanisti," dedicated to his mystical teachings. The ecstatic nature of his doctrine was based on the use of magical talismans, images, and diagrams to draw down the celestial influences from the planets and stars, themselves divine beings, and imprint these on the memory so as to acquire universal knowledge and supernatural power. (The mind as supercomputer? And yet the computer feeds on invisible electric impulses, not images—as poet, I'm deeply attracted to Bruno's absolute faith in images: does it come as any surprise that Bruno was a poet as well as a mystic?) So Egyptian hieroglyphs, which Bruno interpreted as sacred images taken from the natural world, had latent in them the language of the gods. He also invented images of his own; this one, for example, was supposed to draw into the mind the beneficent powers of the divine Sol: "Apollo with a bow and without a quiver, laughing." Contemplation of these images would transform the practitioner into a magus attuned to the monad of the cosmos, his earthly self transcended and reformed to a divine being.

This synthesis of natural magic, celestial effluvia, and spiritual reform seems wholly alien to modern scientific thought. And there's evidence that Bruno lived in a state of mental excitation and euphoria bordering on insanity. But the power to channel divine influences that Bruno ascribed to his images and diagrams strikes me as deeply connected to our faith in certain forms of technology, especially medical technology as it's evolved since the Enlightenment. Franz Mesmer's M.D. thesis, published in 1767, claimed that celestial gravity, through a weightless, ineffable fluid called ether, exerted influences on the human body that accounted for various diseases. He later developed this theory into his infamous notion of "animal" magnetism, a quasi-mystical force charging the nervous system that Mesmer, dressed as a magus, would therapeutically adjust by passing his hands up and down the patient's length, but without touching the person's body.

It's a short step from Bruno's belief in celestial influences operating on the mind for spiritual benefit or harm—there was "good" magic as well as "bad"—to Mesmer's conviction that such forces operated on the human body, also for good or ill. Although Bruno's notion of a living, animistic universe had been replaced in Mesmer's day by a mechanistic one, some of Bruno's mystical cosmology persists in Mesmer's quackery: when treating patients, he would wear a robe embroidered with Rosicrucian alchemical symbols, a practice clearly related to Bruno's use of magical images (some scholars suggest that the Rosicrucians may have been an offshoot of Bruno's mystical sect, "the Giordanisti"). In our less flamboyant day, the white lab coat has equally potent meanings, although perhaps more for the patient than the doctor. And the notion that Mesmer's hands could sense pathology inside the body bears partial resemblance to the X ray. The difference is that science ascribes the X ray's power to see into the patient's body to impersonal natural laws, while Mesmer's power over his patients was due to the force of personality.

Or so it seems from the scientific point of view. But what of the patient's point of view, his wrist encircled by a plastic bracelet with his name, date of birth, and hospital ID number printed on it, his clothes exchanged for a washed-to-rags johnny open at the back for easy access to the doctors' and nurses' hands, his faith in his own body displaced by his hope (and fear) of the IV dripping into his veins, the stabbing pain of the needle inserted through his skin an unceremonious initiation into the society of the sick. Cut off from our associations in the wide-windowed world, the moment we enter a hospital we are changed—our mortality begins to breathe into our faces, everything we experience shimmers with heightened intensity.

When I say "we," I clearly mean "I"—I have a chronic blood disease, potentially fatal, but stable for the moment. Whenever I receive a blood transfusion the slow drip of the blood thinned by saline dropping and dropping through the clear ether of the tube seems every bit as charged with "animal" magnetism ("animal" derived from *anima,* the soul) as

Mesmer could wish. The physiological difference that two units of blood makes is astounding: my mind ceases to hover in a kind of passive clair-voyance in which I feel in perfect communication with the buzzing neon of the overhead lamps, and is pulled back down into my body, out of its trance of lassitude and speculative drift. I literally feel myself becoming de-etherealized, my appetite for living sharpened by the animal fear of knowing that yet again I've survived a close call. Or I'm inhaling radio-active gas so that a close cousin of the X-ray machine can determine whether or not there are blood clots in my lungs; with each breath, I feel my skin fade into transparence until I have a profound sense of the spaces inside my chest expanding and expanding to enormous proportions, my sense of self submerging, even drowning in that slowly opening abyss.

So technology acts on the mind when physiologically you are at your most vulnerable, but also your most receptive to what may seem like mys-tical impressions. Bruno specified a trance that took over the mind as the magus ascended to contemplation of the All, a mental state whose inten-sity had to be carefully controlled by the use of magical images or else the ascending soul could be lost in the All—the result being that the body, bereft of the soul, would perish. Yet I recognize that this loose analogy be-tween the soul's ascent to gain knowledge and my wooziness before a blood transfusion is to a great extent the action of my mind seeking through euphoria to ward off thoughts of death. But this doesn't mean that the magic of my thinking is only whistling in the dark. My mind's acute sensitivity to physical sensation, its ability to animate the oxygen tank so that I literally feel the air desire to enter into my lungs, helps to strengthen my hold on life; yet rationally I know that physiological forces will have to line up with the force field of my will boosted in power by medical procedures and machines if, in fact, I'm going to survive. Several years ago when I almost died from a fibrillating heart, I remember trying to control my panic by focusing on the image of a slice of Wonder Bread that, as the TV announcer in my childhood had resolutely assured me, "Builds strong bodies twelve ways." Talk about faith in images!—at that moment, from a scientific point of view, which of us was guiltier of magi-cal thinking, me or the heretical, Messiah-magus Bruno?

Perhaps my deepest impression of this kind of magical thinking was inspired by witnessing my father's dialysis. Grafted beneath the skin of his forearm was a tube sewn into his artery through which his blood left his body and then returned. Three days a week for four hours a day while his blood was being cleansed, he would sit uncomplaining in an easy chair among other patients in easy chairs, a small-screen television available for him to watch, an earphone plugged into the console, just as it was for all the other patients. When I would let my father off or pick him up in the reception room, a sense of normal human activity pervaded the place. But if I passed beyond the reception room door into the clinic itself, the sight of the patients' blood flowing beyond their veins through a clear tube, then passing through a filter attached to the dialysis machine, always stirred in me a profound unease at seeing what should remain invisible made visible—rich, red, and almost painfully vital in comparison to the patients sitting passively in their chairs.

Although my father suffered from a different ailment than mine, we shared certain symptoms—low red blood cell counts, deficient autoimmune reactions. But how to express beyond the numbers and medical jargon the interior mystery that hid behind those numbers and that jargon! My father and I were indissolubly linked by what at every moment was attempting to dissolve us, to carry us beyond the ministrations of these machines crouched human-sized next to each chair, mere metal boxes with gauges and dials routinely checked by the nurses moving on soft-soled shoes, scribbling down a few numbers and comments on the patients' record sheets, taking blood pressures, the inflatable cuff expanding, then deflating with a long resigned sigh.

My father, who had first made his living by projecting gigantic images on a screen, images that for me had as much reality as my puppets; and who had since envisioned and helped create the thrust needed to break a rocket loose from the earth's gravity, was now at the mercy of the machine beside him, its physical presence weirdly blending in my mind with his own. If my tricycle had once made me feel that my body could fill the sky, now the dialysis machine made my father's body seem like a vestigial, soon-to-be-discarded part of its own functioning. And yet at such moments I felt powerful intimations that ran counter to my sense of medical technology beginning to usurp my father's presence; intimations not as grandiose as Bruno's, but from a scientific point of view, equally hermetic—that my father's life and my life were borne on a current ("animal" magnetism?) that I felt passing all around me throughout the room; that my father's fate and my fate were permeable to each other, and to the lives around us; that in looking at him I'd passed behind a mirror into a place like Adocentyn, mystic city of the sun, from whose glass towers and flashing beacons emanated all the images and representations that human beings are capable of conceiving.

Perhaps this strange conjunction of dialysis machines and quasi-mystical intimations represented a momentary truce between what Stevens once called "the pressure of reality" and the intuitive imagination. My father's physical frailty and my own recondite spiritual perceptions seemed mutually entailing: at such moments I found it easier to accept that my father was mortally ill. But such moments came infrequently and more often than not were the prelude to much less solacing intuitions: the dialysis machine's unflagging tendance to my father's physical frailty made his weakness that much more pronounced—and although I fought against such feelings, I'm ashamed to admit that my father's wasting flesh, in contrast to the machine's seeming indestructibility, sometimes made me a little afraid of him. Hooked up to the machine, he seemed both more and less than human. At such times I reached the limit of my ability to project onto the machine benevolent human intentions—and while I was grateful to the technology that kept him alive, eventually the machine came to dwarf him.

But during the moments of truce when the sinister relation between his body and the machine was transformed into a strange communion between me, my father and his machine, and the other patients and their machines, I felt a spooky form of joy: joy that I could feel so connected to my father, regardless of whether he felt it too: despite his unfailing gentleness and devotion to us, he was always a shy man, often undemonstrative; and the constant exhaustion he suffered because of his illness made him even quieter and more distant. From childhood on, I had been haunted by his remoteness, which I experienced as fear of losing him—a fear that, as a child in Texas, I had controlled by my magical belief in the protective powers of the comedic duo we showed so often at the drive-in theater, Jerry Lewis and Dean Martin: always rising unhurt from elaborate pratfalls, their mutual loyalty prevailing over all dangers, they were my superhuman guardians, powerful as Bruno's star demons moving harmoniously throughout the living universe as they kept watch over their respective corners of infinitely expanding space. So Lewis and Martin watched over my sleep while my father and mother were off attending to the popcorn machine or rewinding the first reel so that they could start threading the second.

But there in the clinic those guardian powers seemed neutralized by forces of equal magnitude. My father's physical fragility made it hard for me to separate the lifesaving function of the dialysis machine from my haunted sense that he was flickering out right before my eyes, his face pale and wavery as sunlight through water. No amount of medical technology

· · · · · · · · ·

was going to keep his flesh steadily burning. In another, more animistic part of myself, I believed that I could keep him alive by sheer force of will. If I kept his image firmly in my head, animating it with my own vitality, and watched over him in the same way that Martin and Lewis had watched over me, I could keep him from gradually vanishing from my sight.

There were times when my animism and the operations of the dialysis machine seemed weirdly parallel, the physical work of the dialysis machine in keeping my father alive transmuted into the mental work of preserving his image. So the same tubes, pumps, and filters that I found dehumanizing also served as an imaginative springboard, a creative impetus that partially patterned my mental response to my father's health. The adaptability of the imagination, first to generate the technology on which the dialysis machine was based, and then to transform it in this idiosyncratic way, shows just how omnivorous and unpredictable its powers are. But from a more personal perspective, at bottom what I needed was a sense of control over my father's fate. As he gradually grew sicker and his need of me increased, I discovered in the imaginative work of trying to preserve my father's image a source of solace and some small measure of control — fragile, illogical, but as vital to me emotionally in a quiet day-to-day way as the dialysis machine was to my father physically.

From a less magical vantage, I can see that my attendance on my father at the clinic routinely put me in those extreme states of consciousness that pondering on mortality induces. Although I experienced that state over and over, each time I passed behind the waiting-room doors the mystery and reality of the clinic seemed always new, even as it came relentlessly closer — the most unfathomable part being that every few weeks a patient would suddenly stop coming. At such times I knew with a helpless desolate shock that this patient would one day be my father.

And so it's fallen out. On my desk, kept Ziplocked in a plastic Baggie, pure product of technology, is all that remains of my father — a half handful of ashes I saved out from when our family scattered them on my mother's parents' graves, on my father's parents' graves. At first I thought of making a box for his ashes, but in the year since his death the plastic pouch of the Baggie, in its cruelly casual, utilitarian, almost wounding indifference, has come to seem a more effective goad to memory. Just as mystics like Bruno took to suspending a colored figure of the cosmos from the ceiling, so that the figure of the universe and not just single things would meet their eyes, so the plastic Baggie brings to my inner eye the image of my father superimposed on the myriad surfaces of the world.

As I've mentioned earlier, Bruno's absolute faith in the power of images to transform us seems to me similar to the poet's desire (at least the poets I admire) to give each passing thing its living name, to illuminate inside our abstract technological web the face of each particular. It's tempting to speculate about the fate of art in our time, launching into jeremiads against that web's accelerating autonomy from moral reflection on the one hand, or singing dithyrambs to it accompanied by electronic synthesizers for its attempts to ameliorate human suffering. Instead, let me say that techology's essence as the ability to create and organize freely could also describe the making of art: under the aegis of such a definition, art and technology are mutually entailing, each suggesting to the other new directions of creative endeavor.

In other words, I'm less worried about technology per se than I am about our loss of an anthropocentric sense of life: the uses of technology threaten to usurp our images of ourselves, which in part explains my unease with the benevolent workings of my father's dialysis machine. But I could gladly live with such ambiguities if, in its less benign manifestations, technological utility, and the social and economic forces that sustain it, didn't keep shifting the spotlight of history away from the human face, and onto their own ever more abstract, increasingly autonomous processes. That's why I find so appealing the manner in which Bruno's mystical images work on the imagination, a specific image channeling a celestial force to bring a particular benefit to the human mind. The sensory concreteness of his system insists that images aren't empty shadows that can be arbitrarily manipulated, but are as physically real as the divine properties that they have the power to attract, the *materia* of the world able to capture and store the *spiritus* material emanating from the stars.

This power to draw down the divine seems similar to what I experienced when, as a child on the verge of sleep, I watched the superhuman men and women on the drive-in theater screen. The parking lot with its hundreds of speakers all whispering at once, the images succeeding each other so rapidly that the flurry of frames seemed able to register each least detail of human life; the flickering projector like the flashing towers and beacons of Adocentyn endlessly fecund in shooting out images across the night; all these influences, plus the feel of my blanket, the exhilaration of being at a drive-in movie while other children were tucked in at home, my ritual bedtime story literally filling the horizon, induced in me a sense of quiet exhilaration that I came to associate with the giants before me working out their black-and-white fates while my parents were busy working the projector and the snack bar. In my mother and father's absence, I linked the quavering voices coming from the speaker with my reverie of flying in a rocketship built by my father, my humbler, technological version of Bruno's aspiration to penetrate the armature of the spheres and show to nature the beautiful form of God. At this moment, the moment when sleep and the projector's power to make images operated on my imagination as strongly as Bruno's magical diagrams, I flew among the stars shining on the curved window glass, my mind racing in anticipation of what my dreams would bring as I turned my head away from the lit screen in order to make the constellations gleam more brightly. Since I never saw more than a few minutes of a movie before I fell asleep, plot and dialogue dissolved into the comforting sensation that these celluloid beings were my companions through the night.

As I said before, I know now that I must have used this reverie to quiet my anxieties about being abandoned by my parents, especially my father, lost not in the All but in the warm night of Texas, the parking lot deserted, every car gone home but ours while they shut down the snack bar and cashed out. I remember how even through my dreams I could sense their voices and footsteps, and how their approach freed me to let myself go even farther into the deeps of space, the immense Texas panhandle shrinking to nothing from my vantage among the stars. But perhaps this anxiety also added fuel to the near ecstasy I experienced during those moments just before sleep when I lay alone in the back window well, the shadowy images of the star demons so protective of me in their superhuman size and benevolence. At such moments even my fear of losing my parents temporarily vanished in my contemplation of the distances I journeyed through, the blackness opening and opening to my closing eyes.

REFERENCES

Yates, Frances A. *Giordano Bruno and the Hermetic Tradition.* Chicago: University of Chicago Press, 1964.

Koestler, Arthur. *The Sleepwalkers.* London and New York: Penguin Books (Arkana), 1989.

Collier, Michael. *The Neighbor.* Chicago: University of Chicago Press, 1995.

Nerds, Technocrats, and Enlightened Spirits

. . . .

by
ROBERT PINSKY

The subject of computers, particularly computers in relation to culture or politics, has personal associations for me. One of these is memories of collaboration. In the early '8os, when I was writing *Mindwheel,* an interactive text-adventure for computer, I found myself working with a team of computer whizzes about the same age as the Berkeley undergraduates I was teaching. We had been assembled into a team by Ihor Wolosenko, the president of Synapse Software, a company Ihor sold to Brøderbund, which issued *Mindwheel* in 1984—reviewed by the trade press as a considerable advance in its genre.

It was always a pleasure to leave the familiar landscape of the Berkeley campus, with its vague architectural references to the accumulated gropings for meaning of human history, putting behind me Telegraph Avenue's weary evocations of Free Speech and Flower Power, and drive over to Synapse, an ungarnished industrial building overlooking the freeway and the Bay. The anonymity of that building and the youthful spirit inside made me think of the featureless buildings on Long Island and in Los Angeles where young wiseacres, grunts, and entrepreneurs invented the motion picture industry.

As with movies, the overlap of technology and art had an exhilarating quality of group improvisation. The programmers might ask me to write a sentence for each of two hundred verbs of action being executed by our interactive, second-person protagonist-reader. Or we might have a philosophical discussion of narrative: narrated "rooms" or spatial creations were important to our product, as were narrated "scenes" in time—is a scene in a room, or is a room in a scene? It was necessary to make the "look-at" messages of *Mindwheel* (text that appears on-screen when a reader chooses to "look" or to "look at" some specific object) consistent with the "scene" messages, and to write the random, textural background narrative for which we coined the terms "weather" (text that occasionally scrolls down to lend emotional texture, without affecting action) and "drivel" (amusing or confusing text that scrolls down without affecting action or emotion). Another day, all work might stop while everybody tinkered with a cheap version of that year's fad toy—the wristwatch that unfolded into a robot—that had something wrong with it. We were all contract workers, rather than employees, which meant that the boys in the pit, as they were known, had no fringe benefits and no regular hours.

My strange young collaborators seemed at first to be charmingly without histories, as if they had been invented by the industry they were inventing. We lived in the task at hand, which for me was writing text and for them was writing code. Of course they did have histories, lives in California tract houses or suburban high schools where many of them had been ungovernable geniuses or social outcasts. One of them told me about going to college for a few weeks and leaving when he realized that he knew considerably more about the subject than his computer science instructor. Plus, he felt homesick. These dramas were invisible to me at first because I lacked the experience to read them the way I could read the approximate histories of students and street types on Berkeley's Sproul Plaza.

One day, I was sitting at a computer terminal at Synapse, with my two main collaborators and some of their fellow programmers gathered around behind me. That was the normal configuration at Synapse: someone at a keyboard, several other people staring at the monitor. I was performing the kind of writing-on-demand that tickled me because the programmers admired my knack for rapid writing (and overwriting, to tell the truth) on demand. On this occasion I was touching up a scene where the reader-protagonist has been immobilized from the waist down—a rather Freudian image I had raided out of the *1001 Nights*—and can escape only by insulting a couple of animal-headed children who are standing by with sticks. By taunting them, and getting them to offer violence, one can escape.

We were making a list of bad names and epithets that the program would recognize as triggers. Giggling, in adolescent high spirits, we added to the obvious obscenities: "wartsniffer," somebody suggested—"dirtpouch." Somewhere on our way from "motherfucker" to "dweeb," I had the bad taste to ruin the party with a small faux pas.

· · · · · · · · · ·

"Nerd," was all I said. My friends grew silent, as if at a racial epithet. Nerd, I realized, was a word that had wounded them in high school—it wasn't funny. It implied hypertrophy in one direction, and failure of a social, physical kind. In their experience the word—desexualizing, contemptuous, exiling—had been a blow to their sense of themselves at a tender stage of life. They did not like it.

This little incident recalls other stereotypes of the engineer or scientist. The Nerd's retaliation, in this mythology, is to grow up to become the heartless Technocrat, menacing all of our familiar arrangements while luring us into dependence on new ones, forcing us to live according to demands impersonal and alienating—repaying social banishment or slights by reducing society itself to a kind of internal banishment, effacing the old connections and dependencies among people. Or there is the image of Strangelove, the technical genius or functionary so in love with his devisings, so eager to dazzle his bosses, that he lacks rudimentary humanity. He makes the elegant missiles without worrying about individual people they might kill or what destruction they might inflict.

Older than either of these ideas, as well as nobler, is another idea: the scientist as enlightened spirit, the advocate of sanitation and vaccination, the fighter for clean water and decent schools. In the nineteenth-century European novel, he is the liberal spirit who argues with the village priest; in the plays of Chekhov—and in the person of Chekhov—he is the medical doctor who works for a better world, a society illuminated by knowledge and resistant to the prejudiced past. The builder of bridges, the healer, the researcher, the enemy of infection and poverty, the scientist or engineer in this avatar is an enlightened spirit.

All three types or stereotypes—the nerd, the technocrat, and the enlightened spirit—play a role in my perception of another personal association: a life that in its dignity as well as its sadness calls up many of these failures and possibilities.

My father-in-law, Sam Bailey, was an engineer who worked on missiles. He was also a writer of fiction, published in the "pulps" of the '20s and '30s: a man of unusual gifts. As was possible in his generation, he became an engineer without getting a degree. He developed the first medical diagnosis computer, decades before the idea flourished. In the '60s, just before the Vietnam War took over national consciousness, he proposed a computerized system of sorting and understanding the vast amount of data that came into the State Department, which I can recall Sam describing to me as "the largest post office in the world."

. . . .

Timid as a person, bold as an imagination, never making much money or establishing a métier, he was a valued workhorse and innovator for a series of employers. He devised the idea of frozen food before its time. To the day he died, three years ago, at the age of ninety, he was familiar with the most current developments in digital technology and software, particularly in the area of control engineering. Like the boys in the pit at Synapse, he was resourceful and unworldly.

The son of a New Jersey farmer who was also a rural postmaster, Sam possessed a New Jersey version of Yankee ingenuity, a tinkering wit capable of fixing broken appliances cheaply, inclined to make a gate-closer out of a bit of salvaged shoe tree, an alarm-clock housing and three roller-skate wheels. He had other kinds of ideas as well. The pulps, named for the cheap, mealy paper they were printed on, the TV of their day, came in genres such as Western, Romance, Urban Sophisticated, Adventure, Fantasy, and Crime. Crime was the specialty of Sam Bailey—a good name for an author in that field.

The pathos and charm of Sam's life, his lonely accomplishment and frustration, bear analysis. I think the old ideal of the enlightened spirit beats its wings feebly in his career, which in ways characteristic of his time forced him into the roles of nerd and very minor technocrat. He had a long career in what became the aerospace industry, going from firm to firm and project to project, a respected engineer, never getting paid very much.

He was not a happy man in his work, for a reason he often alluded to: virtually all he worked on for forty years was weapons, mostly the development of guided missiles. He objected to this use of his intelligence not on anything that could be called political grounds, and certainly not from sentimentality about human nature. Sam in fact did not like people in general; and when he did master the difficulty he had liking any individual, he did not find his affection easy to express. True to stereotype, he was not comfortable with people or feelings, a trait I associate with the death of his mother in a flu epidemic when he was quite small. In any case, it was not a love of humanity that made him loathe spending his stringent and ingenious spirit on the development of one weapon or weapon component after another.

I say "spending" because it was a matter of personal economy. He hated working on means of destruction because he was to the bottom of his soul a creator, a maker. For a meticulous, fanatically orderly man who was skilled with his hands, the idea of applying imagination and resources and organization in order to create devices whose function was to destroy structures, to maim and kill, to deliver disorder, panic, and death, was a peculiar violation. Warfare offended his imagination as the ultimate *mess*. Partly because he grew up on a farm, he had a variety of creative skills. He installed wiring and plumbing, he repaired leaky roofs, and knew how to repair stucco, plaster moldings, pavement, roofing, sump pumps, motors both electrical and internal combustion. He built a rustic house and several cabins with his hands.

He selected the house he bought in suburban New Jersey because he liked its unusual construction, of concrete slabs brought to the site on heavy trucks, rectangular holes for windows and doors already molded into the thick slabs that were piled together on the site like Stonehenge. I used to call it, after the North Jersey town it was in, Teaneck-henge. Sam spoke of it with a peculiar sardonic pride as a bomb shelter.

The house was a museum of inventively eccentric gadgets: hidden speakers and intercoms, self-illuminating picture frames made of hardwood salvaged from the dump, door-closers and laundry chutes and mail slots assembled and insulated and automated by a barely decipherable anthology of cannibalized and deformed salvage, parts recognizable and enigmatic. When his flagstone walk deteriorated, he made a wooden jig to support the stones as he replaced them, and for the mailman to walk on, and by slow progress and with a minimum of effort, removed and replaced the flagstones by degrees, pushing the jig down the walk the way Egyptian slaves and taskmasters brought stones for the pyramids. His daughter observed that someone could make an effective short film called *How an Eighty-Seven-Year-Old Man Repairs a Sidewalk*.

His favorite materials were wiring and wood. His wedding present to his daughter and me—a marriage he came to approve of only gradually—was a chest-on-chest of pine: two stacks of dovetailed drawers, his and hers, that we have used daily for thirty years. Among several other relics we have inherited is the first piece of furniture he made, at the outset of his own marriage: a two-door cabinet constructed from salvaged tongue-and-groove flooring and scrap from a dismantled cherry staircase. The cabinet is made entirely with hand tools. With incised geometrical designs, stained ebony red, it looks like something from the tradition of William Morris—which I suppose it is. And indeed something of Sam's wasted energy, his sense of his own failure, reminds me of the irony of Morris's career: the Marxist reformer who wanted to give pride and dignity to labor, and beauty to the masses, and who ended as an interior decorator to the upper middle class.

· · · · · · · · · · ·

The most satisfactory period of Samuel Bailey's life in technology, by his own perception, did not begin until he was nearly seventy years old, when he began his true career—a career that, against reasonable expectation, lasted for over twenty years. For a while after he retired from the last aerospace job, he tried freelancing for whatever vestigial magazine world resembling the pulps he could find. Sam even had a little success. He sold a very short piece, for example, to one of the minor imitators of *Playboy*, a little fantasia about a married man who goes clandestinely to a computer-dating service, using an alias, and gets set up with a date, and the woman turns out to be his wife.

This sense of technology biting the hand that uses it seems to have been an aspect of his thinking: in one of his stories from the pulp days, the murder weapon is a house, prepared by the killer with so many unsafe booby traps, each separate one undetectable by the police, that the aggregate of hazards dooms the victim as surely as a bullet to the forehead.

But in another sense, the computer-dating-service plot reflects the author's sentimental attachment to computers and systems, to rational ideals like the input of accurate data leading to the output of accurate decision making: the man and his wife belong together, inexorably, and the computer knows it. Technology, in Sam's little marital parable, both exposes the two would-be adulterers and tells them they were meant for each other.

The prose of these stories is serviceable, colorless, conventional, uniformly correct. In language, Sam was a largely self-taught stickler, a devotee, for example, of the distinction between uninterested and disinterested. Sometimes he hid from emotion in the habitual formality and precision of his language. Objecting to his only daughter's too-early marriage, he emphasized that his view was principled, not a matter of—he emphasized the Latinate word—*consanguinity*.

He was a frugal crank, a homemade pedant, a failure, a gadgeteer, a New Dealer, a square, a liberal, an Enlightenment Man. Then, at the age of seventy, he went to work for a magazine whose very name epitomizes much of what Sam stood for deep in his heart: *Control Engineering*. At first commuting to the offices in Manhattan, he compiled and wrote articles about Controls, both freestanding and integrated. He wrote about Controls pneumatic and hydraulic, mechanical and electrical, and—this with perhaps the greatest enthusiasm of all—fiber-optical. He conducted extensive surveys of clients and producers for lead articles. When the magazine moved to Chicago, he became a telecommuter at the age of seventy-six, and for twelve years, with the official title "East Coast Editor," he churned out so much excellent copy that often he chose to leave an article unsigned because, with two or three others already slated for the same issue, it might look peculiar to have still another carrying the byline "Sam Bailey." Few readers of the magazine would picture an octogenarian writing these intense, exhaustive discussions of the most recent developments in this or that area.

But so immense was this late flowering of energy, buoyed by liberation from the designing of weapons, that the man began writing fiction in his spare time. He spawned a couple of crime novels—not accepted for publication, perhaps because unlike the technical writing his fiction was dated.

One day, during a visit, he actually asked me for advice. "Robert," he said, "I want to write a book, and I need a topic. Maybe you could suggest a subject for me."

I am, after all, a professional teacher of creative writing. But such questions usually leave me blank. This time, for once in my life, I had what I felt was an extremely good idea—maybe one of the best ideas of its kind I have ever had. As I talked about it, I got excited.

"Sam," I said, "you should write an autobiographical account of twentieth-century technology—your personal experience of the changes and advances you have seen in your lifetime." I pointed out to him that within his lifetime we had gone from the earliest airplanes to manned space flight—to the moon. "And you *understand* it," I said: as a child, he built gliders and made models of Spads. Then he worked on missile guidance and propulsion systems. He made a crystal set and he saw the nationwide commercial networks develop; he designed transistors and circuit boards. I reminded him that he had stories in every one of these areas—like his father's Model T Ford, how the floorboards were designed to be set in loose, so that when the car got stuck in mud the motorist could lift the separate boards up to wedge under the drive wheels. I suggested to Sam that he could have a separate chapter on each technology—flight; radio and TV; the digital computer—mixing explanations with personal anecdotes. He could write about lasers and fiber optics and tell the story about his physics instructor who, in 1920, when Sam told him he was interested in optics, said no, don't waste time working in optics because it was a dead area, just about everything about it was already known and exploited.

And so forth. I liked my suggestion and Sam seemed to like it too: an autobiographical account of twentieth-century technology, informed and anecdotal, covering the greatest sweep of material progress in history.

. . . .

"That's a great idea, Robert," he said. "I'll see what I can do."

Months passed. Once in a while I wondered if he was working on this project, and one day Sam brought it up: "Robert, you remember that idea you gave me for a book?"

"Yes, Sam, I do."

"Well, I've been working on it."

"That's excellent news, Sam—it really is. I think it could be a truly wonderful book."

"Yeah," he said, and then he broke my heart: "I'm doing it as a mystery novel."

This little story is among other things a parable about creative writing, or maybe about advice in general. But I believe that Sam's failure (from my viewpoint) to rise to the bait of a lifetime reflects a social and political defeat, or if not a defeat an abdication. His unwillingness or inability to imagine the story of the technology he had seen involved all the frustrations and disappointments of his own life. In my own mind, this failure reflects the larger failure of the post–World War II culture: the hopeful world of my childhood, with its housing construction boom, its elegant skyscrapers, the U.N. buildings and the Pan American terminal, the thrilling cars in bright colors, the interstate highways, and the rich new playground of television, a medium simultaneously homey and glamorous.

While inventive people like Sam were devising the cloverleafs and construction techniques for the highways, the materials for the buildings, the electronic advances that made TV sets ever cheaper and better, all the refinements and revolutions that have made the world of the '50s and after look the way it does, most of those inventive souls were as bewildered as anyone by what their imagination and intelligence had made possible. Perhaps many of them were, like Sam, *more* bewildered than most Americans by the new world of desirable marvels and their undesirable corollaries: highway development and TV stars, dying downtowns and fortress suburbs, rapid communications and declining schools, the expansion of land-grant universities, the suburbanization of many small towns, the morbidity of many small cities, explosive abundance and the brutality of unzoned growth, the menace of nuclear war and the prosperity of auto workers, the Cold War paranoia, the new giddiness of sexual mores, the ghettoization of inner-city neighborhoods, high-rise public housing projects, the parking lots so filled with workers' cars that on his visit to America Khrushchev assumed they were faked for his benefit, the dazzling, quasi-public space of the shopping mall, which courts have legally determined to be private space, where the rights of public free speech or assembly do not apply.

Our somewhat disturbing wonderland has gotten some of its energy from advances in technology: little improvements and economies in making air conditioners, bridges, cars, elevators, hydrogen bombs, home music systems, and elevators. But although he had an informed, accurate notion of these improvements, Sam was more bewildered than most people because the sensibility that made him a scientist also made him a square. Although the house of slabs in Teaneck was a few yards away from North Jersey's Route 4, the most horribly overdeveloped highway in the world, he loved the woods, retreating there when he could. He rarely watched television, listened all day to Mozart and Rossini. A timid man socially, he lived in his house and in his own mind, a quiet region governed by Newton's laws, by concepts like input and output and the distinction between *who* and *whom*.

The people who designed, say, the earth-moving machines that built Route 4, or the machine tools that built those machines, were specialists in a way. But in another way, like my father-in-law they were generalists and tinkerers, people who understood better than most of us a wide range of technological developments. In a technical sense, they understood the story of the making of the contemporary world. But perhaps, like my father-in-law, they were not quick to think of it as their story—unlike the character in "Buddy, Can You Spare a Dime," who sings the words, *Once I built a railroad.* Rather, it was for Sam the story of entrepreneurs, investors and politicians, corporate planners and real estate developers.

In his creative efforts, in his variety of skills, even in his political values and racial outlook, Samuel Bailey harked back to that tradition, in however feeble or diluted a way. A lifelong New Deal Democrat, he seemed devoid of racial prejudice, just as he tried to be free of all other irrationalities, a category that for him included religious belief or practice, gambling, rock and roll, and romantic love. He was raised a Methodist but married a Miss Ginsberg, whom he met at a party in Greenwich Village. Together they avoided all forms of worship scrupulously, raising my wife and her brother to revere not God but the values of efficiency, decency, not making a fuss, neatness, and the general Engineering of Control whenever possible.

This way of life represents a flawed, all but nostalgic survival of that old idea of the scientist or engineer as an enlightened spirit. In that tradition, Sam's success in fiction—and dabbling in poetry, he once confessed—appropriately embodied the way in which an understanding of the physical world fosters humanistic, artistic, and progressive concerns, far from the opposite. His love of music and poetry was not a contradiction of his allegiance to the era of rural electrification and the Tennessee Valley Authority. Like Mark Twain's Pudd'nhead Wilson, fingerprinting the twins, he believed that the light of scientific truth ought to dispel bigotry.

His resignation and timidity, his unstated expectation that the large community decisions were made by the likes of devious lawyers, rascal corporate executives, and real estate sharks, reminds me—I am sad to say—of the passive, fatalistic role of my young programmer colleagues in the pit at Synapse. Some sixty years or more younger than Sam, they too had a dreamy, cocooned quality, an assumption that the story of the products we were creating was, on some important level, not their story or mine, but that of Ihor Wolosenko and the others in the front office. (This attitude was confirmed when Synapse with all its products was suddenly purchased by Brøderbund.) Though I found the programmers more charming than most of my English department colleagues at Wellesley or Berkeley, the professors took a strikingly more autonomous approach to such matters; what the college or university did seemed to them properly a narrative of their own intentions and values. The brilliant young programmers tended to be passive and fatalistic about what the managers might bring to pass.

When Sam in his concrete fortress, full of wood and plaster and metal that he had worked with his hands, listened to the traffic on Route 4, rushing through a vital, garish retail and wholesale world, in a technical sense he understood that traffic with unusual clarity. But the social organism that rushed and proliferated, gorging itself on cars and stereos and air conditioners, that charmed itself with the computer animations that sold them, left him with one of his favorite expressions: "I don't get it," he would say, turning away from the newspaper or the television news.

Meanwhile, downtown Teaneck, which had been a crisp, lively meeting place with a movie theater, a famous deli, and attractive shops, came more and more to resemble a game boxer who has been hit too many times. The crime rate and the vacancy rate kept going up. Sam cared about these things; how much he related them—or how much they should be related—to the story of progress I had urged him to narrate, I do not know.

The stereotype of the techie or hacker who is ignorant outside a narrow expertise, like the notion that scientists, engineers, doctors are conservative in their personal tastes, outlooks, politics, may be a relatively recent notion. The group working on the Manhattan project, playing their string quartets and chess games out on the desert, discussing great books and great ideas, may represent a kind of cusp or watershed: the products of the technological imagination may have become too ambiguous or disturbing, or too far-reaching in their consequences, for the old liberal, enlightened-spirit outlook quite to survive.

In Sam, and maybe in my programmer colleagues, I see the melancholy of American tinkering, gadgeteer optimism staggering on without the Enlightenment confidence. The once proud American term "know-how" has become largely ironic. Amongst the Founding Fathers of the country were surveyors, surgeons, doohickey designers, architects, and inventors, many of them agnostic or deist or atheist, reading their Horace, Martial, and Virgil. I took Sam's failure to understand the book project to be a measure of his distance from such spiritual ancestors.

But on the other hand, aside from his engineering articles, the detective novel was a genre Sam had mastered. Maybe it is as simple as that. Certainly, I prefer to think so. I prefer to think that in the present generation of technological maestros there are some souls able to pick their way through the terrible and beautiful possibilities ahead, with something of the old moral sureness and confidence—as I cannot. It would be reassuring to think that some citizens of that kind were among the gentle souls in the pit at Synapse, Inc.

Shortly before he died, Sam was working on a particularly troublesome article. The software involved had a glitch; he cursed and fumed and labored into the night, upsetting his wife. Finally, he wound up speaking to the designers at the firm that developed the program, and over a few days of phone conversations helping them revamp the code. Finally, after one last evening of work, he finished the article and printed it out: texts and labeled diagrams, neatly stacked next to the addressed envelope and camera-ready. The next morning, he had a stroke that deprived him of speech.

Before the second stroke that took him away a month or two later, Sam laboriously learned to speak again, almost perfectly. The therapist at the hospital was astounded by his persistence, the systematic intelligence he brought to his task. The day we brought him home, he told me that he might possibly write one more article for *Control Engineering*. I wasn't positive that he remembered much about the magazine; the stroke had disoriented him considerably. Still, he said he might write one more piece, a retrospective essay looking back at his previous work: it was not, he said, "beyond conceive."

. . . .

Touched by the intelligence and concentration that survived to help him climb back from darkness into speech, and by this sad, revealing imperfection of idiom, I could not help thinking about my creative writing assignment. Yes, it had been stupid of me to think that Sam could somehow tell the partly appalling story of technology in his lifetime, a daimon as rampant, as capriciously benign and terrible, as the old Olympians. But he was a shy, covertly articulate engineer.

What else would one expect? Well, enlightenment, maybe: an old tradition embodied by those scientists and engineers and medical men in Ibsen and Chekhov, that figure in nineteenth-century novels who believes in draining the swamps and cleaning up the slums, progressive ideas in the practical world that extend themselves into ideals like universal suffrage, education, social democracy.

That figure believed his enemies were ignorance, superstition, unquestioning allegiance to the past. What if his real enemy was the profitable allure, the revolutionizing, obliterating power, of his own imagination? What if traditional structures turned out to be in some ways his only defense against his own mind and its devices? (This is an aspect of the rather conservative story told by Mary Shelley in *Frankenstein*.) If some such reversal is even part of the story, then how insensitive I was to propose that Sam Bailey might set out to tell it. Maybe his words "as a mystery" have more force than either of us realized.

Screens:
An Alchemical Scrapbook

. . . .

by
ALICE FULTON

1. October 1992, Ypsilanti, Michigan: Sunscreens turn to smokescreens. The furnace, dormant since spring, fires up and fills the house with the snake cologne of burning mold. A fibrous resin from the Defiant woodstove thickens the air. This farmhouse, built in 1876, has no upstairs heat. My small study is warmed by a portable space heater—a nostalgic, homely looking object. Like many pre-high-tech appliances, it has a countenance: a metal grill that resembles a catcher's face guard shields its humming, blaze orange element. When I first turn it on, a whiff of mortality fills the air: scent of vacuum and dust. The farmer's grain drier roars distantly; a month from now he'll fix a white electric star to its top. How luminous his utilitarian citadel will be when crowned by that simplicity. Most of the farmers have day jobs. The lights of their tractors tunnel the fields after dark with the urgency of harvest; they peel out, do hairpin turns, wheelies, at the end of the rows, worried about finishing or perhaps feeling the puissance of being their own boss. Pheasant cocks, driven from the harvested fields, squawk and fight over their new territory in our meadow. Mice take shelter inside; at night their gnawing sounds like the scrape of scriveners' quills. Corn snakes wintering in the walls make a rope-through-dry-leaves rustling. The pock-pocking of shotguns signals hunters nearby. The house is swaddled by harvest in all of its guises: triumph and yield, realization and renunciation. After the committees of inertia, book blurs, wreck letters, I want to screen the day with the quiet that leads to words.

When I'm lost in the Thou-art-That of composition, the screens dividing each from each dissolve; the separate self vanishes into an undifferentiated state, which—who knows—might be similar to the "suchness" of Buddhism. Yet to enter this seamlessness, I have to screen out distractions. The effort to do so creates new complications. We have two phone lines: one for ordinary calls and one for emergencies. Each phone rings with a different signal so we can tell them apart. The workaday phone is answered by a machine that's an intrusion in itself, a kind of electronic flypaper. As long as we have the emergency phone, we feel safe in turning off the machine attached to the nonemergency number. Going one step further, I also switch off the ringer of this workaday phone. As the days go by, I discover an odd fact: even with the ringer off, the phone emits a vestigial trill when calls come in. As the quiet deepens, I can hear this tiny siren wherever I am in the house. At times, I wonder if I'm imagining the ghostly ringing. But no. My husband Hank hears it too.

I'm thinking about textures, dreams, mooncakes, and writing poems that remember the death of my nineteen-year-old niece, Laura, two years ago. Grace Lee, a Chinese American student, has given me a mooncake in celebration of the Autumn Festival. Traditionally associated with women, the Autumn Festival takes place when heat gives way to coolness, brightness to winter darkness, and the female principle ascends. A harvest fête, it is celebrated at night. People compose poems, tell stories, drink, and eat mooncakes made of lunar-colored flour. The cellophane wrapper of my mooncake features a yellow harvest moon, two tree peony blossoms, and a bar code. It says "made in Hong Kong by Tai Wing Wah Restaurant. Ingredients include Lotus Seed, Peanut Oil, Sugar, Flour." The wrapper enhances the pastry, as the moon is improved by cloud cover. Inside, there's an "oxygen absorber" packet, the desiccant packed with cameras. As I eat a dense sliver, I read about the structure of spider silk and how we dream to forget. It seems dreams are an erasure; a way to ease obsession; strategies for survival. Dreams are like writing.

When I need a break from the screen, I step to the window, see the cornstalks whittled into winter blond, a wizened forest against the unjustified margins of midwestern sky. If the University of Michigan has a home game, I might see the silver football of the Goodyear blimp advertising itself in the blue and maize surround of sky and trees. But most of all, I like to see the old silo that anchors our backyard. The silo's glazed blocks are the size and shape of computer screens. Each terra-cotta tile is rich with variations of patina, tarnish. I name the colors: *warmly sorrel as a Guernsey, weary igneous, dun sunset, almost hemoglobin, hard hard cider, tiger lily, garnet lac.* Built to shelter grain from the elements, the silo has a run in its side

like a laddered stocking where the grainshoot once stood. Previous owners must have used it as a target, because its blocks are riddled with bullet
holes. Its cap has been sacrificed to the wind. Sometimes I leave my room
and visit the silo. Climbing through its ripped side, I consider why some
screens are more lovable than others. Why do I find it easy to admire the
testy elegance of barbed wire? Easy to like the silo, a screen in the round.
Can I extend any of this affection to electronic screens? Inside, the silo is
cool as a root cellar, although its walls drip with ossified pitch, the furnace
remnants of hot tar. Keats's personification of Autumn "sitting careless on
a granary floor" comes to mind, although my appreciation of the silo does
not, I think, arise from literature or a romantic fascination with ruins. The
silo has a sculptural loveliness. I think I hear the faint electronic summons
of the phone, but it must be a wasp living—or dying—in the gauzy mortar
of the blocks. And that sudden sound—pillowcases flapping on a clothes-
line, a row of ceremonial flags—must be low-flying Canadian geese.
Looking up, I see the silo's open crown is sealed with clouds like boiled
paraffin. Summer's Paraclete. What farm wives poured on their preserves.

2. *Screen* descends, etymologically, from "shield": a safeguard or palladium. Like the element palladium, a screen is often silver. The Latin
corium— "skin, hide"—is somewhere in its history also. Protective wind-
screens and sunscreens have to be transparent in order to work. But visi-
bility, surface, is intrinsic to the shielding properties of the smokescreen
or mask.

3. The veil is a prosthetic face. The electronic screen is a prosthetic mind.
    The destruction of a prosthesis isn't as devastating as the destruction of
what it replaces.
    Which is why I'd like to have the option of veiling when I go out. I'd
like to give readings from behind a scrim or screen. Isn't it time to revive
the handheld parchment fan? Not the stare, but the glance, is revelatory.
The space of between, where meaning is neither completely revealed nor
completely concealed, is the space of possibility.
    Men have natural veils, beards, which come from within and are
painstakingly removed every day. Female veils are imposed from outside;
they are cultural rather than natural: makeup. Women want to appear
transparent though they are veiled: makeup tries to be invisible.
    Men have the option of removing their veils, but in some cultures,
women do not. Enforced veiling is a sign of the sexual control of women

by the state. It follows that violations of veiling are a means of disruption. Writing of Middle Assyrian Law, Gerda Lerner notes that when veils were worn only by respectable women, ". . . a harlot who presumed to appear veiled on the streets was as great a threat to social order as was the mutinous soldier or slave."

The long hair and beards of poets are a form of veiling. Behind the veil lies something too shocking, too vigorous, too ghastly to be seen: disease, wounds, mourning. A veil can be a bandage. Or it can be erotic.

If I can't have a literal veil, I'd like some metaphorical screen, please.

4. Enhancing screens have the teasing quality of veils. The threat of opacity lingers within their meshes and shawls. They enforce distance between the viewer and a coveted resolution. Sublime by association, the enhancing screen is imbued with the qualities of the desirable it conceals. And in circular fashion, the screen bestows its power on whatever lies behind it. Reading through an enhancing screen of language, I spend more time with the work. The screen holds my attention more effectively than the bareness of clarity or the confusion of opacity.

> Sunset that screens, reveals —
> Enhancing what we see
> By menaces of Amethyst
> And Moats of Mystery.
> EMILY DICKINSON, poem 1609

5. Does the electronic screen have to be leaden? Why not screens that look like gems at rest? Amethyst. A little sunset in the house. A little blue-green algae. A little—you name it. Does technology have to be ugly to be functional? People aren't wild about the looks of their computers. Have manufacturers thought of this? Are they missing a chance to have computers fetishized as cars are? All other things being equal, would a Jaguar of computers sell better? Old radios—made of colorful Bakelite—are collectible. A friend whose field is artificial intelligence writes, "I do feel some nostalgia for my first home computer (a beautiful chrome-plated box in the basement). . . ."

6. My antique Wang is as unprepossessing now as when I first acquired it, in 1983. Hank and I were renting an apartment in Ann Arbor, Michigan. We had taken the place because of its thirteen windows. We veiled most of them with Japanese rice-paper shades. My study was lit by tube lighting said to mimic sunlight and cure the winter desolations. But the high-tech wand was in itself a desolate-looking thing. We encased it in a Japanese paper lantern. The kitchen window was screened with matchstick blinds. A robin built her nest on the front porch that year, and peering through the tiny fissures of the matchsticks, I followed her progress. When a friend visited, I encouraged him to view the robin as I did, by pressing his eye to the hem of light between slats and making of the seam a frame. The oddity of this struck me later. Why didn't I raise the shade? Offering a guest a stingy slice of sight was like offering a stingy slice of cake. Yet the obstruction made the robin more elusive. Screened and piecemeal, she took on treasure. Picture windows are too easy. I like windows with mullions that frame the details and create peripheral compositions; they honor the margins.

We lived with three kinds of windows: transparencies that pulled in light; electronic screens that gave off light; and paintings that lived on light. The TV was a mirror window, darkly reflecting us when off and brightly distorting us when on. The opaque windows of the abstract paintings bestowed stasis on motion and substance on color. I was grateful to them for staying still. From reading, I raised my eyes to their non-referential world; they were screens that didn't insist on narrative, figure, or landscape. They were absolute music. Their subject was paint just as poetry's was language. The dark peephole of my new Wang computer was something else again. The keyboard was quieter than a typewriter, although not as stealthy as a pen. The type was the spiky green of lawns raised on weed killer. From now on, I'd be writing in golf course, in Astro-Turf. I'd be writing in Emerald City.

7. What are the aesthetics of electronic screens? Superficially, these appliances bespeak a pragmatic world in which aesthetics have no place. But if I press that suggestion, the aesthetic residue of electronic screens unveils. Their aura is suburban: charcoal briquettes and nice driveways. Commercial: they resemble the tray table that opens to support the processed food served in the clouds. The screen connotes utilitarianism and industry: a home equipped with the latest resembles a museum of pavement, a gallery of wet macadam framed in plastic-composite. Electronic screens aspire to invisibility: like the two-car attached garages of subdivisions, they are surfaces of strenuous neutrality. They long to disappear. And yet, the garage door has raised neutrality to visible—hence objectionable—heights. The trend in the more costly subdivisions is for side-facing garages. The mid-

.   .   .   .

dle classes don't want their houses annexed to enlargements of their computer screens.

8. Although many people contrive to hide their TVs, computers usually are allowed to see the light of day. Are they more aesthetically acceptable? Our own TV is housed within an antique oak chimney cabinet: a screen for the screen. Isn't there an inherent vulgarity in hiding a high-tech intrusion within a nostalgic surround? Concealing the TV might show a certain insecurity in regard to taste. And yet, I don't veil the TV because I'm ashamed of owning one. I cover it because I think it's ugly. I can embrace modernism—in principle. But in practice, high-tech design holds associations—of office, commerce, Xerox—that oppress me. I also am repulsed by unintended suggestions of nature in high-tech design: the computer monitor on its stalklike support resembles a skeletal insect. The "mouse" reminds me of a large waterbug rather than a furry rodent. I would like to hide my computer. It has as much aesthetic appeal as a window-unit air conditioner or a NordicTrack. But computers, at this writing, are harder to conceal than TVs. There's the keyboard, the printer, the monitor, the mouse. Computers could be clothed. I see a large tea cozy with tassels on top. From the pragmatic point of view, a fire hazard. From the aesthetic? The well-dressed appliance is funnier than the naked.

9. Manufacturers, aware of the impersonality of technology, want the phrase "personal computers" to trip off the collective tongue. In fact, the adjective "personal" has crept like a blush through the language of advertising. Does fear of the impersonal lie behind this locution? I give you three smarmy sentences: "I want a personal pan pizza." "I want a personal trainer to help me achieve my personal best." "I want a personal computer." The words "I want" are autoerotic. But it's "personal" that sticks in the craw. "Personal" cloys. It's infantile. "Personal" infects computers with the warm fuzzies, a condition no appliance has had to bear before. "Personal" transforms cultural narcissism into a source of pride and self-affirmation. "Personal," it would appear, sells product.

10. Tools can be beautiful. But I don't think computers are destined to become lovely sensual presences. Thus begins their difference from books. There's a romance to the physicality of the book, a tactile pleasure to be had in its constructedness. Of all the objects associated with writing, books are potentially the most beautiful. Potentially, because books in numbers can look messy—even garish. My shelves layer the walls with horizons. Windows get in the way. The titles are an intoxication in themselves, suggesting compressed worlds, visible and at hand. Within the horizontal shelves blaze the slim verticals of the books. The room is a welter of stripes, a riot of primaries too hectic for my taste.

Readers often save a book's protective dust jacket from wear by removing it while reading. A friend of mine has disposed of the wraps entirely. His shelves are saturated with the garment-washed, wet stone glow of cloth bindings. It's as if the dust the jacket was meant to forestall has gentled the books. But I can't strip my books down to the spine. Taken together, the paper-wrapped books are a visual cacophony. Taken alone, a book in its wraps has more interest and texture than one without. It's an aesthetic version of the one/many problem.

11. Soon after the Wang arrived in 1983, I used it while working on a memoir. My resistance to writing the essay was private and weighty. After agonizing for days, I overcame andirons of resistance to pull forth—as if from my entrails, self-eviscerating—several finished pages. Toward the end of this day's work, absorbed, I touched a combination of keys and the Wang emitted a loud, unstoppable electronic scream. The screen was petrified in place. Hank had to pull the plug to get the computer to shut up, and I lost all of the day's writing. A friend who worked with Wangs said I'd hit "a screech bug." I don't have a good record with electric appliances. Is it possible that my own electromagnetic field upsets them? Are we physically incompatible?

12. I'm seduced by a book's ability to preserve physical traces of its readers. Readers of electronic books leave no ink behind in the margins. Although electronic books might allow for marginalia, the notes would be typed rather than handwritten, and they probably would not accumulate as the book passed through many readers' hands and minds. This last would be seen as an improvement. The marginal notes in library books serve as hecklers, upsetting the authority of the printed text, or as echoes, noisily parroting the meaning. But I'd miss the ink of them. As an adolescent, I discovered my sister's college texts in the attic. Sandy had been an English major. I feasted on *Jude the Obscure, Adam Bede, The Confessions of Saint Augustine, Immortal Poems.* And I devoured faddish, unas-

signed books—by Ayn Rand, Kahlil Gibran—with equal appetite. Sometimes the margins were wildcrafted with blue ballpoint notes in Sandy's
hand. Between the pages of a paperback, I found a single red hair, unmis-
takably hers. A bookmark of the body, it seemed supernatural—recherché
as the two recessive genes needed to express *auburn* and my sister.

13. I have a wardrobe of old, ink-covered clothes reserved for writing. Pen
in hand, I'm a menace to the blank slate of everything in reach. The pen has
become such a constant extension that I no longer remember I'm holding
it. I stretch, and the movement is inscribed—on the sofa, the sheets, the cat.
If invited to a literary costume party, I'd like to dress as Caddy Jellyby of
Bleak House, whose "inky condition" parodies my state: ". . . a jaded, and
unhealthy-looking, though by no means plain girl, at the writing table,
who sat biting the feather of her pen, and staring at us. I suppose nobody
ever was in such a state of ink. And, from her tumbled hair to her pretty
feet, which were disfigured with frayed and broken satin slippers trodden
down at heel, she really seemed to have no article of dress upon her, from a
pin upwards, that was in its proper condition, or its right place." Caddy
serves as "amanuensis" to her mother, Mrs. Jellyby, a self-serving philanthropist and tireless generator of letters. In my reinscription, I cast Mrs.
Jellyby as the draconian Muse. "Where are you, Caddy?" she says with a
sweet smile. My copy of *Bleak House* belonged to my sister. Certain passages have been underwired with red ink, filaments delicate as hair.

14. Gatekeepers, judgmental structures, screens are invested with the
power of entry and exclusion. They discriminate; censor; discern; play favorites. They have an agenda. They're critics. Or artists, functioning as
silkscreens. In silkscreening, ink is forced—through a silk mesh with both
pervious and impervious areas—onto a prepared ground. The artist's
open and hidden interests are the blotchy screen through which the work
is pressed.

15. October 1992: Well into work, I was floating around the silent house
in a creative stupor, bumping into objects. Though the ringer was off, the
phone continued its spectral trilling. We'd decided that the mechanism
must vibrate slightly even when disconnected. The emergency phone was
silent—as if all the fumble-fingered dialers of wrong numbers had entered
a state of digital grace. I'd spoken to no one but Hank for who knows how
long. In this somatic daze, I slumped in front of the screen and summoned

my e-mail. Something from the English department appeared. What bureaucratic white noise—what evaluations, colloquia, surveys, forms—lay in wait? "What fresh hell is this?" I yawned, blasé as Dorothy Parker. But the adrenaline message on the screen pierced my nonchalance: my sister Pat was trying to reach us. It was urgent. I should call her immediately. I braced myself for some awful intelligence.

Pat had been phoning us for days. She'd been unable to get through because, as we soon discovered, the emergency phone had come unplugged by accident. As she talked, my mind filled with images like film rushes, nonsequential, nonverbal: Marleen, my sister Sandy's twenty-year-old daughter; a club in Argentina; disco dresses; drinks; a holdup; film noir; smoke; gangsters; no shots fired. Marleen had lost consciousness. Marleen had died. Wait. No. A *health* club; tennis; juice drinks; a robbery; Marleen at the register; no shots fired. Marleen had lost consciousness. Marleen had died. Unbelief. Sandy's nineteen-year-old daughter Laura also had died suddenly, from natural causes, just two years earlier.

16. October 1992: When Laura died, Sandy and her husband George had tried to create a ceremony that would speak to that incommensurate loss. Everyone struggled to invent expressions for an event that had no precedent. Amateurs of mourning, we foundered in the new and terrible terrain. At Marleen's funeral, however, the sadness was magnified by a feeling of being overrehearsed. We knew the ritual all too well. Familiarity—usually a comforting sensation—took on a horrific aspect. Repetition gathers its own significance: recurring nightmares are the most frighteningly portentous.

While we were gathered for Laura's funeral, Marleen had shown everyone a photo album filled with snapshots of herself and her boyfriend, Mauro: bright occasions screened in laminate. Every time Mauro's name came up, Marleen would say, "I love him," with the same inflection: trusting, insouciant. Sometimes the voice tries to be a screen and fails. Sandy and George tried to sift the anguish from their voices, since their suffering would leave others at a loss. Although their composure was heroic, they sounded most distraught when asserting that they wouldn't be sad: Marleen was in heaven. The struggle between stoicism and emotion, between brave face and hysteria, creates pathos. The screen opens and closes. Burning and dodging. What's glimpsed in the hinge moment is most mov-

. . . .

ing. *Burning in* increases the density of a photograph by exposing certain areas to extra light during enlargement. *Dodging* reduces the density of selected image areas by shading and masking the light. Both techniques create greater detail in the print.

Once women in mourning wore long black veils. These days, the face must serve as screen, and it fails. It leaks, rips, and before you know it, you're crying over your smile. At the wake, I felt sorry for Marleen being shown off when she was so dead. It was like being naked in front of every-one—except that she definitely would have looked better naked than dead. She was so attractive in life, and so unlike herself in death. In Scotland, a large head scarf is called a *screen*. I wanted to throw such a screen over her, anything to ease the exposure. But we don't do what we want to do on such occasions. Since Marleen's letters to my mother often began, "Hey Crazy Lady!" my mother wanted to put "Crazy Lady" after "Grandma Fulton" when signing the funeral home's guest book. In deference to propriety, she refrained.

Funerals are mirror images of celebrations: they require announcements, programs, flowers, new outfits, photographs, and the preparation of a feast to be eaten afterwards. On the day of Marleen's funeral, the sky glowed like white organdy, silkscreening the light. Her handsome Mauro spoke little English. His presence dramatized the insufficiency of words. A little snow drifted down like pale confetti. If funerals are inverse celebrations, this one was a wedding.

17. A volatile folding word, *screen* encases dual meanings within one another. *Screen* implodes and so allows its opposite to exist.

While the noun *screen* connotes an outer, visible layer, the verb *to screen* means "to hide." Yet to screen a movie is to show it, rather than obscure it. Screens are partitions that conceal; but they also collapse into portability, revealing all. As walls go, they're flimsy—temporary, nonweight-bearing. When a screen is a sieve, it's both porous and impermeable: allowing and preventing passage. A screen can be necessary or ornamental; solid or pierced. The opposing definitions of *screen* remind me of stellar pairs, binary stars in close proximity to one another orbiting about a common center of mass. Astronomers have noticed a feature common to all binaries: the closer the two members lie to one another, the more rapidly they swing about in their orbits. So *screen* oscillates under consideration.

18. November 1992: I called my mother. She said that last Saturday was Laura's birthday. I remembered that we'd been gathered to celebrate my mother's birthday when Laura died.

This year on Laura's birthday, George and eight-year-old Ali were in a bakery. Ali said, "Why don't we buy her a cake?" So they did. My mother said, "It's better that they remember her birth than her death."

19. Iced with pastel Crisco, the glassed-in bakery cakes might remind a child of Snow White in her casket. Did Ali feel beyond such fairy tales? The see-through slipper, poison apple dramas. The wolf that huffs and puffs. And George, what did he feel? I imagine him breathing the hydrogenated fragrance of the bakery — of pastries dry as marble dust — and hesitating. The cakes stare him down like frosted clocks. He considers. Thinks yes, why not celebrate his daughter's birth? Let them write "Laura" in a wreath of hemoglobin roses. Once home, the cake is an amazement of candles and mussed icing. Everyone inhales and thinks a wish. Everyone wishes that the radical hospitality of paradise has not been exaggerated. But no one has enough breath to extinguish the candles' little fiery bricks.

20. I wanted to write this in monument, but I just had ink.

21. I have a vested interest in the aesthetics of science. Since the sensibility of engineers and hackers affects the medium I use to compose my work, I'm curious about their worldview. What tastes have informed and created computer culture? And what spoken or unspoken aesthetic makes itself felt in writer culture? Do the twain ever meet? Some of the same stereotypes have been used to characterize both groups: the mad scientist and mad poet; the science nerd and the bookworm.

"Elegance" is the most well-known component of scientific aesthetics. The elegance of science is connected to simplicity, an investment that seems in conflict with science's ever-increasing complexity. Yet what seems elaborate to nonscientists can be a model of elegance to the expert. The hapless home computer user must purchase "upgrades" or find herself in possession of an obsolete system that cannot be repaired or replaced. Should her antiquated computer break, all of her files will become inaccessible. In order to keep up, she must spend hours installing and learning to use costly "improvements" upon a system that already seemed sufficient for her purposes. To me, the upgrades are extraneous: devised by manufacturers in order to sell more products. But to the virtuosos of hacking who created the novations, they are elegant.

In *The Second Self: Computers and the Human Spirit*, Sherry Turkle notes that hackers "built a computer culture around a widely shared aesthetic of simplicity, intelligibility, control, and transparency." The mainstream of American literature shares the same values. Most U.S. writers are adherents of the plain style, striving for transparency of surface and for meanings intelligible enough to be widely understood. Control is shown by a respect for craft or a revival of traditional forms. Turkle also points to hackers' fascination with recursive structures: the Escher stairway that climbs upwards while folding back into itself, the Bach fugue that builds upon its inversions to end up where it began. In like fashion, postmodern literary works tend to be self-reflexive, "about" their own workings; rather than trying to awaken emotions in the reader, they create cerebral delight, the pleasure hackers locate in the Escher print or the fugue.

22. In the early '70s I had a radio show on a station owned by Rensselaer Polytechnic Institute (RPI). Like most of the DJs, I was musically obsessed. The engineers, or "techies," on the other hand, were fixated on the station's broadcasting equipment, which they had built themselves, from the ground up. While I was on the air, an engineer would sometimes enter and gaze appreciatively at the wall of bouncing meters and blinking lights—a sight that to my mind lacked the erotic halo of, say, a Gibson Sunburst guitar. Sometimes after a show we'd all go out to their restaurant of choice, the International House of Pancakes (IHOP), for a late dinner. The techies got to choose the restaurant because they owned the cars—rusty, oil-dribbling Volkswagens that smelled of sour milk and vinyl. Despite the marginal health of their vehicles, the engineers held an annual road rally. Rather than prizing the automobile's mechanism, they were excited by cars as a means of navigating a labyrinth under the constraint of rules and clues.

My future husband, Hank De Leo, was the station's program director and, unlike me, an RPI student. While at RPI, Hank had two roommates. The first, Strike Perlswigger, hoped to earn his living as a professional bowler. Strike seldom went to classes; he seemed to distill the requisite academic information from the thunderous air of the Troy Bowl, where he spent his days. Strike went from September to mid-November of 1970 without bathing. He evaded laundry by refusing to change his sheets or clothes. Many of the more gifted engineers ignored their own physicality. Flesh was not their concern. They were cerebral beings, who one day would give birth to virtual reality and cyberspace. Learning of another student, Rob Rozecki, who also had roommate problems, Hank arranged to move in with him. Rob had very good hygiene; in fact, he was compulsively neat. He was besotted with Doris Day, and he knew every episode of *Star Trek* by heart. The engineers yearned for alternate worlds where technology reigned. As readers, they prized inventiveness—a sci-fi author's ability to resolve dilemmas without breaking self-created laws. Such writerly concerns as character and language were incidental. While many RPI students shared the *Star Trek* mania, Rob's former roommate, Claude Gideon, did not. Claude was obsessed with bridge. He never studied, but stayed up all night playing cards with a group of like-minded buddies. I'd never suspected that young men could be addicted to bridge—a game I associated with Junior League matrons. But bridge, like the road rally, offered the chance to master complex patterns while obeying clear-cut rules and working toward a trump.

More than simply serving as exemplars of dorky science nerds, these RPI engineers foreshadowed the values of computer culture. Their interest in mazes and the conquest of recondite structures would find its ideal expression in programming. Strike's apathy toward embodiment has been extended to the computer's body, whose physicality seems unimportant. Rob's Doris Day obsession was admittedly an uncommon affliction. Perhaps he was attracted to the reliability of her wholesome image and to her unavailability, which forestalled rejection. When Sherry Turkle asked hackers what they found in their relationship to the computer, their answers could be summarized as "safety." The relationship with the machine was more dependable than a relationship with a human being.

23. In my observation, writers are as fond of safety as engineers, although writers' quests for security take different forms. Hackers, according to Sherry Turkle, embrace "an ethic of total toleration for anything that in the real world would be considered strange." Writers are much less accepting. In fact, despite declarations of aesthetic risk taking, writers seem afraid of nonconformity—on the page or the body. They limit their couture to camouflage. By courting invisibility, writers affect to transcend the superficiality of surface concerns. Yet rather than fashion innocents, they are disciples of a conservative, unspoken dress code that associates serious stature with earth tones. Better shabby than flashy. Better figuratively

·   ·   ·   ·   ·   ·   ·   ·   ·   ·

dead than literally red. The wish for plainness has no ethical dimension; the "Sackville-West Vest" from J. Peterman costs six times the price of the neon knit from Kmart. Romanticism tamed by folkloric elements is also a safe bet: all writers own those oatmeal-colored Irish fisherman sweaters. While I'm being reductive, why not go all the way? If hackers are obsessives, writers are narcissists. If engineers are pragmatists, writers are connoisseurs—of wine, books, opera. Hackers gather at no-nonsense IHOP for physical sustenance; writers loiter in coffeehouses for imaginative fodder. Engineers decorate with Escher prints; writers choose Asian scrolls, Edward Hopper, Joseph Cornell. Engineers play bridge; writers play poker or blackjack. Hackers are Bach fans; writers are Rolling Stones fans. Hacking is the computer freak's drug. Drugs are the writer's drug: alcohol, nicotine, caffeine. The composite impression? Engineers are cerebral and analytical; writers are sensual and intuitive. And yet.

"When you are programming, you just build straight from your mind," a hacker tells Turkle. When lost in their work, writers also exist in a cyberspace of the mind, unaware of sensuality—screened from heat, cold, flies, hunger, darkness, e-mail, phone calls. A. R. Ammons, a poet who began as a scientist, ends his poem "Summer Session" with lines that acknowledge the biological and mechanistic underpinnings of imagination and unsettle the scientist / humanist binary:

> the head is my sphere:
> I'll look significant as I deal with
> mere wires of light, ghosts of
> cells, working there.

"I'll look significant" admits a self-conscious questioning of personal authority unknown to science. And rather than assert himself as prophet elect, a chosen conduit for the Muse, Ammons constructs the imaginative sphere in terms unknown to poetry: the poet's head as mysterious computer of flesh.

24. November 1992: My heart has always made me nervous. I don't like to contemplate my dependency on the common time it keeps so well, faithfully repolarizing itself between beats, muscling blood through the body. What an automaton the heart is. What a genius of insistence, mechanistic yet animate, the pulse like an insect trapped under the wrist's skin. Unthinking replication is a staple of the horrific. One ant might be an interesting subject for study, but thousands swarming together, identical,

unfeeling, robotic, alive, would give many—give me—the creeps, the willies. The aesthetic deadliness of electronic screens arises in part from their likeness to one another: the thousands of computers as interchangeable as ants. And, like insects, computers raise questions concerning consciousness: at what point does a brain, "mere wires of light," come alive? When it becomes self-aware? When it shows a will to live? The heart scares me because I can feel its importance physically. Most of the body's major organs are more reticent: the brain hums along so quietly that the ancients believed *thought* lived in our noisy hearts. Now, of course, the heart symbolizes emotion, not analysis. Each beat offers another chance for revelation. Repetition can take on a powerful beauty if it manages variation while retaining the residue of its original meaning. The recurring lines in blues songs create fresh implications with each saying—unlike the drilling of the phone. After Marleen's funeral, we turned the ringer on again. Sandy called and told me about visiting her friend Rosa, who'd had a stroke and lost the ability to say anything other than "I love you." By shading this phrase with different tones, Rosa managed to convey a wide range of emotion and meaning. She could say "I love you" so that her family heard, for instance, "don't do that," "open the door," "I'm angry with you," or "I love you."

25. I once heard a psychologist remark that obsessive-compulsives were the most boring patients. I can see why. Yet the opposite is also true: obsessions—because they hint at vast stores of passion and laser focus—are fascinating. Computer junkies are a source of concern: an Internet Addiction Group has formed to help the screenstruck. (This group "meets" on-screen, a choice that seems akin to holding an AA meeting in an open bar.) It's easy to imagine the lethal powers of electronic objects. Books, in contrast, seem more benign. "When you go to a bookstore after work, thus arriving home late at night, do you lie about where you have been, telling your spouse you were at a bar?" Tom Raabe asks in *Biblioholism: The Literary Addiction*, a book that parodies the self-help market. What's the term for someone who fetishizes the materiality of the book itself: who wants to crawl inside it, feed upon it, dwell in it. Bookworm? Bibliophile? Are there negative effects of book addiction? "I started reading *The Catcher in the Rye*, and I couldn't put it down until I got to the end. And I read it again. Then I held it between my hands. I put it against my face, and inhaled deeply, drinking in the aroma, that sort of faintly antiseptic smell of a new book, through my nostrils and my skin. And I felt: 'Here is

. . . .

a way. . . .'" Mark David Chapman, the man who killed John Lennon, describes his favorite book.

26. November 1992: My heart has let me down more than once. I've learned a technical vocabulary to describe its fickleness: *syncope* (loss of consciousness), *prodrome* (sensations experienced in the seconds before fainting), *epinephrine* (adrenaline). The sudden deaths of my nieces sent me back to analyze my own medical history. When Laura died, doctors reassured Sandy that her other children were safe. They were wrong: Marleen. As soon as we returned from her funeral, Hank began researching the causes of sudden death in young adults. I began archiving the times I'd fainted or nearly fainted, scrutinizing the circumstances and adding to Hank's composite portrait of the undiagnosed condition. Along with necessary external details came unwanted images of the internal struggle to hold fast to consciousness. I remembered the times I'd fallen far into unbeing and come back terrified by a new knowledge of the nothing screen. How dreamlessly unlike sleep it was. How zero. I came back terribly impressed. Awareness has a sculptural, 3-D quality: the sensorium is experienced in the round, as if the depth, pitch, texture, taste, and scent of intelligibility were welded to the insides of our heads. I recalled the deflation of this sphere, the flattening of dimension to a screen of fiery pixels, snippets, vermiculite glittering, as vision swarmed to buzzing snow, a prodrome like the blizzard screen of no reception on TVs. Back came the loss of face that is loss of world, as I assembled my collection of helplessness.

In 1977, I almost passed out while trying to make a case for my aunt with her psychiatrist over the phone. "But my dear little girl . . ." he said, and the patriarchal maw of medical authority seemed to devour all the oxygen in the room. My aunt was at the mercy of this institutionalized egotism. For her sake, I fought to repress my anger and remain polite, an effort that almost made me black out. If I fainted, her shrink would brand me a hysteric. This realization kept me conscious while my mother's kitchen shifted and fizzed in place.

My nearest near-death experience occurred in grad school. I'd gathered my nerve and spoken to my advisors about the male domination of academe. "Women are motes of dust around here." I hadn't expected this pronouncement to be met with sympathy, but it was. "I think I'm going to faint," I said. Was this some kind of joke, the angels-of-desire-poetess swoon? I surprised them by dropping to the floor, deeply unconscious. I had every test available at the time, but the doctors were mystified.

This is just a short list of *losing it*. There were many other instances. To my own profile, I added those of Laura and Marleen. Laura had experienced a single episode of unconsciousness before the one that took her life. After the alarm sounded one morning, her roommate noticed that she was struggling to breathe. The paramedics were called; she was revived; tests were done; but as with me, nothing was found to be wrong. A year later, she died in her room, apparently while sleeping. The phone was ajar, and Sandy wondered if she'd been trying to call for help. Before Marleen's sudden death during the holdup, she had never lost consciousness.

As I reviewed these memories, Hank gazed at the computer screen, looking up abstracts on Medline, a database. By searching under *cardiac, sudden death, syncope*, he came up with a huge list of articles. About half were available as abstracts on the computer. He read those and looked up others in the University of Michigan's medical library. He studied textbooks, seeking symptoms that matched the constellation surrounding Laura, Marleen, and me. By piecing details together, he was led to something called Jervell-Lange-Nielsen syndrome. But there was one confounding detail: the condition existed only in deaf children. Using this syndrome as a lead, Hank searched further on Medline and came up with four articles on an inherited disorder called Long QT syndrome. After reading these, he called Sandy and told her to be sure to have her doctor rule out this disorder. "I think I've found it," he said to me.

Long QT is a rare, genetic disease in which the electrocardiographs of some sufferers show an infinitesimally prolonged "QT interval," hence the condition's name. The medical histories of afflicted families reveal instances of fainting and inexplicable sudden death. In normal people, both exercise and the fight-or-flight mechanism cause a release of epinephrine (adrenaline), which increases the heart rate. In the case of long QT sufferers, however, an electrical defect prevents the heart from repolarizing after a massive influx of adrenaline. The resulting arrhythmia leads to fainting and, in some cases, cardiac arrest. Fainting episodes occur under physical or emotional stress. Loss of consciousness also is triggered by sudden noises, particularly if the subject is startled while sleeping. The articles recommended "that affected individuals avoid . . . exposure to abrupt auditory stimuli. This can be accomplished by eliminating alarm clocks, door bells, and phone ringing from the household. . . ." Hank speculated that the phone had startled Laura from a nap; this would explain why it had been found ajar. In Marleen's case, as in mine, the emotional component of the disease was telling. The literature cited instances of children in

. . . .

the nineteenth century who dropped dead while being scolded in school. Fainting resulted from a feeling of powerlessness; it was a response to an oppression that allowed for neither fight nor flight. Like a holdup. Like misogyny. "But I can't be right," Hank concluded. "I'm not a doctor."

When Sandy relayed Hank's suspicion to her cardiologist, he said it was as if a light went on. It seems Hank had diagnosed the disorder, and he couldn't have done so without the computer. The condition can be treated with beta-blockers, drugs that protect the heart by building a chemical screen in the body. They block the beta reception sites so that epinephrine cannot reach them and make the heart race. Some beta-blockers work only on the heart, and some cross the blood-brain barrier, a screening device that allows certain chemicals into the brain while refusing others. But these are clumsy descriptions of intricate effects, beyond current comprehension. *Behold, I shew you a mystery; We shall not all sleep, but we shall all be changed.*

27. Consider the leafiness of books, the peeling that is reading. Consider the peeling that is writing. By the end, I feel exfoliated.

Writing this, I was blinded by the paper, the screen, the events recounted. The material called for shades. Called for language to screen the emotional loudwork. Language as acoustic shadow: an area that inexplicably retains its reticence despite a great noise nearby.

28. I wanted to write this in diamond, but I just had blood. I used the hand's most important attribute, opposition, to hold the pen, scissors, glue. I marred the page, wrist pulsing against the notebook's cool seersucker, its ticking checking my drifting sentences and chilling my recklessness. I used paper sacrificed from the gold fingerprints inside trees: high acid foolscap with no watermark, I see, holding to the light a scrap of flimsy, its edges grunged with dust.

The Conversion

. . . .

by

WENDY LESSER

I resisted e-mail for at least two or three years. Many of my Berkeley friends are academics, so they got it automatically as part of their jobs and then annoyingly sang its praises. "It replaces long-distance phone calls!" "You can dig up old recipes from libraries across the Midwest!" "It allows you to communicate instantaneously with colleagues from South Africa!" None of these seemed like things I particularly wanted to do. Moreover, I had strong if somewhat irrational reasons for resisting. I did not want my computer talking on the phone to anyone else's computer, because who knew what could happen once you opened up those lines? I wasn't just worried about viruses, though those were indeed a concern; but how could you be sure that someone wouldn't sneak through the e-mail door and thereby penetrate your hard disk, stealing or at any rate messing up your closely held documents? I preferred to keep my computer chaste and self-contained, aloof from all potential communicants. And then, I didn't see the point of getting those unreadable little messages that seemed to go on forever, with little or no punctuation. To judge by the e-mail I had read in newspapers and magazines (the kind that was always reproduced to show how fun and liberating this new mode of communication was), these emissions were somewhere below the level of the worst unsolicited manuscripts I habitually receive in the course of editing a literary maga-zine. Why should I want to read *more* of the stuff, especially on a barely legible computer screen? What was the good of a technological form that erased the boundary between intimate friends and total strangers, reduc-

. . . .

ing everyone to a digital printout? Where was *handwriting* in all this? Where was *personal style?*

I should interrupt my screed to say that I am not a complete antitechnologist. I watch more television than just about anyone I know, and believe that *Hill Street Blues* and *NYPD Blue* are among the major artistic achievements of late twentieth-century America. I use the latest (well, the second-latest) desktop publishing equipment to put out my magazine, and rely on a rather complex database software to organize its subscriber list. I adore the fax machine and have long considered it the single greatest invention since the telephone — the fax machine, after all, respects and transmits handwriting, just as the telephone conveys the nuances of the individual voice. I am not, that is, a hermit. I constantly employ and enjoy electronic transmissions of all sorts, and I do not feel that they in any way sap my capacity to be an Emersonian individual. On the contrary, they enhance it: without all my little machines, I could not make a living as a self-employed, self-designated arbiter of cultural taste. In Emerson's time, you had to inherit a comfortable income if you wished to subsist as a man of letters; in our day, technology can substitute for and even generate the freeing effects of wealth.

But for some reason this dashing perspective, this resolutely cheerful optimism about mechanical progress, did not make a dent in my fear of e-mail. From the perspective of one who has now crossed the great divide, I can see that my phobia stemmed in part from a category error. That is, I thought that "e-mail" and "the Internet" were identical: I believed that in order to communicate with my friends and colleagues, I would have to place myself squarely in front of all the oncoming lanes of traffic in the Information Superhighway. Worse: I was persuaded that those snippets of generic e-mail clipped from the bulletin boards of the Internet represented what my own friends would sound like if I had to talk to them by computer. I wrongly supposed that the machine controlled it own content, that the medium (as we used to say, *pace* McLuhan, in the '6os) would be the message.

Why I should have believed Marshall McLuhan in this respect when I had long since discarded his views on television is a question that perhaps requires a cultural psychotherapist to answer. (I don't know that there *is* such a thing as a cultural psychotherapist, but since I have recently learned of something called "ecopsychology" — which is designed to help us bond with Mother Earth — I assume there are no limits.) For some reason, fear makes us believe in false prophets, the more apocalyptic the better. Clinging to the printed pages of my old-fashioned literary quarterly and my beloved cloth- and paperbound books, I thought that e-mail spelt the end of reading as I knew it. After all, you couldn't do it in the bathtub.

Well, there are lots of things you can't do in the bathtub and even I have to admit that doesn't make them useless or unacceptable. I wouldn't want to read a novel or even a ten-page story on e-mail, and faced with that little message screen, I probably couldn't compose an essay worth printing. But for daily correspondence, electronic mail has become my essential instrument. And like all tools, it is more than just a simple replacement of the previous technology—it acts on you as well as you on it, and it acts in ways you can't always predict. In effect, e-mail has restored the personal letter to my life.

If you are like me, you went through a phase when personal letters occupied a central place in your existence. You were probably in your late teens or early twenties. Possibly you were living away from home for the first time, or perhaps you had just embarked on your first long-term (and long-distance) love affair, or maybe you were traveling alone through Europe, or all of the above. The mail became your lifeline, and you honored it accordingly. You poured everything into your letters—the engaging details of daily existence, the special sights, the serious emotions, the witty observations—to such an extent that even journal-keeping, by comparison, seemed onerous and redundant. You tailored each letter to the personality of the recipient, delightedly imagining the eventual response to the in-jokes of a shared history. You received as good as you gave, and each day's mail delivery marked an emotional high or low point. And then, at some point, you grew out of all this, and household bills, business letters, magazines, and fund-raising pleas came to fill your mailbox instead.

Just as personal letters define a phase in an individual's life, so do they also define a period in Western history. I didn't realize this until I read P. N. Furbank's review of the *Oxford Book of Letters,* wherein he remarks

> ... how deprived the ancient world was, not having discovered the secret of personal letters—long, spontaneous, chatty letters, as funny as they can be made but not always just funny, and coming nice and often—the sort of letters you might have got if you had known Henry James or Bernard Shaw or Philip Larkin. You would have been expected to answer them, and that would have been marvelous too, at least for oneself. It would be like enjoying a second life.

.   .   .   .

Exactly. And, as Furbank goes on to say, "The ancients knew nothing of this. With what leaden spirits one would have received a letter from Cicero! One may hazard that this best kind of letter-writing began in the eighteenth century and really came into its own in the nineteenth." Not coincidentally, this was just when the postal system was reaching a pinnacle of service, in terms of frequency and reliability.

For one of the keys to the pleasure of letters lies in that half-buried little phrase, "and coming nice and often." In London, where P. N. Furbank lives, mail is still delivered twice a day, and a letter posted first-class will reach its destination anywhere in the United Kingdom by the next day. It is still possible to keep up a satisfying personal correspondence under such circumstances. For the rest of the world, however, mail is generally too slow to gratify the needs of the moment. You might choose to rely on the stamp and envelope on special occasions, or for particularly delicate communications, or if (like a young person in her teens or twenties) you live on a very limited budget; but when you have something important to say, you're much more likely to pick up the telephone.

The crisis in my attitude toward e-mail occurred when I realized that I would no longer be able to afford the telephone. I was about to leave America for four months, and to indulge in long-distance calling from Europe would be ruinously expensive. Nor could I tolerate waiting the two weeks it would take for the round-trip communication by post. It was e-mail or nothing.

One problem with e-mail, though, is that it takes two actively willing participants. Anyone in the modern world can receive a postal letter, but only those with an e-mail hookup can receive e-mail. So I had to get my near and dear to join up at the same time I did. Among those I had to persuade was a writer in New York, a friend of twenty years' standing on whom I normally lavish at least one long-distance phone call a day. As he is even more of a Luddite than I am, this was no easy task.

"I feel very resistant to the idea," he explained.

"I know, I know," I said. "I've already been resistant for three years, so can't we take it as done?"

Finally, I just cheated. I ordered *his* CompuServe introductory package when I ordered my own, knowing that when the user-friendly software slipped through his mail slot, he would be unable to resist trying it on. (Or, to put it more truthfully: I planned to make life miserable for him via telephone until he got around to applying his e-mail diskettes.)

It was slow to catch on. At first my friend and I used e-mail mainly as a

toy, in between the more substantial communication of our transconti-
nental phone calls, and most of our electronic conversation was metacon-
versation, in that it dealt with the ins and outs of using e-mail. But when I
left California on a Wednesday night, arrived in London on a Thursday
morning, hooked up my computer, received my New York friend's welcoming message, and instantly e-mailed back—well, that was a revelation
for both of us. Soon we were up to three or even four exchanges a day. The
five-hour time difference meant nothing: he could post a note before he
went to sleep, and I would receive it when I woke up the next day. And
what I discovered, to my enormous pleasure, was that the electronic mode
did not wash out his characteristic tones. On the contrary, he sounded in
his virtual incarnation exactly as he did in real life: wry, observant, dryly
affectionate, subtle, and sharp. Personal style, it turned out, did not get
blotted out by the machine. In some ways it was even enhanced, with new
opportunities for humorous self-expression and literary allusion afforded
by the title spaces in our messages. "Internettled," his title bar announced
when he had been fiddling all day to make the machine do something new.
"Later the Same Day," I called one of my frequent messages, echoing
Grace Paley. And it was inevitable, given the technology, that we would
soon feel inspired to use E. M. Forster's "Only connect."

Even in our differing responses to the availability of e-mail, my friend
and I were faithful to our respective personalities. Something of a self-
styled loner, he built up a tiny, highly selective list of e-mail addresses and
mailed only to those two or three people. (His willful resistance to technological self-education may have had something to do with this. "How do
you communicate with those outside our parish?" he once complained,
stumped by the difficulty of crossing over from CompuServe to America
Online or Prodigy.)

I, on the other hand, verged on epistolary promiscuity. Within my first
week on-line, I had mailed to a number of my Berkeley pals, a long-lost
classmate in Tasmania, three Londoners, my husband at his work address,
my stepson at college, my father, my sister, a good friend who had temporarily moved to St. Louis, and my exercise teacher. I became an e-mail
maniac, checking in every hour or so and collapsing with disappointment
if I got the empty-mailbox beep. I found myself waxing expansive on-
screen, chatting on about virtually nothing. I was responding, I now
think, to the special enticements of the form's mixed nature—at once private and public, solitary and communal, so that it seems to combine the
two oldest types of American writing, the diary and the sermon. With

. . . .

e-mail, you begin with the former, alone at your desk, and end (if you use your "multiple send" button) with the latter, broadcasting to the whole congregation.

One of the first responses I got from old e-mail hands, when I contacted them with my newly acquired address, was scorn at the impersonal nature of my mailing moniker. Everybody else, it appeared, had managed to craft idiosyncratic, sometimes poetic, always memorable labels for themselves. Using the loose conventions set up by most e-mail providers, they had come up with word combinations that were nearly as distinctive as their own names (and that often incorporated those names into the address). But CompuServe allowed for no such creativity: we were simply allocated a number. "Your address sounds like something from the Planet Zog," one of my correspondents wrote. Another mocked me for my long resistance to e-mail. "This is just the kind of address I would expect a confirmed Luddite to get," he noted. "Those who resist the machine are doomed to be punished by it."

Whatever form it takes, your e-mail address becomes a part of your permanent identity in a way that no mere phone number can. For one thing, you can't hide it. You can make an obscene phone call from an anonymous number or mail a poison pen letter without giving a return address, but your e-mail message carries its provenance in its heading. This necessary mutuality is both e-mail's virtue and its curse. That is, you have to consider before engaging in any communication whether you want to hear *from* someone as well as speak *to* him, because he will thereafter possess your address. There are no one-way assaults in the world of e-mail: if you launch a missive, you automatically open yourself up to a counterattack.

And unlike a phone number, which can be as temporary as your present whereabouts, your e-mail address travels with you. I had exactly the same CompuServe number during my European stay as during my normal Berkeley life. People seeking to contact me didn't have to know I was out of the country or even out of the office. Sometimes I would amuse myself by trying to imagine where my virtual mailbox was located. Did it float somewhere in the fourth dimension, rushing into my computer only when it was actually consulted? Or did it hover somewhere over the Atlantic, relaying messages between my temporarily European self and my North American correspondents? I had been told it was in cyberspace—but what kind of space *was* that, exactly? Thinking such thoughts is a bit like trying to imagine how one's voice gets through those little telephone wires into the other person's receiver, only more so. You regress to your childhood

self, for whom all such concepts are made concrete and miniature: the little person inside the telephone receiver, the tiny mailbox inside the computer. And the fact that my computer was itself a laptop (a ridiculously
compact mechanism which, the dealer told me, was more powerful than
the huge computer that had flown the first man to the moon) made the
miniaturization imagery even more credible.

I discovered just how portable my e-mail was when a thief crept into
my house and walked off with my computer. One day I had been happily
communicating with the entire world, the next I was reduced to virtual silence. My anxiety at the loss of my equipment was exacerbated by my
sense of all the messages I was missing. I had become dependent on my
daily fix, and the burglar, as if guessing at this aspect of my psychology,
had even cut the phone wire that led into the computer—a symbolic act,
easily remedied by the purchase of a new wire, but one that drove home
for me my feeling of violent interruption. "I feel as if I'm hemorrhaging information," I told my husband. But information was only the half of it.
All the little pieces of *me* that I had been feeding into cyberspace were
loosed into the world, never to return.

Yet when I got a new computer, hooked myself back up to CompuServe,
and checked my old mailbox, there it still was, just as if no interruption had
ever occurred. My e-mail had been patiently waiting for me out there in
Nowhere Land, the messages accumulating until I was once again able to
pick them up. The beauty of the system, it turns out, is precisely that it's *not*
connected to any physical object. They can steal the transmitting device
from you, but the mail service continues unabated in its ideal Platonic
form—temporarily inaccessible, maybe, but always ready to be picked up.
I had my answer to Bishop Berkeley's question: if the tree had fallen in
cyberspace, the sound could simply have waited decades or generations or
millennia until someone came along to hear it, and *then* it would have existed. In this respect, as in so much else, e-mail's qualities are strangely
mixed. It is both speedy to the point of instantaneousness, and arrested in
a state of timelessness.

So have I lost my soul to e-mail? I think not. Of course, proper use of
it requires some mastery, and particularly self-mastery. One's initial sub-
servience to the medium's surprising delights is inevitably a bit enslaving.
(But this must have been true of all new media, even the cave paint at Las-
caux.) Still, once it has been brought under control and made to function
in the life you have already constructed for yourself, e-mail can be a great
gift. If you keep all those strangers and business connections and mass-

directory people off your screen, it can be, as Furbank put it, "like enjoying a second life." You will be rewarded with all the old-fashioned pleasures of the intimate personal letter. You will be offered, in other words, the chance to *gain* a soul rather than lose one. As an agnostic, I'm not even sure I believe in the very idea of a soul; but if I had to say where it resides, I would point to the thing in us that allows us to be and have intimate friends. And e-mail, by bringing back personal correspondence, reintroduces us to the form of writing that best enables us to know and acknowledge friendship.

Only Connect?

. . . .

by

LYNNE SHARON SCHWARTZ

It was tall, erect Miss Mulcare, in the seventh grade, who introduced me to the nuances of telephone etiquette. Lesson one: never phone a friend and say, "Hello, is Claudia there?" Instead say, "This is Lynne. May I please speak to Claudia?" If we knew the parent answering, she enjoined with a flash of cerulean eyes, we must say, "Hello, Mrs. Jones. This is Lynne," and perhaps even add, "How are you?" depending on our degree of acquaintance and of aplomb.

Miss Mulcare was austere, and with age the rosy skin of her face had grown softly tufted, like certain pillows. Her hair was speckled gray and white. We, her students, were smooth of cheek, young enough to remember the aura of power and privilege attaching to the phone, the infantile thrill of burbling a few words and hearing, by magic, an answering voice. We had longed to grow big enough to dash for its ring, a prerogative of grown-ups.

We had phone privileges now, but they came with obligations. Lesson two: never, under any circumstances, open with, "Who is this?" The caller, the invader of privacy, rather than the callee, must declare herself. "Reach out and touch someone" was plainly not Miss Mulcare's motto. In her civil code, the phone was an intrusion, and the person intruded upon was entitled, at the very least, to a smidgen of courtesy. She was so austere that she might have regarded any social overture as an intrusion.

Today, a shamelessly mercenary promotional flyer urges, "Go ahead and talk, talk, talk." I'll give you a ring, a buzz, a call, we say, and do it on a whim. The evolution of this most casual gesture—picking up the phone—has been swift. It grows swifter each day as new electronic devices promise more efficient "communications," along with dwindling human contact.

In old movies, or new movies and TV shows that portray olden times, we see phones used in a cute, self-conscious manner, as vital elements of the story rather than as narrative aids of no interest per se. I'm thinking of the telephone that entered the lives of the young generation in the televised version of Galsworthy's *Forsyte Saga.* Or the telephone in *Upstairs, Downstairs,* handled with cautious deference by the impeccable butler, Hudson. These phones are clumsy affairs, a tubular receiver and a boxlike speaker on the wall into which the characters shout: sweet campy objects that make us laugh. (Affectionate, condescending laughter at things never intended to be laughed at is the essence of camp.) The Forsytes hardly took their phone for granted: if it rang, both they and we knew something noteworthy was afoot.

Later, yet not so long ago, the aim of the personal call was usually to arrange a meeting where, in the words of the smarmy metaphor, we might indeed reach out and touch someone. The conversation itself might cover every topic under the sun, even ascend—or descend—to intimacy. Still, it was only a prelude, a snatch of delights to come if we signed on for the full experience, like a coming attraction for a movie. Nowadays the phone call *is* the visit, as though nothing essential or significant would be added were the speakers to meet.

Physical presence, the sensory awareness of others, counts for little. What does count is abstracted—hearing a disembodied voice and receiving its data. It's no accident that the phone call as a form of social life has flourished in an era of minimalism and conceptual art, when bare allusions are accepted substitutes for the real thing.

With my obvious bias, how come I'm a devotee of radio, where people exist through voices alone? I have no yen to meet my radio friends, or even to know what they look like. I avoid any opportunity to see them on a screen or in the flesh. I'm not convinced they exist materially, off the radio, just as in school we couldn't visualize lives for our teachers—certainly not for Miss Mulcare—outside of the classroom. They might as well have been locked in the metal closets at three o'clock and released the next morning.

Radio is a hardy art form, which has managed to stay alive and even thrive lately despite the preponderance of television. Its distinctive genius is to distill immediate presence into the voice—all gross matter purged away—and its best practitioners can make the voice, with its variables of tone, pitch, rhythm, and inflection, as rich a bearer of sensibility as silent dancers can make of the body. Just as speech would not enhance a ballerina's performance, a radio voice needs no face or body.

Phone conversations are not quite an art form yet, although they're evolving in that direction. Someday soon we may label people as good on the phone, just as we call them good company or good listeners or good dancers or good in bed. In fact I label them so already. There are moments—too surfeited with work, too restless to read a book—when nothing will serve so well as a long chummy talk, curled up in a chair, analyzing the day's events with an absurd yet regenerating minuteness and concentration. That's when I seek out friends who blossom on the phone. I can feel them settling in, summoning their resources of clarity and empathy, calling forth my own best flights too. (Other friends, equally dear, are no use at all on the phone; they hurry off, saving themselves for the reality of our next meeting.)

So perhaps I've been hasty. Perhaps it's not so much a fraudulent and reduced version of human contact that phones offer, as a different kind or quality. After all, pen pals know each other only by letter and have rich connections, are even loath to meet for fear of disturbing the fragile bond so carefully nurtured. (Users of e-mail may feel the same, though I cannot venture to say.)

Likewise, with certain friends who live too far away for a visit, we talk so well and so thoroughly on the phone that we don't ever long to see them. If they do hit town periodically, we feel a discrepancy, a slight jolt when we meet. We're so accustomed to the unfleshed voice that we have trouble compounding and compacting it with the body it issues from. By the time our neural circuits have wedded the voice and the body so we can speak as naturally as on the phone, the visit may be over, the critical moment passed. We part looking forward to the next phone call; we go home unsatisfied, as if we haven't really enjoyed the friend we know so well. Something was missing. What was missing was the physical absence, the fertile vacuum in which our friendship blooms, a vacuum that bathes our words in its delicate emptiness and suffuses them with a pure, floating grace.

If certain friendships are best cultivated over the phone, certain things are more easily said, too. Asking favors is easier over the phone. So is refusing them, especially for those who find it hard to say no; the phone removes the awkward sight of the other's disappointment. (That kind of vicarious discomfort, of course, is less the sign of a kind heart than the dread of being the object of ill will.) Anger, a sharper way of saying no, is also easier over the phone, at least for the timid, who can hang up when the rising temperature begins to crackle the wires. (The brave and belligerent may relish the heat of confrontation.) The timid, again, profit by the phone when encountering someone for the first time, particularly someone in a position of power, a prospective employer, say. They can sit quaking and unkempt in their bathrobes, attending only to voice and words, heedless of facial expressions, gestures, and all the rest. Apologizing is easier over the phone, although without the sight of a forgiving face, one tends to apologize for too long, hoping to make an abstract absolution palpable. A telephone encounter can be a great equalizer for those who for one reason or another feel unpresentable. (Unless pride makes them flaunt their appearance: take me as I am or not at all.) And none of these maxims applies if you're phonophobic, an ailment more widespread than is generally recognized; perhaps it will soon have its flurry of media attention and support groups, in which phoning fellow sufferers will be the first step in recovery.

Finally, saying good-bye is easier over the phone.

Easier. Easier to avoid the emotion that attends direct experience. One of phone culture's many results—ominous or convenient, depending on your outlook—is to dilute strong emotion, often to the vanishing point. To make everything personal feel, to some degree, like business—a development in keeping with our waning century's transformation of the planet into a giant quasi-corporation. The phone makes us businesslike; it makes us conduct our lives like cottage industries, with appointments, calendar juggling, quick jottings of memos, names and numbers.

In the world of business there are no interruptions. Or rather, interruption *means* business—action, transaction, goods and money flowing. A business with silent phones is on the path to doom. So with our lives; we want the phone to ring. It means we have a life, we're in business. And the ways we conduct our little businesses—from hello to good-bye—illustrate what the late social philosopher Erving Goffman so happily termed the presentation of self in everyday life. Some people feel they must greet the world with a steeled formality. They pick up with an officious, off-putting "Hello," then relax immediately into a colloquial tone.

Others, never having known the likes of Miss Mulcare, dispense with "Hello" altogether and launch into breezy narrative, confident that they're uppermost in my thoughts. How mistaken. Besides, although I have a good ear for music and speech rhythms, I can't readily identify phone voices. More times than I care to remember, I've had to reply to an exuberant rush of anecdote — "So who do you think just resurfaced in my life? That guy from. . . . " — by asking, "Yes, but who *is* this?" And certain eccentrics baldly adopt the business mode for personal life — "John Doe speaking" — and in the space of a breath reshape the borders of public and private.

I've been told my "Hello" sounds a world-weary, "What now?" note — if not expecting the worst, then at least something pretty bad. This doesn't surprise me. Our every gesture shows how we anticipate that the world will impinge on us — for impinge it must, and more and more often right at home, assaulting the open gate of the ear. The world's approach, for me at any rate, is an interruption of the inner dialogue, at once fantastical and mundane, in which I'm forever absorbed. Sometimes I even answer with an intimidating "Yes?," trying uselessly to forestall whatever is about to be demanded. I wouldn't want to be greeted by a "hello" like mine, and luckily I'm not. The great majority, whose comfort in the universe I can barely imagine, pick up with a tone of merry preparedness: what delightful new event is about to befall me?

Endings tell as much as beginnings. The conversation draws to its natural close, but some people cannot hang up. They cherish the long good-bye. Either they dread the silence awaiting them or, less pathetically, they cannot stop whatever they're doing, whether pleasant or painful. The longer they've been doing it, the harder it is to switch gears. A long conversation becomes incrementally longer until the good-bye resembles the drawn-out conclusion of a Romantic symphony. I, on the contrary, am restless to move on once "Well, it's been good talking to you" has been mutually sounded. I begin to hang up, but then I hear the dimming voice come wistfully from the lowered receiver. "Sorry, what was that?" Nothing, usually. Except in cases where the speaker leaves the most salient item, the real purpose of the call, for last — "I forgot to mention, I'm getting married and moving to Spain" — and what might that signify?

The simple contraption into which Don Ameche — as Alexander Graham Bell — so memorably shouted has become a wildly complex global network. And the more varied its options, the less human contact we reap. The telephone's evolution could fill volumes, and soon will: a 1993 *New York Times Magazine* article, "The Telephone Transformed — Into Almost Everything," notes that its author, James Gleick, is writing a book about the telephone, which will presumably include its relations with computers, faxes, et al. In Gleick's piece, as elsewhere, technical wizardry is amply

. . . .

documented and justly marveled at. A Bell Communications Research representative is quoted as saying, "All this accumulated technology and accumulated vision is like a volcano waiting to erupt." What effects will this volcano spew on the human spirit as the millennium dawns?

One of the first jarring omens, which in our innocence we didn't properly read, was losing our beautiful and evocative exchanges, our Butterfields, our Murray Hills, our Morningsides. Obliterated overnight as if by an act of God and replaced by digits. One may not feel attached to a social security number or a zip code, but Plaza, Riverside, and Chelsea were no mere syllables or clues to location on a map. They were treasured possessions, tokens of identity. Trafalgar, Cloverdale, and Esplanade conferred traces of their multisyllabic glamour on us all, but there is no glamour to living in the 468 neighborhood. Despite the monotheistic solidity of 1 or the Christian symbolism of 3, the architectural satisfaction of 4, the Satanic connotations of 6, and the fabled luck of 7, numbers will never have the poetry of letters, whose magic conjunction makes names—music on the tongue—and conjures the winds of association and memory.

We accepted the deprivation meekly; we were taken aback, unprepared, improvident. We should have seen the loss as political as well as aesthetic and fought for our exchanges, kept using them in nonviolent defiance. A handful of numbers in my address book are in fact still listed by their exchanges—sweet nostalgias, bitter reminders. When I'm using state-of-the-art phones from which letters have been banished, I need to translate carefully, letter by luscious letter, into vapid numbers. Inconvenient, but a small price to pay. Total defeat would come only if every letter disappeared from every phone.

And this, it appears, is not about to happen. Ironically, letters—of a different sort—are making an unforeseen comeback. In the present global village, or global mall, of 800 numbers, they are replacing digits in part or entirely. Billboard and bus advertising teems with examples. To feel more at home in your chosen land, call 1-800-ENGLISH. For help getting into college or graduate school, dial 1-800-KAP-TEST. Trouble sleeping? 1-800-MATTRES [sic]. For therapy, 1-800-FEELING. Better still, to reshape your life and prospects, 1-800-BLEMISH. The letters, presumably, are easier to remember. Thus the wheel, newly reinvented, comes round again with the coming of the new century.

In those days of Axminster, Baring, and Shore Road, my parents' friends would unexpectedly ring the doorbell—"We were just passing by"—and be invited in for coffee. The hour might be inopportune, but these were friends, after all, and they were made welcome. With scheduled appointments the order of our day, doorbells are silent but phones clamor. You're settling into the tub after worrying all day about a loved one who's sick or in trouble. What will the blood tests reveal? Will he get the job he needs so badly? The phone rings. You could let the machine take it, but no, love propels you, dripping, toward the news. Hello? you pant. It's Planned Parenthood and they need your help.

The dinner hour has become a free-for-all. Hosts of strangers prod us to become a charitable point of light. Or to take out a new credit card. Or invest in land in Texas. The voices give them away: unctuous, bright, a tad edgy, prepared for your hostility. Naturally they do all they can to avert it, and the worst thing they do—reading from their scripts—is greet you by name and ask how you are. For me, that "How are you this evening?" is the clincher. I don't do phone solicitations, I reply in the flat tone cleaning women use to say they don't do windows, or prostitutes that they don't do cuffs and chains. It usually suffices for all but the most avid. "I understand, but just let me tell you how worthy our cause is, and how dire our need."

Hanging up is the only solution. But hanging up, like breaking up, is hard to do—almost as hard as slamming the door in someone's face. I know people who'll hear out the whole script before saying no. True, there've been complaints about phone solicitors, and yes, there are ways to keep your name off the lists. But since being a good citizen has come to mean being a good consumer, I shouldn't wonder that such cruel and unusual practices are by and large accepted passively.

One step beyond the hypocrites who pretend to care how we are leads to a twilight zone: calls from no one. You're expecting your mate just stepping off the plane, and instead a voice severed from its owner says, "You are the winner of a three-foot rubber raft, suitable for water sports." Or, "This is the principal's office at Urban High School. Are you aware that your child did not attend classes today?" Or, "This is your telephone company. Press one if you still need service, two if the serviceman has already visited, three if the problem has disappeared. . . ." (Don't *they* know?) Those virtual voices intoning virtual sentences jar our notions of what qualifies as talk. Is there perhaps something barbarous about using precious ordinary language—and extraordinary technology—to mimic actual communication? Maybe this other and profoundly offensive thing should have a different name.

Not long after the tragic fall of President, Trafalgar, and Buckminster came the demise of answering services. They were favored by doctors for

· · · · · · · · ·

after-hours emergencies, by actors for the crucial callback, and by those people, ahead of their time, who couldn't stand to miss a call. The diverse and idiosyncratic voices that manned the services are silenced now; also gone forever are comic movie scenes of wires hastily being jabbed into switchboards by rows of operators whose antic garbling of messages drove the helter-skelter plot. Instead we have the answering machine. We wonder how we managed without it, yet manage we did. We must have lived more patiently. We had, perforce, the capacity to wait. But machines shape our nature as much as anything else, and the answering machine has wrought the need to reach out and touch someone—or someone's echo— into a craving that demands instant gratification.

Like aesthetic choices, the messages that greet callers are another Goffmanesque presentation of self. Early messages had a naive transparency, as in any new craft or art; in hindsight they seem touchingly ingenuous, like the great primitive paintings. Some were arch and self-conscious, others gracious— "I'm so sorry I can't get to the phone," or as one friend more elaborately put it, "I'm sorry to greet you with a recorded announcement." One of my favorites, showing a rare existential precision, declared, "This is the voice of John Smith."

How fast we've moved beyond all that. We're sophisticated, adaptable, ready to explore the possibilities of the form. Greetings range from baroque to Mondrianesque: one close friend simply states her phone number. I get the point—this is, after all, only a machine—yet I feel a chill through my bones. Must she be quite so stark? It's not the world at large who's calling. It's me!

In the middle of the spectrum are the playful—snatches of popular songs hinting at the greeter's passing mood, the most famous bars of Handel's "Hallelujah Chorus," the daily-changing homilies from Ecclesiastes or enshrined poetry, and what can only be called kitsch: the family's youngest member piping out a rehearsed sentence, sometimes assisted by a pet.

What a jolt it was, hearing my very first machine greeting. What was this eerie artifice, this absent presence? Did it actually expect me to say something in return? Over my dead body. I was so boggled by the prospect that I just hung up. Later I was told that hanging up mute is a form of rudeness. I didn't feel rude. How could you be rude to a machine? But apparently you could. How odd Miss Mulcare would have found that: machines legislating manners, expecting all the courtesy due to their owners.

I made judgments of character, in those frontier days, based on who had answering machines. But as they sprang up like weeds, my categories broke down. It was not merely the trendy, the anxious, or the self-important, but just plain folk. A select few, though, would surely never succumb: old-fashioned, unimpressed by novelty, temperamentally ill-suited. How wrong I was. In the end, in a revolution that changed forever the nature of human connection and conversation, everyone succumbed.

Me too. I spent hours poring over the manual. Within a couple of weeks I was able to use the machine adequately, although refinements such as selective erasing still strike me as risky. After some months, I learned by trial and error how to pick up my calls from outside. Someday I may even feel ready to erase calls from outside.

I used to come home each day eager to check my mail. Now I have a double desire. I look for the flashing red bar, I count its flashes. I don't feel especially neglected if there are none; in some ways it's a relief to be left alone. What I do miss is the *frisson* called forth by news, happenings, change. Even in the absence of the flashing red bar, I sometimes listen anyway, to be quite sure.

And what do I find? Styles of addressing machines are as varied as voices themselves. Most callers keep their usual speech patterns, and their usual personalities too. But a few are curiously altered—the kindly becoming imperious, the reserved loquacious; romantic, volatile souls turn lucid and precise. Who can say why? Art is a mystery. Listening to one's messages is a study in the varieties of human response to a vacuum. We eavesdrop on a voice alone yet not alone, on a soliloquy played into the dark, in an empty house.

Gone are the amateur days of fumble and stammer. Now, when we make a call, we're prepared for the canned greeting; we have our speeches set. We talk freely, maybe even more freely than had we reached an actual person. Sometimes we even prefer to reach a machine and are startled by a real voice—what are *you* doing at home! And we're inhibited, as once we were inhibited by the machine; we need to revise our words to make them fit for live consumption.

Certain coy messages hint at, but never give away, the essence—"I just found out something really shocking about X"—a transparent ploy that ensures a quick call back. The efficiency-minded rattle off information, while purists leave austere names and numbers. I appreciate their Spartan aesthetic, but their opposites are far more entertaining. I mean the callers who make an imaginative leap and address my recorded voice as if it were my current and receptive presence, telling it everything they would tell me. With those messages, I settle in to listen, chuckling or frowning as I would

. . . .

at any amazingly lifelike performance. Paradoxically, I'm in no hurry to call back, for it seems I've already had the zesty human exchange, and in so undemanding a fashion, too.

As a rule I return most of my calls promptly and willingly. But what of the others? The machine, with its demand for a response, makes the nuances of connection pitilessly explicit. We can gauge our feelings for people—feelings once serenely vague—by how soon we find ourselves calling back and by the vigor we bring to the task. Even worse, our caller can do the same. In the early days of ineptitude, you could say the message was lost or the machine broken, but that excuse won't fly anymore. No, we are fated to discover all there is to know about our attachments, and to those who prize self-knowledge, this may be a boon. Not such a boon, maybe, is discovering how keenly others feel attached to us.

But not all unreturned calls mean we're unloved. Lots of people, never having been schooled by Miss Mulcare, simply take advantage of a new way of being rude. Is not returning calls the same as not answering letters, or is it worse because the human voice—mightier even than the pen—is involved? If we're overlooked, do we call again? How soon? More than once? I'm irritated by the non-returners, yet I secretly envy them. I wish I had that blithe and awful freedom.

It used to be that the only mail I received from the phone company was a monthly bill. But lately they write constantly—clogging the mailbox, raising the rates, toppling the trees—to persuade me that some cunning new phone game would improve my life: Speed Calling, Call Forwarding, Wake-up Call, Reminder Call. Three-Way Calling sounds piquant, a near-relation of the *ménage à trois*. It might eventually supplant more traditional gathering places such as coffeeshops, bars, and park benches. If one of the phone company's aims is indeed to make human contact superfluous, it had better be planning alternate arrangements for procreation in the brave new world: phone sex can't yet go that far.

An undeniable aim is to ensure that the sound of the busy signal is heard no more in the land, since more completed calls mean more revenue. Success is imminent. The busy signal has all but died without the proper obsequies. Brought down by what a 1994 *New York Times* article called "the demands of a frenetic society that increasingly sees the busy signal as a symbol of failure and lost opportunity, a vestige of the past that is no longer tolerable." Lost opportunity? Symbol of failure? What harsh words! The busy signal could be irksome, yes, but it was reassuring, too.

The object of desire was nearly within our grasp—tantalizingly there but not there. The preconditions of story, of romance. (Are they too a vestige of the past?) A little while longer and our efforts would be rewarded. Granted, we might suffer some jealousy and resentment meanwhile, but they were manageable, tempered by anticipation.

Uncertainty gives ordinary life the fine edge of suspense. Just so, the chance of a busy signal spiced the banal act of phoning. Now, with all the automated means of circumventing the busy signal, there's almost always success, of some sort or other. These semi-successes offer a restless semi-satisfaction that, as with sex, food, and sleep, is arguably worse than none at all. (Just as advertising has warped our sense of need, and faxes our sense of urgency, automation may well distort not only our sense of connection but also of friendship, of love, of pleasure.)

If the busy signal has not been suitably mourned, its most common stand-in, Call Waiting, has been too naively welcomed, like the stranger of legend who knocks on the door in a storm and is given a place by the hearth, then makes off with the family heirlooms or worse. Call Waiting titillates the basest of impulses—greed and opportunism. (So sorry, a subsequent engagement, as Oscar Wilde prophetically said.) It plays on our anxiety—the nasty little need to know what or who might be better than what we've got now. More than a need: a fear, tantamount to desperation—given the Pavlovian alacrity with which people respond to the click—that something might be missed. The chance of a lifetime? Or an exciting emergency that requires our participation? And yet no one who's shunted me aside—after having phoned me—has ever returned saying, "I've got to go, my child has taken ill, or, Jeepers, I've won the lottery."

For the interrupting caller, Call Waiting means being swiftly weighed in the balance. Are you more alluring than the person you innocently broke in on? If so, you feel gratification but also a small tug of guilt, as at any impure victory. If not, you're summarily dismissed. The busy signal avoided such minor abrasions to the spirit; it acted as an anodyne.

In the end, whatever role we play in the unholy Call Waiting triad, we talk on tenterhooks. Impending interruption, judgment, and competition hover over our words, draining the bloom of the present moment. The exchange is vitiated, the implicit premise of conversation overturned. The phone company's goal might as well be to unravel the social contract.

Countless examples of phone acrobatics confirm that our lives, our small going concerns, are important. They must be, mustn't they?, to warrant such high-tech attention as Voice Dialing (for the terminally lazy) or

. . . .

the customized Ring Mate Service — "Why rush to the phone . . . only to learn the call is . . . for someone else in your household?" Pay for a distinctive ring that's all your own. Or Repeat Dialing, a tribute to sloth and impatience, which at the touch of a single button rather than the arduous seven, "will keep dialing the busy number for up to half an hour." Or Call Answering, the "revolutionary" message-recording service touted as a lifesaving device, the EMS of telecommunications: "Imagine being in the middle of a call when another call comes in. . . ." Or Call Return, which by the touch of a button reconnects the call you missed while racing from the shower.

One and all, they not only reveal unsightly fault lines in human nature, but widen them. There's something authoritative about a ringing phone, and the new devices encourage us to leap like good soldiers to the sound of authority. (Have we learned nothing from our century's tribulations?) Even more, they appeal to latent desperation, rubbing at the sore need to feel connected, although to whom seems immaterial. How, they collectively needle us, can we afford to miss news that might change our lives? The implication is that our present lives are not quite enough, not quite right. And existentially speaking, that may well be. Insufficiency and imperfection are built into the human condition and are the impetus for art and science, love and crime. But they will not be remedied, or at least only temporarily, by a phone call.

Until fairly recently it wasn't uncommon to ignore a ringing phone, provided you didn't have aged parents or young children on the loose. It was an impersonal act, or personal in the deepest sense — an assertion that privacy matters, that the uninterrupted flow of consciousness is our true life, maybe our only entitlement. But even if we have the strength of character to let the phone ring, the gesture is no longer the same. What was once a refusal has become a mere deferral; the answering machine will take the call. And as we all know, standing by while a plaintive voice addresses our machine makes us feel not private but roguishly perverse — a perverseness tinged with an unsavory sense of power.

That same power is the appeal of the insidious Call ID, which "makes sure *you're* in control." The caller's number appears on a little box near the phone: if you don't want him, don't answer. (This is quite different from ignoring an anonymous ring — no tribute to privacy but an out-and-out snub.) Obviously Call ID might be useful in deterring heavy breathers, as well as children playing phone games: as kids, we'd call the local funeral parlor just for the pleasure of saying, "I'm dying to give you my business." And control of any kind can be a heady feeling. Except in this case the gift of control, along with the theft of privacy, is mutual. Never again would I be sure whether my own unanswered call means no one's home or I'm being forsaken.

Besides sowing the seeds of doubt, Call ID spoils the surprise of a phone call. The ring may be intrusive, unwanted, yet it can't help but set off a tiny thrill. Someone wants us. Who can it be? And for what? We must take what thrills we can get: in return for the interruption, grant us at least our shiver of suspense.

Like entropy, technical ingenuity is unstoppable. The impish new options, embraced not wisely but too well, are here to stay, and already their effects on social life are being felt. Call Forwarding, for example, ensures that your caller doesn't know where you are. He imagines you harmless at home while you're at the racetrack or in a hotel room. Wives and husbands can chat about picking up a loaf of bread amidst any kind of betrayal; marriages remain intact and children undisturbed — a contribution to family values. A boost for privacy, at any rate. Not so Redial. Was your daughter talking to the boy you warned her off? Your son hobnobbing with a drug dealer? Your boss hiring your replacement? Press Redial and see who turns up. TV mystery plots have already incorporated these fertile twists, and since life imitates television, our daily rounds should soon be laced with phone intrigue. As a matter of fact the New York Times ran a rueful little article about a woman who was "humiliated by a telephone." Pleading tiredness, she called to cancel a brunch date, only to find that her would-be host, equipped with Call ID, knew immediately that she was calling from a mutual friend's home. "Even though he said he wasn't mad," she lamented, "I haven't heard from him for two weeks."

Notwithstanding all of the above, I must confess I have great affection for one clever phone game: the Conference Call. Conference Calls are festive — a regular little party, only you don't have to stand on your feet balancing drinks and paper plates, or worry that your skirt is too short or your hair frizzing up in the humidity of a crowded room. Conference Calls make you feel important. They must be set up in advance; your convenience is considered, never the case with ordinary calls. They arrive promptly, at least in my limited experience (I hope my future holds more conference calls). The operators are polite — they too must think the parties are important simply by virtue of engaging in a conference call. There's something amiably civil about the whole process. "Are you there, Lynne? Good. We've already got Bob on the line. Please hold as we get Sue and Jim and

. . . .

Carol. . . . Are you there, Sue? Please hold as. . . ." While you wait for the others to be lassoed from their far-off venues and pulled into the auditory corral, you can chat with the early arrivals, the kind of spontaneous, free-wheeling talk of people off on a giddy spree. Suddenly a new voice is heard. Welcome, Jim. Hi, Carol. The operator, like a suave *maître d'*, bows out and the fete can begin. The habits of group discourse undergo a slight shift, becoming more democratic. The shy are encouraged to speak, for when a voice is the sole sign of our presence, an absent voice is notable. Those who talk too much are cut off more readily than if they loomed two feet away. Time is money, so matters are settled nimbly, with less show-offy wrangling than usual. No travel time is involved. All in all, the conference call is a far more natural outgrowth of the original telephone, the functional phone of Hudson and the Forsytes, than the grotesque mutations of Call Waiting or Call Return.

Or of Voice Mail, the dread labyrinth; I shudder to think of Miss Mulcare ensnared in it. Voice Mail is reshaping the dynamics of daily trivia. However humble, trivia form the armature of our lives. We curse them, yet lean on them for comfort, as well as for relief from more serious matters. And we have—or had—a taut reliance on the anonymous voices, sullen or friendly, that helped us dispatch life's errands. Well, no more.

Voice Mail, whether its architects know it or not, has an august history. It derives from no less than Plato, who in his *Dialogues* used a process of dichotomizing and categorizing to generate the endlessly forking, ramifying answers to philosophical questions. Centuries later the neo-Platonist scholar, Porphyry, analyzed the method so astutely that it became known as a Tree of Porphyry. As a mode of inquiry, the Tree could provide instruction and delight, if you had the time. But Plato would be the first to agree it was never intended for the mundane. For one thing, it takes too long. (If Voice Mail is saving time for anyone, it's certainly not the humble citizen.)

You can't even leaf through a magazine, as in a doctor's office, while you wait—you have to keep a keen ear for your category. Hearing the relentless data drone by might be borne if you could trust that eventually a category would turn up that suits your need. But it doesn't. Your need is sui generis: either the Voice Mail daimon never thought of it, or else it was too singular to merit a slot. Uniqueness is gratifying, yet in this case it cannot mitigate despair. A despair not lost on the telecommunications experts: "I suppose," one speculated in Gleick's article, "in the future we could have devices on the lines that detect the caller's stress level and, based on that, access a prerecorded library of celebrity personalities designed to achieve maximum rapport and manipulate the hell out of us."

Until that day arrives, you wait with mounting panic and frustration, hoping for a human being as a last resort. You place all your waning faith in the kindness of strangers. But more and more, the human option is omitted. The litany is over; you face the auditory equivalent of a brick wall.

Voice Mail is our latter-day Castle. Were Kafka alive, he would write a book about it: *The Phone Call,* or more likely *The Phone Kall,* and the call would never go through. Like all evil empires, Voice Mail seeks to restrict and define the choices of the citizenry. The authoritarian spirit serves only itself; it sets the terms of discourse and proscribes dialogue. It shuns the ragged edges of the unclassifiable. It renders its victims impotent and passive, ultimately ensuring that there is no discourse, which is what happens when all we can do is obediently press buttons or hang up (flee the country). When all business, great and small, can be completed without any live interchange, when proliferating buttons supplant open-ended question and answer, then the dehumanization will be complete.

Well before our age of wonders, the phone supplied adventures in automation, but they were never so unnerving. Quite the contrary. My childhood fun with phones included dialing a number to get the weather report or the time (with the lovely exchange of Meridian). How delicious to hold the receiver without uttering a word and hear: "At the tone, the time will be . . . 1:45 A.M." There couldn't be a woman, could there, sitting by the phone day and night repeating that sentence? No, you could sense a shift in the air, a hollowness, before the time was announced, so that even as a child I knew it was a recording played till the crack of doom with only the number alive and changing, just as the moments on a wall clock tick by unvaryingly, but the lived quality of each has a fresh taste and texture.

No longer can you get your time or weather pure, without a string of commercials. The spirit of free enterprise is alarmingly inventive and wriggly as a chameleon, finding its way into any vacant nook. It makes opportunities for lonely phone adventure quite fantastic. Some years ago, the *New York Times* reported on the case of a Russian immigrant, alone and unable to afford English lessons (1-800-ENGLISH), who spent hours every day calling 800 numbers, not only for language practice, but for whatever frail sense of connection they supplied. Happily, the article flushed out many volunteers willing to help him with simple English conversation.

The hours of movies, the real estate listings and the help-wanted ads

. . . .

may be useful, but how banal compared to soap opera updates, tips on homework, crossword puzzle answers, abbreviated religious sermons, and, last but not least, sex. Phone sex is safe sex in unsafe times, but I think it would have thrived in any case, in keeping with telecommunications' shrewd ways of helping us avoid each other. Not that it's brand new. It's probably been around ever since phones themselves, the crucial difference being that those who were so inclined were far from strangers engaged in a commercial transaction. Rather, they used the phone as a stopgap measure when they couldn't meet. Or sought diversion. I can't picture the Forsytes or Hudson indulging, though, and as for Miss Mulcare, perish the thought. I haven't investigated commercial phone sex, partly out of inhibition but mostly because I have a strong feeling it would lead to junk mail. Anyway, if I must have sex without another person present, I prefer to have it with a book.

Fun *with* the phone prompts the question of what you might do while *on* the phone. A question Miss Mulcare never broached, and for good reason: there wasn't much you could do. (Unless you had that enviable Look-Ma-no-hands ability to tuck the receiver in your neck and hold it there with a raised shoulder, leaving both hands free. Or to use the arc-shaped plastic gadget that hooked onto the receiver and nestled on the shoulder.)

My options increased exponentially when I became the proud owner of a cordless phone. It took only a few hours to read the manual, and after a day or so I was adept. Within my four walls, I can take my phone anywhere I want, like a snuggly pet. Hugging it close, I gaze out the window at passersby, mute strangers whose physicality complements the disembodied voice addressing me. Now and then I have the feeling I'm trailing a long cord or leash behind me, but I expect that will pass. Most of the time I feel liberated, untethered.

But always, new freedoms bring new dilemmas. Alone in our rooms, we claim all the rights of privacy and mobility, yet on the phone we're engaged in a social act too, a form, however bastardized, of being with another. A few open-hearted souls will welcome us to any sort of intimacy. I called someone in Hawaii and heard the sound of rushing water in the background. "You sound like you're near a waterfall," I said. "I am," he replied. "I'm in the shower." On the other hand, I can testify that while my friends—also cordless—might have felt shielded by solitude, I've heard the sounds of dishes being washed, food chopped and stirred, a pencil doodling, and, yes, even the muted tapping of computer keys. Hey, I want to shout. Listen to me!

Have we a right to expect someone's complete attention, as we would over a cup of coffee? We haven't set up an appointment (although some people do make dates for phone calls); we've rung up out of the blue with a demand for talk. I'm no better than anyone: I've hunted for lost objects, checked the contents of the fridge, and scribbled shopping lists, as well as done things I'd rather not talk about. I don't relish the day when Video-phones (or whatever they'll be called) display us all on their little screens, like a come-as-you-are party.

Cellular phones are still enough of a novelty to make us laugh at people ambling down the street all alone, chattering or arguing. You dismiss them as run-of-the-mill lunatics, until you catch sight of the small companion pressed to their ears. And they engender an obscure irritation. Walkers in the city should play their part in the street scene—strangers in a tacit community. But these defectors are both present and absent, split souls not giving themselves fully to either experience.

Unlike most pets, cellular phones can be taken on local outings—restaurants, shopping trips, ball games. They must be a comfort on solitary drives through uncharted territory, and yet it's a pity that the car, once one of the few places out of reach of the phone, couldn't remain chaste. No purist myself, I've called people in their cars, in California, and felt a vicarious thrill, as if I were traveling with them. As in a metaphysical sense I was—ear to ear though we moved through different hours, under different stages of the sun.

Suitable hours for calling were a key feature of Miss Mulcare's phone etiquette. Perhaps she began her career in a hospital or reform school, for she warned us never to call anyone past nine o'clock in the evening. Life in gerneral seemed to take place earlier back then; whenever the phone rang at ten-thirty at night my mother, yawning over her two-cents-a-day rental novel, would groan wearily, "There's Uncle George again," as if he were violating a curfew. Beyond knowing Uncle George's propensities, though, she happened to have a near-infallible phone instinct, a kind of sonic ESP. "That's your sister," she'd inform my father at the first ring. Or, "Oh, good, it's the plumber," as if hearing his individual timbre (the opposite of today's Ring Mate) or sensing incipient vibrations from a voice not yet dancing on the air.

Even in adolescence I was a night person and broke Miss Mulcare's rule. The day's winding-down hours, ten to twelve, still feel like happy times for social phoning. This preference (maybe I share a gene with Uncle

. . . .

George) has naturally irked people who keep infantile hours, or infants. So I tend to favor friends who are willing to be phoned late at night—as sound a basis of affinity as any other: it means we're sharing the same diurnal round.

For much as we'd like to think of ourselves as a human family, brothers and sisters under the skin, the disparity in phoning hours points up what far-apart galaxies we inhabit. Lots of callers, for instance, feel that 8 A.M., a savage hour, opens the official phoning day. And I must pick up, for what but disaster could seek me out so early? "So sorry, did I wake you?" they address my sleep-clogged voice. The proper reply is, "Oh no, it's quite all right." But it's not all right. I'm still tangled in dreams, while they've dressed and had their coffee; their every cell is alert, carrying forward the affairs of the world. I can accept that this is true for Australians, but when it happens right across town—hardly long-distance—my sense of community is shaken.

Making a long-distance call was once a major procedure, undertaken only in unusual circumstances—dire news or grand news. It meant placing yourself in the hands of a long-distance operator, specially trained like an intensive-care nurse, who appreciated the gravity of the act. She would patiently ask for data and offer a choice of treatment—collect, or maybe the more elite person-to-person.

Depending on your temperament, getting a long-distance call was cause for either alarm or joy. (In my childhood household it was commonly alarm. "Long Distance calling. I have a call from so-and-so. Will you accept the charges?" My mother turned pale as she breathed an assent.) Apart from announcements of death or disaster, though, long-distance calls were a brief exotic treat, like some delicate morsel. And similarly expensive. You didn't chat or loll but stuck to the matter at hand. Duration was not so important in any case. A small helping might be even better than a large, lest the richness begin to cloy. You made sure to savor every mouthful. That unique flavor seeped away, of course, with the advent of direct dialing, a treat in its own right. A small miracle, even—getting through all alone, no operator required! But very quickly it became commonplace.

Not yet so commonplace is the international call, the only phone experience that can duplicate the savor and intensity of yesteryear's long distance. An international call requires planning and forethought. First of all, you have to figure out what time it is in another country, and the arithmetic can be daunting. (Why can I never remember time's direction—

backward to the west and forward to the east—but have to look it up with each call? It's the same sort of riddle and ritual as the semi-annual shift of the clock, and my resistance to both, I think, is a resistance to the artifice of turning time into numbers, as well as to the intractable fact that the earth moves, not the sun.)

Patterns of life in other countries are mysterious, and of individual lives even more so: we don't easily picture the daily routines, the comings and goings. Reaching a voice oceans away—hearing it live and palpitating—comes to seem a victory over nearly insuperable odds. Sometimes we don't reach the voice directly but an operator, and find ourselves embroiled in bureaucracy in a foreign tongue. Or we reach a machine offering what must be the usual message. How odd it sounds in those foreign syllables, yet it gives a warm flush of recognition too: Aha! So their lives are like ours; this is what their friends hear all the time.

At last the goal is reached. We speak. And until recently there would come that puzzling little time lag between our speech and the reply, the half-second it took for each voice to stretch its way across the waters. We would speak, but every reply was preceded by a minuscule delay. The far-away person seemed to be hesitating ever so slightly, the sort of hesitation that in ordinary talk means disapproval or detachment or some ambiguous feeling barring the way to a willing response. The conversation had an awkwardness, moving as it did in tiny fits and starts. We felt our words were not being well received, or not being received in the way we intended them. We quickly grasped that this was an electronic, not a personal, lag, but the blight remained. And the feeling was surely mutual: our response never quite satisfying, our timing off.

This small lag embodied the true and broad meaning of distance. However wonderful the magic of electronics, it hadn't closed the gap entirely. Time and space were between us, claiming their reality. You may feel close, they told us, but you are not close. Now that small gap has been spanned, thanks to more efficient magic. At least I didn't hear it while talking to Italy last week. I missed it. The artisans of Persian carpets, we're told, left a small error in the weave to signify human imperfection. In the same spirit, it was good to be reminded of our separateness and of the uncrossable spaces, not merely between our bodies but between our voices and the words they tenderly, mutually, wistfully bear.

In Praise of Silence and Slow Time:
Nature and Mind in a Derivative Age

. . . .

by
MARK SLOUKA

> Besides, nature, by virtue of all the feelings that it aroused in me, seemed
> to me the thing most diametrically opposed to the mechanical inventions
> of mankind. The less it bore their imprint, the more room it offered for the
> expansion of my heart.
> PROUST, *Swann's Way*

Picture this. On a morning in mid-September, you wake early to the vertical blinds lifting and falling in a new breeze. Light plays across the sheets,
and with each key pressed into light or shadow, the open window above
rattles quietly. Sharp wedges of sky, cut by the angles of wall and blind,
show with each hesitant gust. Reaching up, you draw the blinds aside to
reveal the trees; the room pales. Watching the branches shake and sway
and still, your mind wanders freely over the landscape of your years, over
a purely personal, utterly idiosyncratic terrain of places and names, of
lovers known or only dreamed. Stories rise and run and fade, faces return
and leave once more, and all the time the precise hues of shade and light,
the coolness of the air, and the faint clattering of aspen leaves gently draw
you back to the moment you are in, then set you free once more.

In the house / apartment / duplex next door, a radio goes on. ". . . so
call 1-800 336-8266 aaaand looks like we've got a call, hello? You're on."
Male voice: "Yeah, I just wanted to say that . . ." (someone tunes in another station—static, snatches of melody, verbal collage: "before it's too
late," "sale," "right now . . .") ". . . we're talkin' 100% pure ground-
chuck patty topped with melted cheese on a sesame-seed . . ." (static)
". . . up on another thirty minutes of NON-STOP music right here on

KCCP but first let's check in with . . ." (static, woman's voice, laughter) ". . . that's right Bob, looks like a stall in the number one lane, pretty much bumper to . . ."

You roll out of bed, start getting dressed. Partly out of habit, partly to drown out the radio from next door, you turn on the TV. Katie Couric and Bryant Gumbel look groomed and happy. You start making breakfast. The trees, the wind, the landscape outside your window have disappeared. The voices of your private life have shut down.

■ ■ ■

Erosion and encroachment, forces generally associated with the natural world, with the slow-motion wearing of rock and earth, or the burial of a meadow under asphalt or scrub, apply to the supernatural one as well. At the close of the twentieth century, the terrain of the spirit—by which I mean the domain of silence, of solitude, of unmediated contemplation—is everywhere under siege, threatened by a polymorphous flood of verbal and visual signals (electronically generated, predominantly corporate), that together comprise what we might call the culture of distraction. The gradual erosion of the soul's habitat, however, has been marked, all along, by a parallel effect in the physical realm: the ever-diminishing role played by the natural world in our lives. Nature and spirit, we see now, 113 years after Emerson's death, are indeed joined at the hip; as one fades, so does the other. The artist and the environmentalist are leagued in the spirit of preservation. And resistance.

What are they preserving? Life, I would argue, in all its drama and diversity; the irreducible thing in itself. On the one hand, the roughness of wood, the smell of piñon and sage, fritillaries settling on a rotting trout. On the other, the untrammeled landscape of the imagination; the trackless and often terrifying wilderness of the individual soul. What are they resisting? In a word, electronic mediation. Whatever distracts or distorts, whatever distances us from the color, the authenticity, the *aura*—to borrow Walter Benjamin's term—of the primary and the real, whatever threatens to strand us (even more completely than we've already been stranded) in that strange middle ground one technophile so accurately referred to as "the terrain of simulacra."

The argument against mediation, of course, is hardly new. "Our age," wrote Emerson in 1836, "is retrospective. . . . The foregoing generations beheld God and nature face to face; we, through their eyes. Why should not we also enjoy an original relation to the universe? Why should not we have a poetry and philosophy of insight and not of tradition, and a religion by revelation to us, and not the history of theirs?"

Substitute technology for tradition, Bill Gates for the forefathers, and the questions still apply. Our age, of course, is derivative in a different way. Although we, too, get nothing firsthand, although we, too, are continually offered the chewed-over, reconstituted versions of someone else's history, although we, too, might wish for an original relation to the universe, in our case the mediating effect is due not to the anxiety of influence, but to a pervasive and well-nigh inescapable layer of technologies that connects us— ever more irresistibly—to the electronic marketplace, while isolating us from nature, from others, and ultimately from ourselves.

Instead of talking to one another, we're watching the ubiquitous television hovering over the bar, or the jeans racks, or the checkout counter. Instead of spending time in what remains of our impoverished natural landscape, we're watching wolverines mating in the PBS wilderness. Instead of meeting one another face to face, we're customizing like-minded "communities of interest" in cyberspace, thereby avoiding the daily grinding of differences so necessary not only to the democratic process but to individual growth.

Increasingly, in other words, we're spending the hours of our days Elsewhere—inhabiting an abstract space, a simulacrum, which mimics the forms of social life even as it confirms us in our isolation. The result is twofold: a growing alienation from what I have called the inner landscape, and an essentially derivative, increasingly voyeuristic relation to the outside world. As an ever-greater proportion of the physical world is transmuted into digital code ("Now is the flesh made word," proclaims one technoevangelist), we find ourselves (at least in part because we *are* uncomfortable with our own inner silences) peering at the life we used to know through a series of screens sold to us by digital entrepreneurs who believe a fully englobing, electronic environment is not only possible but desirable.

Strangely enough, the rapid encroachment of the wired world on our lives is a subject about which the technologists themselves are surprisingly eloquent. Already today, writes Kevin Kelly, executive editor of *Wired* magazine, "Every fact that can be digitized, is. Every measurement of collective human activity that can be ported over a network, is. Every trace of an individual's life that can be transmuted into a number and sent over a wire, is." Already, writes author Gregory Stock, our technologies have bound us into "a dense network of communications links and trade systems . . . Without noticing it, we walk above pipes and cables, beneath airplane flight corridors and satellite broadcasts, through radio and television transmissions." In fact, he concludes, "if all communication . . . left behind a conspicuous threadlike trail, soon everything and everyone would be ensnared in a dense tangle of fibers."

Stock's "dense tangle of fibers," of course, evokes the metaphor of the Net, whose strands are invariably shown radiating from the ganglia of New York and L.A. and Seattle. A visual cliché of the digital age, spread, ironically enough, by the electronic media whose spread it depicts, the image is suggestive for two reasons. First, like a single, frozen image culled from a high-speed sequence showing burgeoning clouds or flowering orchids, it implies a process underway. The ganglia will blossom and multiply, we understand; the fiber-optic radii thicken and spread. Second, as the Net grows (and the analogy to the spread of, say, penicillin mold in a petri dish is apt), the terrain it covers, increasingly ribbed and intersected, gradually disappears. In life as in metaphor, wires obscure the landscape.

To a great extent, they already have. Every year, after all, more and more of the things our eyes show us are electronically generated facsimiles. Every year, the time most of us spend actually *seeing* our world—our actual forests, for example, rather than representations of forests on television—grows smaller. Every year, Kevin Kelly points out, individuals throughout the industrialized West spend an increasing portion of their day "immersed in hyperrealities: phone conversations, TV viewing, computer screens, radio worlds." Gregory Stock sums it up nicely: "No wonder the emotional links between humans and the 'natural' environment are weakening; an ever-growing fraction of human experience is in an entirely different realm."

The same conclusion could be made, I believe, for the individual inner landscape. If the emotional links between human beings and the natural environment are weakening—and every indication suggests that they are—so too, and in perfect counterpoise, are the links between human beings and that 'other' natural environment, the terrain of the individual mind. Hyperreality, it seems, is a double-edged blade: with one stroke it renders unfamiliar the two worlds that nurture us—the twin solitudes of forest and thought, meadow and mind.

Unfamiliarity, of course, breeds contempt, or, at best, indifference. As the wires continue to meet and mesh, as the culture of distraction grows more pervasive, more familiar, the unwired will come to seem first quaint

. . . .

and then unreal. The copy and the original will reverse roles. Our own thoughts (when we have time for them) will remind us of something heard on *Oprah* or *Geraldo,* and the actual meadow, the empirical forest, will recall their facsimiles on CD-ROM. In time, like an endangered animal population that finally shrinks below the threshold of genetic viability, the unwired world may simply fade out altogether. It will still exist, of course, but our interest in it, our capacity to nourish and cultivate and appreciate it, will be gone. Along with Gregory Stock, we'll be in an entirely different realm—the placeless, ahistorical, market-saturated middle ground of the television sitcom and the cyberspace chat group.

The danger inherent in this is as much psychological as environmental. Identity, in no small part—both personal and communal—depends on our identification, in time, with the specific features of a particular landscape: that's the stoop my mother liked to sit on; there's the tree I fell out of when I was six. Like Arctic travelers lost in a whiteout, like Melville's *Pip,* overboard in the wide Pacific, we need to locate ourselves, to plot our coordinates in the physical world, in order to know where we've been and, therefore, who we are.

In cyberspace, though, neither place nor time exists. Increasingly isolated from both the inner and outer landscapes (and thereby deprived of the enormously important correspondence between them), we are left stranded in an "eternal, uncrystallizing present," a world detached from history. What will be the legacy of this creeping abstraction? An increasingly unmoored populace, a people severed from one of the fundamental roots of identity. Alone in our interactive bunkers, we may find ourselves (like the Sarajevan young man in this morning's paper, who, lying in a hospital bed, gets to watch—and watch again—his own shooting on videotape) obsessively pausing and rewinding and playing again the disembodied images offered to us, hoping to locate ourselves in that digital hall of mirrors, hoping, that is, to reconnect to that moment beyond the electronic middleground, when place and time were one.

■ ■ ■

Resisting the encroachment of the wired world on our lives, already damnably difficult, is rapidly becoming more so. A recent experience of my own, though admittedly insignificant in itself, may help make my point.

Last July, my wife, Leslie, and I decided to revisit the Pacific Northwest; we put the kids in the car, packed junk around them like protective wadding, and headed north. To pass the long hours between Motel 6 swimming pools and John Birch Society road signs, I spun tales of dense, primeval forests, melt-swollen rivers, and herds of elk grazing in the rain at dusk; every now and then, I told Zack, our six-year-old, a bull or cow— as though electrified—would shiver a pale halo out of its sodden hide. There were bears and mountain lions in those forests, I said, and, best of all, huge, tiger-striped banana slugs fully five inches long.

The slugs won. In no time at all, they had vanquished all rivals in wonder. By the time we hit Stockton, they had in some measure *become* the Northwest, a sticky synecdoche. Up the long, baking pan of the San Joaquin Valley, through a corridor of billboards and housing developments and radio frequencies, they ran neck and neck with Pocahontas as the backseat subject of choice. By the time we reached Mount Shasta, beloved of German tourists and New Age healers, two things had happened: my three-year-old daughter, Maya, had cracked the billboard color code and could now identify fully a dozen restaurants, gas stations, and motels by the distinctive color of their ads ("Motel Hix! Motel Hix!" came the periodic chant from the backseat whenever the red, white, and blue oval appeared among the forest of signs), and the lowly banana slug had become, for me, anyway, both inspiration and antidote: the symbol of essence in an increasingly virtual world, of nurturing silence in an increasingly noisy one, of fuck-you slowness in a culture enamored of fiber-optic speed.

Dazed by the heat and the unceasing noise of the interstate, I found myself longing for the unwired and apart, for a glimpse of life still tuned to a different frequency. Lying awake in the motel room set down among Mini-Marts, fast-food franchises, and Kwik-Stop gas stations, listening to the mad chant of television voices coming through the walls, it seemed to me that the slug at the end of the road would make an appropriate grail for our pre-millennial world: a being utterly removed from the babble of "information" and the traffic of commerce. An ur-snail to set against an e-mail culture. A rivet for our centrifugal age.

This is how it played out. North of Hoquiam, about an hour out of Humptulips, we entered a devastated landscape of stumps and brambles and impenetrable briar thickets—all that remained, for mile after mile, of what used to be the Olympic National Forest. The much advertised "replants," authentic-looking enough to those passing at cheetah speed along the highway, were worse. Nothing moved, nothing lived in these simulated forests: no snakes, no mammals, no birds in the understory. And no slugs. "There's one! I think I see one!" my son kept yelling, running off through that purgatory, his little sister in tow.

We quit for the day. We found a motel room. The kids clicked on the TV. And there, by one of those weird coincidences capable of bringing on a kind of postmodern vertigo, it was: the banana slug, or a facsimile thereof, courtesy of PBS. In the race between the thing itself and its electronic representation, the representation had won. I pressed the OFF button. The slug disappeared.

■ ■ ■

"In Wilderness," wrote Thoreau, "is the preservation of the World," by which he meant, of course, the spiritual world, the world of the soul. In the new age, the dictum may have to be reversed; today, the soul may represent the last hope for the preservation of the physical wilderness. Like some key species whose success determines the health of the entire ecosystem it inhabits, the individual soul—if thriving—may help restore that physical correlative of its own domain, the *actual* wilderness, by reawakening our interest in it, our need for it. As things stand (for a growing majority in the industrialized West, at least), there is neither the interest *nor* the need: living by remote, increasingly comfortable in the terrain of simulacra, insulated from the relentless current of history by the wonder of the instant replay and the miracle of the OFF button, we seem, as a group, to have arrived at the point where the virtual is not just *as* good but in many ways preferable to the original it replaced. Deerflies don't bite in the electronic wilderness.

The movement into our own "surround," it seems to me, is worth pausing to think about. One of the great migrations of the twentieth century, after all, it suggests a willingness on the part of the émigrés themselves to literalize the metaphor, to accept the *virtual* community, the *virtual* landscape, as actual and true. It should come as no surprise, then, that the majority of émigrés thus far have been American, that the Net—although spreading like Levi's or Coca-Cola to other lands—was made in America.

Throughout our history, after all, the empirical has served as a springboard into metaphysics. From Massachusetts Bay to the Michigan Militia, the actual, physical landscape, for example, has functioned as the all-purpose tenor for the national metaphor of the moment: the land as a stage for some ritual of socialization; the land as New World arcadia; the land as prophetic scroll. Our real investment, in other words, has traditionally been in worlds elsewhere. The conclusion seems clear: the virtual world of the Net, hawked by everyone from Al Gore to Timothy Leary in the hyperbolic terms usually reserved for millennial sermons and declarations of war, is as American as advertising and apple pie. Only a century after Frederick Jackson Turner eulogized the closing of the western frontier, another, electronic frontier, is open for business. America, as we always suspected, goes on forever.

The new American frontier, however, differs from its predecessor in an important way: it lacks what one technovisionary has called "the ballast of materiality." On the old frontier, after all, the hard facts kept poking through the metaphorical strata; in the airy precincts of cyberspace, there *are* no hard facts, or they lie so deeply buried, we can safely ignore them. Swaddled in layers of technology, having shed our ballast, we are free to recast avoidance as emancipation, and pretend that the electronic malls and gated communities of cyberspace are something more than elaborate, electronically generated metaphors. In cyberspace, the sun never burns, the wheel never breaks.

What to do, then? How resist (if resistance is our aim) the encroachment of forces fueled by both the unconstrained power of the free market *and* historical precedent? To whom do we turn, in a time when the McDonald's jingle echoes even in our dreams, for some viable alternative to the culture of distraction?

For better or worse, the burden of resisting the copy, it seems to me, of breaking through the terrain of simulacra, falls to the individual artist. Why? Because art, ultimately, is always a work of the individual creative imagination, and because the imagination—strangely silent, profoundly personal—represents the natural counterforce to the noisy, homogenizing power of the wired world, that increasingly corporate, largely metaphorical middle ground dominated by the sound byte and the sales pitch. Art, to resuscitate a romantic truism, works against the grain of the dominant culture.

Of course, asserting the traditional anti-structural role of art may seem quaint given the extent to which art itself has been appropriated by the corporate world. Today, after all, Beethoven's Ninth, appropriately amputated, sells Exxon, van Gogh and Rembrandt sell cars and jockey shorts, respectively, and rock and roll (spayed and neutered, no longer interested in painting *anything* black), hawks everything from soft drinks to software. The appropriation of individual works by the marketplace, however, does not necessarily undo the disruptive potential of art as a whole; used correctly, it can—as the writers of the American Renaissance, among others, so eloquently maintained—strike through the mask, pierce the rotten diction of the age. At its idiosyncratic best, art can drive a wedge under the sealed rim of the simulacrum we inhabit.

What I am suggesting, as should be clear by now, is a revival of the distinctly nineteenth-century notion of art as simultaneously subversive and liberating, both capable of cutting through the layers of mediating technology that surround us, and reattaching us to the worlds we've left behind. In this scenario, the fingerprint of individual style—whether expressed in print or pigment, marble or musical notation—plays an essential role. Applied to the tissue of verbal, visual, and musical clichés that surround us, to the hackneyed expressions and formulaic sentiments characteristic of the vernacular of electronic advertising, for example, it functions as a corrosive, quickly cutting to the bone of unmediated experience.

If all this recalls Wordsworth's nostalgic hankering after original participation, or Thoreau's anxiety "to front only the essential facts of life," or Carlyle's desire to turn our attention away from the distractions of the Age of Mechanism to the inner landscape of the individual soul, it should. At the same time, the late twentieth-century neoromanticism I am advocating is significantly different from its predecessor in that it does not posit a golden age—no transcendent realm, no idealized past characterized by some supernatural correspondence between self and other. All it does is evoke (summon up, one might say, as at a seance) the ghost of the unmediated world.

It may turn out that for many of us, the unmediated world will already seem vaguely supernatural, that the silence beyond the Net will seem as otherworldly, as idealized, as any arcadia, that our own, unwired past will appear to us in the glowing lineaments of the sublime. Perhaps, in the not-too-distant future, the completed, unmediated thought, like the bracing otherness at the heart of nature, will seem as foreign to us as anything in Bullfinch. Quite possibly, we will let them both slip the rest of the way into extinction and myth.

Until that day, however—and that day is not yet—we need the resisters, the poets of silence and slow time. Along with the ranks and battalions of individuals whose own particular, uncontrolled thoughts help restore the climate of authenticity, whose own actions cut loose the wires that bind us, they may yet succeed in rescuing some territory from the spreading net, in shoring up what remains of our natural and psychological legacy. It will be a great, and, to my mind, joyous labor, and its success will hinge, I believe, on what may come to be understood as an essentially religious gesture: the twist of the wrist that turns off the TV, that clicks off the computer, that restores us to our world and to ourselves.

Along the Estuary

. . . .

by
CAROLYN GUYER

> . . . isn't it what always happens when you're with other people? that's
> when things get complicated. . . .
>   "Buzz-Daze"

I live these days on the banks of a river that was once called *water flowing
two ways*. Or at least, favored lore claims that Native Americans named it
so. At any moment the Hudson contains some proportion of both salt-
water and fresh, mingled north then south then north again by the ebb
and flood of Atlantic tides. Right here is where I am. On these gentle, ancient banks, extravagant swag of hills still called mountains for what they
were, I know this to be a heart's place, because I have known others. One
of those—a different estuary—is the Potomac, just where it touches the
Chesapeake before breathing ocean. But I have also lived for a vast hori-
zonal time on a Kansas prairie, where sky and earth mirror each other in a
delirium of opposition.

It is easy to see that I measure things, the earth itself, with my body. Insisting on a swag and a delirium, turning geography to my own physical
style, making landscape intimate, its presence more present. I anthropo-
morphize because when it comes to what we really know, our bodies are
what we have to understand being alive. The present is a place as much as
it is a moment, and all things cross here, at my body, at yours. It is where I
consider the past, and worry about the future. Indeed, this present place is
where I actually create the past and the future.

Not alone, of course. Which is always the snag. There is no way to
know who I am, without also some way to understand where it is *not* me

anymore. There must be an Other in order for there to be a Me. Bodies bump, both in the night and in the street, colliding across the impasses, rivers, oceans, and continents. The proximity of yours and mine is the situation of difference and influence. It is how history is versioned, parceled and joined, invented as much as lived. And just the same in the other direction. We dream our future by incremental passes, carom into the unknown by tangent and gap.

As a girl on the Potomac, my concerns were rarely so high-flown and abstract. I didn't even know that my river was an estuary, or that not all rivers have tides. Instead, I was interested in learning to feel heavy so I could swim underwater. How to place a too buoyant self into that other world of seaweed tendrils, jellyfish, and fractured green light. Good practice, I think now. How better to understand a tidal mix than to swim in it? Under the water not far from the pier in front of my aunt's house, I knew something, and can easily recall some forty years later the pleasure of moving through – or trying to move through – a not entirely welcoming milieu. (Oh, *milieu*. The perfect word for underwater. A word without end, open and softly waving like the seaweed itself, holding hidden dangers.)

> or sometimes . . . the tallgrass which billows along her flanks, viridian swell
> of skirt in the wind
> *Quibbling*

Specific attractions drew me to the use of computers. The first and easiest, and indeed, the seduction for most people, was mutable text. Just the words themselves become fluid, more on a beam (motes on a beam) with the way language is in me. Word processing is a dry distance of a label for what is, more accurately, writing with light. But once that became possible, once I found I could think better when the words reforming on the screen in front of my eyes began to approach the speed of the ones behind them, I found myself wanting the synchrony to increase. My growing ease with electronic text catalyzed a desire to be able to write in dimensions that reflect a more complicated human experience. Nothing new in that really. The truth is that people have always had this same wish about language, needing more than past and future tenses to indicate how we actually know and create such abstractions of time. We have all sorts of literary and storytelling devices to try to achieve the effect of simultaneity. But what I wanted was to be able to spatialize text; I wanted a changing, changeable form. Not the animated march of Holzer marquee aphorisms, although I like those very much. No, something further, a way to instanti-

. . . .

ate the temporal leaps and slides we make just getting through a day. I wanted hypertext. An electronic medium* that theoretically can include and allow everything, and so finally allows only that we find our own perspective. Hypertext works tend to be so multiple, they reveal what is individual, ourselves, writers of our own story. When I discovered that this possibility existed, I hoped I had found the perfect medium for the creative process I had always known, the yielding, waving, pushing taction of form and formlessness. The way we can know that holding the paradox of existence is to *be* the cathexis, *be* the synapse. Human creativity is the dynamic of change, where difference is meaning, and where Self and Other are in tensional momentum. Beyond survival, and perhaps even as part of survival, this may be the most primal human impulse.

> Mother and Father. Earth and Sky. Like children, we try to make bridges between them, bind them together, never understanding the inextricable bond of difference. We sigh with relief and pleasure when they hold hands. We sigh. The comfort of rain, joy of glinting pond.
>
> *Quibbling*

During my first decade of living in the wide spaces of prairie, I was still young and didn't notice what happens there. When I finally awakened, it was to the breathtaking swoop and curve of grass hills, called Flint Hills, continuing forever, rhythm on rhyme, matched in scope only by the sky itself. Matched and opposed, this was the first way—dramatic and clear as bones—that I began to understand the importance of difference. Recently, a friend told me the story of young nieces and nephews from the Midwest visiting his home here in the Catskills. They complained that

---

* Hypertext is a category of software intended to allow links to be made among various kinds of information, including text, graphics, video, and sound. As a generic term, *hypertext* does not refer to writing alone, but rather to the linguistic and associative nature of human thinking processes. (Frequently, the word *hypermedia* is used instead, with an idea of reducing emphasis on text.) Hypertext is intended to allow information to be put together in such a way that a reader or user can move around in it however she likes. This has obvious and much utilized applications in orientation, training, and education, but hypertext is also employed to make many different kinds of interactive art.

There are two types of hypertexts, defined as: *Exploratory,* in which the reader explores a body of information and discovers the connections placed there by the author; and *Constructive,* in which the reader can enter the work and change or add to it herself, thereby becoming a co-author.

The most densely populated portion of the Internet, the World Wide Web, is designed as a hypertext, though almost completely of the Exploratory type thus far.

they couldn't see anything here because "the hills and trees are in the way." And just so, the tidewater child of the Potomac, swimmer under water, foreigner to the Midwest till she married, began finally in her late twenties to look up and out, to see that it wasn't empty there, and to see that horizon was not just dividing line but also connection. A kind of fitting marriage, if you will. I began to observe how extremes turn into their opposites, and so beginnings and endings, firsts and lasts, the things we believe so specific and significant, are always refusing to be just themselves. Instead, in changing, they point to the real significance, the shoreless variety of mixtures of difference.

> Power ceases in the instant of repose. . . .
> EMERSON

The great cultural question of our time is how to accommodate our growing recognition of multiplicity. It is easy enough for any of us to make weary, snide remarks about "being PC," but the weariness is really due to the frustration of being expected to provide equal significance and respect for a seemingly infinite number of segments of society. It is a frustration resulting from our self-induced illusion of standing still. We may long for the simplicity of generalized core values, of a mainstream more important than its streams and creeks, but the reality is clearly not that way, never so singular as the perspective of a rationalized hegemony. We think we believe in the individual. The solitary soul, self-reliant, removed from pedestrian life, a singular voice rising above the rabble. Yet we know that even our beloved Thoreau could not escape persistent visitors by the pond. It's a strange vision, this heroic separateness. For there is no human momentum that is purely self-generated; we are and must be connected to others. Which does not mean there is no such thing as a distinctly identifiable individual. Great personalities will continue, and perhaps this is what we have meant all along. Every person is a conglomerate of influences, aspects, and conflicting notions, the coherence of which is personality. This kind of individual, a teeming culture unto herself, should actually be quite prepared for the leap to a vast multiplicity in the larger society, where a constant shifting among perspectives is necessary and enforces the need for a strong, flexible psyche; an individual who retains identity while recognizing that the sources of her own development are never singular or completely separate from herself. This is not easy to do, or even to say. The energy required to stay actively engaged, heart and mind creating without cease, makes the temptation of simplicity great. But the truth is as ordinary as a river metaphor and, because of that, as needful of reminder. We so easily forget that the only real simplicity is some ultimate balance among all things, a "quietude" that comes, not when directly sought, but of its own accord when we experience the most profound creative instant, everything at once and in equilibrium. The only way to keep my balance is to keep moving.

> murmuring along the ridge a lip a line a brink of marriage soft spoken meet and heard our edge
> *Izme Pass*

It turns out that the boundaries between people, between groups of people, are permeable. There is no completely solitary individual and no homogeneous group. Each opposition is made of the other. The way we generally accommodate this wholly ungraspable reality, I believe, is the very essence of human creativity. We do it by the largely unexamined means of interiorizing disjuncture. That is, we gather the scraps and shards of interrupted conversations, overheard gossip, sound bites, photo ops, advertisements flowing by right through everything else, and we manage to arrive at a coherence of some sort. Yesterday was this way, last week was so, and then, spring and creek, a river of days, changeful and cyclic, but eventually a life, all made of mixtures that "don't belong" together. This nearly invisible and indecipherable meshing of differences may be the most creative thing humans do. And we do it all the time. Might it be useful to become more aware of such a pervasive process? What if we were to turn an inundation of multiplicity deliberately to the grace of tides, to the waltz of a fitting marriage?

By multiplicity, of course, I don't mean something like an ethnic street fair. But I do mean all the kinds of human dimensions and factors, all the most difficult, personal things. How to assess the quality of someone's work when everything can be considered valuable from some perspective or other. How to collaborate with someone with whom I simply cannot agree. How to live morally and ethically, really believing in my own principles, and still not assume they are also the best principles for everyone else. This is the hard stuff. But if we can imagine a way of doing these things, we can do them. Indeed, we have already in our electronic realm a medium where we can rehearse the leap and slide, where we can begin to work out the perverse problems of creating ourselves in a necessary paradox.

When I first began using hypertext almost ten years ago, I believed it was "natural," designed to work associatively, as the human brain does. I still believe something like that, but amplified, and with the plentiful hitches of a young technology thrown in. From those first days till now, I have continued to see this medium as very lifelike. I see it in the form of a quotidian stream. The gossip, family discussions, letters, passing fancies, and daydreams that we tell ourselves every day in order to make sense of things. The unconscious rhythms we incorporate—literally embody—as a reliable backbeat to our self-narratives provide familiar comfort as well as essential contrast for the changing turns of disjuncture. We live and make our stories in a line of time that wraps and loops on itself, trying to contend with the geometries of space we also inhabit. Affected by nearby hues we cannot or will not understand, we follow our influences, oppose, match, and continue, even in an electronic milieu, to measure with our bodies.

Some people have done things with hypertext that cause me to ache. The best have been the worst writers, the ones who have joined collaborative ventures with undeveloped skills and plunked what they felt right in the middle of someone else's sinuous prose. These I am grateful to for revealing to me my own biases, and for showing me the perspectival quickstep. Value is a contextual element, and contexts overlap. The worst, however, have probably been the best logicians in some world. They can take a living web of ideas and press it firmly into notched hierarchies, clearly linking exactly the path one is to follow. No straying, no trouble, this way to the castle. Let go the leash, I want to yelp. It is very hard for me to find the angle of vision by which I can see the value of this authoritarian approach. In the effort to get to such a perspective, I can, perhaps, grant that there may be times when guides are useful, and indeed, that most of us are so accustomed to being herded about that there is often a high preference for direction over finding one's own way. But oh, doesn't our best future swirl about somewhere beyond this scrim? I keep hoping that we may look up, or out.

> Dual channels give way to something more like the permeable flow of meaning between sometimes veering, sometimes nearing, banks of a single river.
> MICHAEL JOYCE

The tiny river hamlet where I live is situated right at the place where a creek enters the Hudson. At this juncture, Wappinger's Creek appears to be misnamed, for it is as broad as a small river itself, and there at its wide mouth, it too is an estuary where the local citizenry sometimes fish for Atlantic blue crab, dropping baited lines straight down from the short curve of a bridge. In the autumn, white swans enter here from the Hudson, I suppose to live in the more protected reaches of water they know, swimming in a mile or more to dot themselves picturesquely about on a slender lake formed by the creek. This tributary extends for miles inland, gradually becoming more like its name. Away from the river, where it meanders steeply, people have built homes near it, and their lives inevitably take on something of the creek's character. Something more of sudden delight, or intimate celebration, dappled and quick. Whether trickling between high banks and dense trees, or fanning broadly to meet the flux of the Hudson, it is a beautiful body in all its parts and changing nature. For all its complexity, it has a particularity I crave. Each of the creeks and streams along the river has this effect on me. Like personalities to learn or invent, each its own neighborhood, arrangement and trajectory. Where does it go by the time it moves into the larger stream? No longer traceable as it flows south and north, then south again, day by day the tidal promenade to the sea.

You can't tell me this isn't significant. You can't tell me anything. Ask the people who know me. It's true. This was all under water once.

Izme Pass

When I walk down the slope of my backyard, past the black walnut trees, and the old toolshed, down to the rocky garden now blooming in the late season of asters and mums, down to where I can see the river best, there I stand with my hills and stream in the same green tradition as anyone. They are for me a way of directly understanding my soul, gleam on water, blue of distance. From that same yard I can look back up at the house and see the window of the room where I use my computer, the site of a similar kind of exploration of existence. There is a difference between these two ways, but there is no reason for them to be anything other than an integrated process. Nature is what we are, and so cannot be opposed to, or separate from, humans and their technologies, even when we push our inventions to the point of self-destruction. Our newest and possibly most powerful technology, this electronic, known mostly as Computer, a word both comforting and spitting in its sound, promising the ease of things we do together (collaborate, cooperate, congregate, collect), and at the same time sharply forcing the challenge of individuality to find its center, this newest great invention is not yet at the point of self-destruct and still holds the potential for encouraging and supporting full human multiplicity and creativity. Of course there is no certainty, nor even a strong likelihood, that computer technology will fulfill that potential. Because of cultural realities surrounding its use, a patriarchal, white hegemony, and an economic system which has come to represent greed far better than social connection and responsibility, these and other factors will probably have their predictable influence. It takes little to realize for instance, that those of us who are already subordinated—women, people of color, developing countries—are the ones less likely to be participating in technology, and that as computers influence human society more and more powerfully, those same groups will be even more reduced in status than they are now. It is quite possible that all the inroads made in recent decades for social justice could be simply wiped away. Knowing that to be true is precisely the reason for more of us, concerned with the human condition, to become involved. I believe that this is indeed the most powerful and affecting technology we have ever contrived, and that there is no denying its hold on our lives and consciousness. As we form it, we are being formed. This is true for all of us, whether we use a computer or not. In the largest and most genuine sense, this is our future. Right here is where we are.

REFERENCES

Emerson, Ralph Waldo. "Self-Reliance" in *Essays: First Series*. Cambridge: Riverside Press, 1903.

Guyer, Carolyn and Martha Petry. *Izme Pass*. Hypertext fiction in *Writing On the Edge*, Vol. 2, No. 2. University of California-Davis, 1991.

Guyer, Carolyn. *Quibbling*. Hypertext fiction. Boston: Eastgate Systems, Inc., 1992.

Guyer, Carolyn. "Buzz-Daze Jazz and the Quotidian Stream." Panel on Hypertext, Hypermedia: Defining a Fictional Form, MLA Convention. New York, 28 Dec. 1992.

Joyce, Michael. *Of Two Minds: Hypertext Pedagogy and Poetics*. Ann Arbor: The University of Michigan Press, 1995.

Mr. Peabody and His Athenaeum

.   .   .   .

by

DANIEL MARK EPSTEIN

As I set out to learn the mysterious art of poetry twenty-five years ago, I got along in Baltimore on a weekly salary of forty dollars from part-time work in a jewelry store. I lived in a third-floor walk-up apartment on Cathedral Street just off Mount Vernon Square. Once H. L. Mencken occupied a lavish suite of rooms just up the street, overlooking the statuary and fountains of that city park he called the most beautiful in America. There the statue-topped pillar of the nation's first Washington monument passes its shadow over a brick mansion designed by Stanford White, the Greek Revival pediment of the Walters Art Gallery, the columns of the cacophonous Music Conservatory and its venerable, silent neighbor, the George Peabody Library.

I say that I lived in the apartment, but the tiny efficiency in which I slept and wrote in the mornings was hardly a space for living. I lived, really, in the neighborhood of Mount Vernon, which twenty-five years ago still kept the serenity and something of the gentility of a southern town. In the summer, businessmen crossed the square wearing seersucker suits, bow ties, and straw hats. They shopped downtown in haberdasheries their grandparents had patronized. This was before the real estate boom and bust filled the streets with brokers, mortgage bankers, and nouveau bureaucrats. Baltimore had a stable middle class that used the public schools. Old women in flower-print dresses and white gloves strolled arm in arm on Charles Street in the evening, without fear.

The old city was quiet and lazy, hospitable to ghosts and visions and reverie, a perfect place for a poet. I haunted the elegant, slightly seedy streets of Mount Vernon. The deserted marble salon of the Walters Art

Gallery was my living room, hung with paintings by Ingres, Botticelli, and Monet, the dusky bar of the Alcazar Hotel was my dining room. And the great Peabody Library was my study.

There is no other library like this in America, or anywhere else, excepting the parallel universe of Jorge Luis Borges's fiction.

From the cobblestones of the Square you ascend marble steps between fluted double columns, pass under the arch of a classical portico and through the cubic vestibule. The lofty reading room with its low shelves and card catalogs looks out on the green park through three enormous windows. Like ancient censers, eight ceiling lamps hang on chains, illuminating gilt-framed portraits of long-dead librarians.

In the middle of the interior wall, beneath a high archway of dark wood, an unwound pendulum clock hangs silent under the keystone. Through the doorway under the arch you see the white marble floor shining, set with black diamond "tesserae." As you pass under the arrested pendulum into the open space, your eye is drawn up slender columns sixty feet to the latticed skylight with its gilded finials, the pale sky supported by a mountain range of books, 250,000 books under the roof's painted vaults, whispering, humming a mazy fugue, a bibliographic Tower of Babel. Books are shelved to the sky upon five tiers of cast-iron balconies, ladders of lacy grillwork railings running all around the four sides, friezes and columns glittering with rosettes and gold scallops. Double globe lamps hang from the columns on brass stems, lighting oaken library tables in the alcoves of the lower stacks.

Once the globe lamps were gas fueled, now they are electric. Nothing else here has changed in a century. The collection is noncirculating: these books have never left the building. The space breathes such a dignified air of antiquity, it is hard to believe the library has not been here since the founding of the Republic, ours or another state more imposing, more deeply rooted, a Republic of humane letters. But the library opened its doors to the public in 1878, as part of the educational institute founded by George Peabody.

A cameo portrait of George Peabody shows the prosperous silver-haired bachelor in his sixties, with muttonchop whiskers, kind, wide-set eyes, broad forehead, a large patrician nose, and a determined mouth that flickers at the corners with wry humor. He was born poor in Danvers, Massachusetts, in 1795. The boy served an apprenticeship to a grocer for five years, then he worked in a drapery shop. Peabody served in the army during the War of 1812, where he met Elisha Riggs, a merchant. In 1815, when the war ended, the men set up a dry goods business in Baltimore under the sign Riggs, Peabody & Co. Peabody, the younger partner, cranked the business up into an enterprise with branches in New York and Philadelphia. By 1829 the firm's name had become Peabody, Riggs & Co.

In Baltimore George Peabody made the small fortune that would provide the cornerstone for the great one he would pile up later as a financier. The center of the financial world was then London, so Peabody left Baltimore for London in 1837. But he never forgot his home here, or the friends he had made in his youth; and he vowed that someday he would return to do something worthy of the city that had given him his start.

No one could have predicted this tyro's success in that treacherous world of bankers and bond factors. By the beginning of the Civil War, George Peabody was so rich that he single-handedly rescued the endangered credit of the U.S. government in England. Sensitive to the plight of the working class in Dickens's London, the energetic American built more than 40,000 housing units at his own expense, and gave them away to needy families. For this heroic act of charity, Queen Victoria offered Mr. Peabody a baronetcy. He declined the title, explaining that it might only come at the expense of his U.S. citizenship, which was dear to him. The philanthropist gave tens of millions of nineteenth-century dollars to Harvard, Yale, Philips Academy, to his hometown of Danvers (now Peabody), Massachusetts, and to the South for public education after the war. Thus he became the prototype for other great nineteenth-century philanthropists—Andrew Carnegie himself acknowledged his debt to Peabody's example.

The charity Mr. Peabody is best known for today, however, was his endowment of the cultural institute in Baltimore that bears his name. The founder's letter dictated that the Institute should have four elements: an art gallery, a lecture series, an academy of music, and a library "which I hope may become useful towards the improvement of the moral and intellectual culture of the inhabitants of Baltimore. . . ." The fastest-growing city in America in 1857 had no university, no library, no art museum— Baltimore was a cultural wasteland. It took the ex-grocery clerk, who had not the leisure to read fifty books in his lifetime, to see the need and provide the basic elements for a civilization.

■ ■ ■

I am sitting in an alcove on the ground level of the stack room, under a mountain of books. To my left, shelves upon shelves of huge quarto volumes of *The Victoria History of the Counties of England,* red bindings, gilt-stamped; to my right the *Calendar of Charter Rolls 1226–1516.* Sadly, some of the bindings have unraveled and pages are crumbling away, turning to dust.

These books and a quarter million others are more than packages of information. They inhabit space, as well as time, bearing a very specific spiritual charge, a metaphoric gravity. English history is here, and the history of France and America, Greece and Rome, as well as the thoughts and memories of millions who have lived and died leaving little above ground but black print on white pages.

I may pull a quarto from the shelf of a hundred tomes on the English counties, and read at random: in 1713 the headmaster of the Petty School adjoining the Church of Basingstoke, one John James, was indicted for caning a boy to death. I have read one page out of fifty thousand. Think what a vast human drama abides there, silently, perhaps never to be discovered! In the next alcove is the *War of the Rebellion,* the records of the Union and Confederate Armies, in two hundred volumes. All I have ever read of the Civil War is contained in twenty books that cannot begin to convey the dimensions of that national tragedy; yet it is here, figured forth in the heft and breadth of this wall of history, a wall of printed facts I may walk around or enter through a door of pages, but which I may not, in this sanctuary of the human conscience, altogether ignore.

It is very quiet here. There is no one in the library but me. That is, there are no other patrons. Somewhere behind the scenes there is a librarian, and a clerk who will rise from the dust if I call him, and fetch the books I request from the card catalog. But I am the only reader in the library. That is more often true these days than it was twenty-five years ago when I first sat here looking out the west window on the brick wall of the Conservatory. I remember how surprised I was that the other desks were vacant, and how I wondered whom the library was meant to serve.

I sit at an oak desk with an arabesque book rail. Years ago, a librarian whispered to me over my shoulder that John Dos Passos had once occupied this desk. "John Dos Passos," she whispered reverently, and then tiptoed back to her hiding place. And I thrilled at the thought: he, Dos Passos, was the last patron the library was meant to serve!

Now there is a little brass plaque on the book rail that says, "John Dos Passos, Novelist and Social Historian (1896–1970) / he spent many hours

. . . .

in research at this desk." I suspect the trustees placed this plaque to honor Dos Passos not so much for his writings as for his iron perseverence as the library's solitary reader.

He is gone. Am I the last reader in the Peabody Library? I sit alone with this incalculable treasure, like a character in a Jack London story who outlasts the rest, to discover a gold hoard so vast, hypnotic, and remote from civilization that no man who has ever seen it can go home again. The triumphant prospector is destined to add his bones to the pile.

What would Mr. Peabody think of this use, and this disuse, of his books? It is my guess that this very practical man of affairs would not be looking down from Heaven to monitor the turnstile, as if his library were a dance hall or baseball stadium. Mr. Peabody knew about commerce, and he had a feeling for culture — and he was not about to confuse the one thing with the other. His founding letter of 12 February 1857 is quite specific in its description of the sort of library he had in mind: "An extensive Library, to be well furnished in every department of knowledge, and of the most approved literature, which is to be maintained *for the free use of all persons who may desire to consult it . . .* it should consist of the best books on every subject . . . *to satisfy the researches of students who may be engaged in the pursuit of knowledge not ordinarily obtained in the private libraries of the country.* It should be guarded and preserved from abuse . . . *it shall not be constructed upon the plan of a circulating library."* The emphasis is mine. The founder understood that circulating libraries serve their own democratic purposes, not to be confused with the function of a bona fide research library or athenaeum, whose volumes not only store information but represent, as significant vessels in hallowed space, the memories and impressions of humankind.

Peabody himself did not have the education to create such an athenaeum, and knew he would not live to see it. So he charged the trustees and the provost, Nathaniel Holmes Morison, with instructions to procure the best books *"no matter what their age or cost,* for scholarly research and reference in the arts and sciences."

Now what this means, in effect, is that if you are a budding dramatist, or critic interested in the Restoration comedy of manners; if you should decide, on a bright summer morning, that you would like to look at William Congreve's first play, and ring for the shelf clerk and give him your order from the dusty card catalog, in ten minutes he will descend in the rattling elevator with your book: *The Old Batchelour* by William Congreve, 1694. That's right, 1694, the year after the play was produced in London under John Dryden's supervision. Holding the original text in your hands, turning those foxed pages, you can almost hear the dry laughter of the Cavaliers. The book is only three hundred years old. Columna Franciscus's *Hypnerotomachia Poliphili* was published in Venice in 1499, Paracelsus's *Works* in Geneva, 1658. Are you interested in Francis Bacon? You shall have his *The historie of the raigne of King Henry the Seventh* as it was first published in London in 1622, or the first translation into French, done in Paris five years later.

Most of these books were available after the Civil War in reprints at only a fraction of the cost of the first editions. But money was no object. Mr. Peabody's purpose was to gather books that had made history and first recorded the thoughts and passions of humankind, in the belief that a book is something more than a locus of data, paper, glue, and ink; a book has supersensible power, and a great collection draws down a resonance endowing the reader of any book in it with special faculties of understanding.

If you are an aspiring author and want a shot of Henry James, you shall have *The Wings of the Dove* as it first appeared, in two volumes, in 1902. During three months, many years ago, I spent an hour a day reading that novel, parsing the master's labyrinthine sentences in the shadow of 250,000 books, most of them older, unwilling to let go of any paragraph until I had understood Milly Theale and Merton Densher as well as I could. What higher tribute could I pay this author than focusing on his book to the exclusion of those other classics clamoring for attention, eager to comment, to argue, to be heard?

And if you are John Dos Passos, perhaps the greatest epic novelist of America's empire, you have the substance and spirit of human history as the grist for your mill.

■ ■ ■

Dos Passos was a passionate defender of individualism, all the more passionate because he nourished a diligent social conscience. In the 1960s he was still fashionable, the subject of a flattering essay by Jean-Paul Sartre. When I was in high school, my friends and I read Dos Passos's *U.S.A.* trilogy in lively paperback editions illustrated by Reginald Marsh, epic novels in which a host of diverse characters play out the drama of their lives against the panorama of history from 1900 to the 1930s.

He was our Homer, without a hero. His carefully observed hoboes, soldiers, waitresses, and financiers are forever measuring the scope of individual freedom against the rule of law and the needs of the *polis* as a whole, i.e., *each other.* The protagonist of this sprawling narrative is no single character but the whole ensemble, the aggregate soul of America. Dos Passos saw his work as following the English tradition that begins with Chaucer and ripens in Shakespeare, Fielding, and Dickens, a literature dedicated to the description of people not only as individuals but as eccentrics bound to suffer one another's company on the hard pilgrimage of life on this earth.

If the novelist of today serves any social purpose—apart from perfecting objets d'art and advancing human perception—it consists in such luminous study of individuals and their affairs as will inspire a reader to understand men and women unlike himself. It is thus we begin to comprehend society as a whole. Of Chaucer, Dos Passos writes in praise of his "down-to-earth knowledge of vulgar reality, the gift for jocose narrative, the appetite for freedom, the sharp satire mellowed by fellow feeling for a great many varieties of men."

Our English word "individual" comes from the Latin *individuus,* not divisible, of one essence. As Walt Whitman knew, the individual is *individuus,* paradoxically, because he is of one essence with all people.

At the bottom of the well of the Peabody Library, Dos Passos mused darkly on the fate of the individual in a society based on industrial mass production. "Life has become so cut up into specialized departments and vocabularies, so hard to understand and to see as a whole, that most people won't even try. Even people of first-rate intelligence get so walled up in the particular work they are doing that they never look outside of it." He recalled Ralph Waldo Emerson: "Man is not a farmer, or a professor, or an engineer, but he is all . . . There is One Man—present to all particular men only partially, or through one faculty; you must take the whole society to find the whole man." And then Dos Passos dipped his pen to write novels upon Emerson's advice, books that would deserve a place in the athenaeum that nurtured his vision of the whole man.

This is the novelist's consummate role, to reunite the fragments of the subdivided social state in his vision of the whole, the original unit, the fountain of power. The celebration of family histories and egocentric memoirs is useful and salutary, but it must not become the foundation of an aesthetic. These must not be taken as the ideal of literary art. Nor is it art that restricts itself to elaborating any single viewpoint, of the disenfranchised, the dispossessed, the bookish, or the privileged. This is a form of journalism that has its own standards of excellence. But it must not be confused with the art of Henry James, Ralph Ellison, or Virginia Woolf, whose vision contrives to relate elements of society that have lost sight of one another.

I have heard the solemn critics say, again and again during the last decade, that there is no story, there are only stories; there is no truth, there are only truths; there is no human character, there are only characters. These deconstructionist slogans may or may not pass muster in the metaphysics seminar. But when Gabriel García Márquez succeeds in appealing to a worldwide audience, reuniting diverse readers in the clear light of a fictional universe, it is because he has told *the* story all can share, because he has discovered *the* truth that is the ground of understanding between reader and writer, because he has revealed an essence of human character that is universal. Insofar as J. M. Coetzee deserves his laurels as a novelist, it is not because he bears witness to the persecution of his people — for this he deserves credit as a journalist. He is important as a novelist to the extent that he has told the story of his family within the larger context of human history, with irony, including characters unlike his own, not monsters, but equally human. It is significant that the greatest American novel about the Holocaust was written, not by a Jew, but by the southern gentile William Styron. And the genius of *Sophie's Choice* was to show that the tragedy of the Holocaust did not begin and end with the Jews in Europe, but could be reenacted by three young people, more and less Jewish, in the microcosm of an American rooming house.

■ ■ ■

I would guess that Mr. Peabody, with the clairvoyance granted to angels, is pleased with the use of his library.

He sees who comes and goes, what they read, and what they think. Maybe ten people will come here in a day, or maybe one person in ten days who is more perceptive than ten taken together. With every Dos Passos come a hundred critics of the author; for every great novelist there are a hundred historians whose lucubrations on the recent past will inspire the next epic novelist, and so on. Add a few thousand thoughtful readers and there you have a civilization, which is a society conscious of itself (much as a person is conscious), of its history, thoughts, and feelings, the interrelations of its sundry parts.

Mr. Peabody understood that to have a civilization, you must have an athenaeum, just as to have a school of fish, you must have a body of water. In your pond or lake you may have fish or you may not, but without water you surely will have none. This magical library, in this charmed space, was designed to be used by a few men and women who could learn how to live in it. This is the necessary environment for private education, the encounter between a person and a book. It is free and private. That is why there are so few tables and chairs. That is why it is always so quiet. Mr. Peabody endowed not only the books and the cast-iron architecture. He endowed the silence in perpetuity, in a space where time stands still. Here the individual can begin to locate his soul in the sprawling galaxy of human experience symbolized by the books on the towering shelves.

Now there is great concern in Baltimore, as in all major cities, about the decline in literacy. It is no longer possible for most children to learn to read and write in the public schools. Since the end of the Vietnam War, public education has descended to a level so pathetic that even the cruelest satire cannot exaggerate it. Bells ring in schools where there are no textbooks, no lightbulbs, no windows. Children cannot use the lavatories for fear of being robbed and beaten there. Increase of funding is fruitless where incompetent teachers are not fired nor recalcitrant students expelled, where the "C" grade is given for failure, and teachers no longer routinely correct grammar or spelling, for fear of injuring their students' self-esteem. This has come about largely because of a debasing of academic standards to flatter the lowest common denominator, so that no teacher or student should appear more intelligent than another. The passion for a utopian equality has caused originality of thought and excellence of scholarship to be vilified, and a bestial uniformity to be valued above conscious individuality.

For my generation, the decline of the public schools is especially frightening because we remember the system in its golden age. Democracy giveth, and Democracy taketh away. New Deal politicians pumped up funding for circulating libraries and public schools in the '30s. The electorate's passion for mass education reached its sublime expression in the GI Bill of Rights of 1944, financing higher education for millions of veterans in an era when colleges had not yet bartered away their standards of excellence. That was real progress. The sons and daughters of these middle-class alumni went to the public schools where their parents taught, in the city and suburbs. Schoolteaching was a respected profession, the only one besides nursing that favored women, and women enriched it beyond measure.

American public schools were never more effective than in the 1950s and early 1960s. They had sufficient if not generous funding, serious educators, and most important, a strong basis of support in the communities they served. That was the golden age. Never was education more widespread and high-minded in this country—certainly not in the 1920s or 1930s. As for the nineteenth century, let the mistier sentimentalists glorify the one-room schoolhouse and its knuckle-rapping schoolmarms and masters. Most boys and girls too poor to attend private school, like George Peabody, went to work.

Yes, post–World War II America enjoyed the apogee of mass education and witnessed unprecedented literacy, and we thought it would last forever. But in the late '60s, federal and state bureaucracies melted down the community-based public schools at the bidding of an electorate determined to drag the best students down to the level of the worst. They have succeeded, horribly. Now most of the city schools are no more than detention centers—poorly managed ones, because their guardians and detainees persist in the delusion that they are somehow involved with education; this distracts them from their only remaining purpose, which is to secure public safety within and without.

What is to be done? Without mass education our universal suffrage will surely lead us to demagoguery or tyranny. "When society has entered on this downward progress," wrote the English historian Thomas Babington Macauley in the 1850s, "either civilization or liberty must perish. Either some Caesar or Napoleon will seize the reins of government with a strong hand or your Republic will be as fearfully plundered and laid waste by barbarians in the twentieth century as the Roman Empire was in the fifth; with this difference . . . your Huns and Vandals will have been engendered within your own country by your own institutions."

What shall we do for the Baltimore schools? They need books. Shall we sell the rare books in the Peabody Library at auction? Here is a Double Elephant Folio and Octavo set of Audubon's *Birds of America* worth at least half a million dollars, and hardly anyone ever looks at it. Why, the Peabody book collection must be worth millions and millions of dollars, and think of how many social studies textbooks and computers the schools could buy with all that money. And then, when the library is empty, see what a splendid indoor stadium it would make for wrestling and gymnastics!

"You will in such season of adversity as I have described," says the prophet Macauley, "do things which will prevent prosperity from return-

. . . .

ing; you will act like people in a year of scarcity who devour all the seed corn. . . ."

By the mid-1960s, the Peabody endowment had so far dwindled that the trustees, in dismay and desperation, offered the athenaeum to the city's library system; in 1966 the George Peabody Library became a department of the Enoch Pratt Free Library. And as surely as night follows the day, the city promptly announced a strategy to auction off the rare books, shuffle the rest into the public library system, and convert the building into a study hall for high school students.

Such a cry of pain and outrage arose from the scholarly community thirty years ago as has never been heard since, and the city's plan never materialized. A fund-raising campaign to restore the building, install air-conditioning, and rebind a few hundred books carried the library through the '70s. But as the city's budget tightened, the Pratt decided it could no longer justify the expense of the Peabody Library. In 1982 it became a department of the special collections division of the Johns Hopkins University Library. The transfer agreement states the university's desire to honor Mr. Peabody's original intent.

■ ■ ■

So, for the time being, the library is safe. We shall not sell the books at auction or turn the stack room into a skating rink. But look how close we came to that folly only five years before I made the library my study! Had it not been for a handful of scholars, who understood the athenaeum's intangible value well enough to explain it, appealing to the public's highest instincts, then that sanctum in which I found my voice would have been no more than a romantic legend, like the libraries of Alexandria and the Palatine.

But will the academic dons and cashiers of the Johns Hopkins University have the integrity and the providential foresight to maintain the library as they have promised? I would like to say that this is certain, but I cannot. Thirty years ago, the Hopkins had a top-notch classics department, whose members were dedicated to the study of Greek and Latin authors and ancient history. Scholars like these defended the Peabody Library when Baltimore city bureaucrats armed themselves to plunder and despoil it. In the 1980s, the Hopkins classics department was virtually dissolved because of poor enrollment—a sad concession for a private university, to bow to the economics of mass education. When the accountants explain, as they must, that the maintenance of the Peabody Library for a few hundred eccentrics is less cost effective than a new computer system that will be used by thousands, who will stand up to defend the library?

Who will be left, in the next millennium, to defend the idea of a civilization? Not, surely, the graduates of Baltimore's public high schools, unless some of the more curious children are drawn to the athenaeum or someplace else where there are books and an atmosphere of reverence for their human contents. Does any thinking person believe there is *less* need for a great library today than there was in 1857?

What would Mr. Peabody say and do, if we could have him and his old fortune (at 7 percent interest) restored to us in the year 2000? Strolling up Charles Street in his frock coat and looking around him, he would doubtless be pleased at the sight of the Walters Art Gallery and the sounds of the Baltimore Symphony, flowers from the seeds he planted. Surely this is progress, he would say. Then of course he would want to know about the schools, and we would have to tell him.

And what would Mr. Peabody do with his millions, in the best interest of society and civilization? It stands to reason that he would do what he did in the nineteenth century, when he gave roughly equal amounts to found the Peabody Institute and to jump-start public education in the ruined South. For a free society is not monolithic—it depends upon a harmonious interaction among its diverse constituents. Leave it to the rags-to-riches philanthropist, who has known society from the bottom up, to understand this truth: civilization may flourish or rot from the top down, but in a democracy it can only endure by consent of an educated electorate. Five poets at work in the Peabody Library and a thousand readers studying their verses may constitute a civilization, in time, given the time. But if half a million others cannot understand print on a page or the humanizing value of poetry, these will burn down the library sooner or later, in a rage over what they cannot understand, furious over the beauty that has been denied them.

The philanthropist, his judgment none the worse for a century's holiday among angels, would divide his fortune as before, between a research institution for the few, and public education for the many. By public education I do not mean the city public school system as we know it. I mean only to distinguish public education from the sort of private education that goes on between a man and a book in the athenaeum. Mr. Peabody was a realist, not a man to throw good money after bad. He would grant his money only to schools, public or private, maintaining standards of excellence and the power to fire inept teachers and expel disruptive pupils:

parochial schools, charter schools, magnet schools, and "private" schools open to needy students through scholarship programs. This is the best that any philanthropist can do at present to foster literacy in the public. Perhaps in the future a literate minority will once again persuade the electorate that schools funded by the public best serve the public when they recognize individual intelligence, reward academic excellence.

Of course, Mr. Peabody would not leave Baltimore until he had fastened down his athenaeum, a constant source of human progress and enlightenment. He would round up a posse of conservators to rebind his crumbling books and oil their leather hinges. He would telephone I. M. Pei and Robert Venturi and hire them to build a new tower nearby for a hundred thousand new old books that would bring the athenaeum a little closer to the twenty-first century. Then, with a smile of modest satisfaction, the philanthropist might return to that blessed world of light where questions have easy answers and virtue is rewarded, knowing that all he could ever do for civilization he has done.

The Lemmix

.   .   .   .

by
ALBERT GOLDBARTH

1.

It's 1995, and a recent paperback's silver, raised cover text promises
"wildly exotic love in a harsh and beautiful land." This is the ambience,
too, of the famous 1921 Rudolf Valentino movie *The Sheik*: the rhythmic
dunes, a counterpointing caravan line, all deepened in a gorgeously
bloody sunset, all imbued with the romance of the pretechnological. But
Agnes Ayres, who stars opposite Valentino, is shown in the clasp of the
desert warrior wearing a very 1921 wristwatch—one of the earliest bloop-
ers, though of course the term was unknown then. In the 1926 sequel, the
error repeats: this time it's Valentino himself, burnoosed and passionate,
who sports the contaminant timepiece.

This is why my Grandma Nettie had to die, I believe. She'd arrived in
the Land of Liberty from a world of village donkey carts—in basic ways,
was permanently fixed by that world's ethos and tempos—and, having
lived through Kitty Hawk, and both world wars, and into the age of Sput-
nik (I can picture her, dimly, as one small patch on the backdrop of my life,
as my transistor radio's static curtain admits the top hit "Telstar" into the
room), she became an embarrassment to Time, an outmoded unit.

She couldn't speak English. Her thick shoes laced up with a button-
hook. She knew what it was to sit in the kitchen and pluck a chicken bald
to its stippled skin. She might as well have attended the world premiere of
this year's microchip Rolexes wearing a heavy miniature hourglass
strapped to her wrist. And so, when the last of the cotton underthings had
been stained for the last time, we buried her.

There aren't any photographs of her childhood; there were no cameras there and then, period. Really there's only one image of her that I know (her face less photographed by far than faces of certain pampas herdsmen or New Guinea weaver women, or that neolithic-level tribe that *National Geographic* was snapping so gleefully, about a decade ago).

The occasion, my parents' wedding. Already this woman who's nine months short of being a grandmother looks like an emptied pouch, although I'm also tempted to read a weary kind of dignity into her bearing. My father is beaming goofily through the 1947 tones of black and white. My mother is contentedly placid; her hat aspires to emulate an orchid plantation. Everyone must have been festive—I imagine my father czardashed to a neighbor's accordion far past sober accomplishment—but the clothing is that of the rising poor; and the table's offerings, similarly thin; and the room is some plainly fixtured neighborhood hall within walking distance. No one in this photograph drove. In 1947, with the world accommodated by then to visions of atom-powered Flash Gordon rocket travel, the car was still a luxury to these people. It waited somewhere out there with moonships.

So I'm puzzled at this fuzzy demimemory I have of Grandma Nettie appearing, surprisingly enough, in a jittery fifteen seconds or so of actual movie film. Unlikely, given her retrograde vibes. And yet it's certainly *possible;* Uncle Morrie was an engineer (by virtue of having any degree past grammar school, he declares himself in this narrative as someone unrelated by blood, who married into the family) and he toyed around with a clunky prototype camera-and-synchronized-tape-recorder attachment intended for home use. In the last of her days, he might indeed have captured her, with rounded chopper in hand, above the great wooden bowl in her lap, in which the chicken liver and hard-boiled eggs and sprinkled nuggets of chicken grease and fist-sized onions were being made one. She looks up, and she says one blurry, Yiddish-phlegmy sentence that sounds to me like Ahlaf seyna dokwanda—"I have seen a dark wonder" is how I remember it.

She'd be dead soon after. Morrie is dead. His cutting-edge-of-a-movie camera is long since superseded. Nothing stops the future from eating us alive, and recombining us. Those zippy Flash Gordon astrocruisers are still the stuff of fantasy, but fifteen seconds of Nettie Goldbarth is beaming, along with *Gunsmoke* and *Your Hit Parade* and *The Honeymooners,* past the outermost ring of the planets and onward—a face (and a bowl of chopped liver) composed completely of photons now.

2.

When Flash and Dale and Zarkov land on Mongo, what they find is a despotic ruler and subjugated peoples, what they find is violence, sexual passion, avarice, selfless sacrifice—the range of human doing that would be at home in Dickens, and that plays its capabilities out in a recognizable narrative progression. If the eyrie-spired city of the Hawkmen floats above Mongo on a pillar of "strato-thrust" . . . its halls are peopled (even if wingédly peopled) with character types whose motivations, foul or noble, are bred in the very chemicoghostly neural works that power the corner cop and the supermarket cashier.

Although the genre's best practitioners *can* be psychologically savvy, the commonest sci-fi (surely the pumped-with-wonder adventuresome stuff I read as a kid) predicts on the level of Nifty Scientific Doohickeys only, and assumes what I call the Electric Can Opener Noneffect: the move ("up?") from a manual to an electric model, even to a model with lights and ergonomic Velcro grips and buzzers, is a matter of pure convenience; the actual *thinking* of the user doesn't alter. For most of us, and most sci-fi, a rocket ship is a can opener.

The cover art of my 25¢, 1953 Signet edition of Asimov's *The Currents of Space* (which looks to my lay eye to be by Saunders or Valigursky, although it's uncredited) shows us a plucky hero and heroine on the run through a future spaceport thrillingly filled with the visual cues that say Tomorrow. Other planets have been conquered: an impressive needle-with-thrusters spaceship sleeks straight up from a billow of rocket exhaust. A sister ship stands by, for clearance. A third ship scores an off-white feather of propulsive trail diagonally across the sky. Two small security rocket patrollers are zipping after our fleeing twosome at nearly ground level. The hero wears a grapely purple flight suit with its traditional fishbowl helmet, and the heroine's blouse's shoulders are given an aerodynamically futuristic three-tier look.

But our hero is also holding an oblong of carry-on leather luggage no different from what was heaved to the docks in the golden age of steamship travel; in fact, it's colorfully covered with stickers that likely say Mars Dome 1 or Saturn City, but could be claiming Istanbul or Cairo just as well. Around his neck is the same damn traveler's camera my father would have brought along in 1953, when I was five, and we vacationed at the Indiana dunes.

. . . .

We almost always think that future eyes—whatever electroluxury or nuvo-Boschian hovel they review us from—will marvel at our objects (*they had "cans"!*) and maybe customs (*and "vacations"!*) but connect to brains that necessarily function in a sequence and with oversensibility we'd recognize as kindred.

That assumption may be tested in the next few generations. No, can openers will not rewire the paths of the species' circuitry. The electric can opener *is* an easier opener, and our life goes on. But the car *isn't* simply an easier horse; and, after its invention, *different* life goes on, and different eyes are required to be its witness. The shape of the planet and how we understand it—change. Ideas having to do with needs so basic as sex and privacy—change. The speed of the car and the speed of a roll of movie film demand new speeds from change itself. Then okay, maybe even a can opener becomes part of a cultural complex. And we come to fit the shape of the exoskeleton that—by cathode ray and silicon chip and laser and fiber optics—we've made.*

"Embedded in every tool is an ideological bias," Neil Postman writes, "a predisposition to construct the world as one thing rather than another."

And our next change? —Evolutionary. Not in a metaphorical sense, but a literal Darwinian one. The beings of the cyberhive, linked up in their achronal, nonsequential, and unspatial cyberatmosphere, will surely repattern their brains' own storage and sparkage in terms of such context.

I don't think that this is "bad" any more than it's "good"—any more than the cosmos operates in terms of "up" and "down." But I do know where my fondness wells. I know that a certain orderliness, and a certain sense of individual definition, are passing away.

On page one of Asimov's *The Currents of Space,* somebody visits an office of the Interstellar Spatio-Analytic Bureau. (Whew!) He's in another galaxy. (Double-whew!) And yet the stellar agent he talks to is waiting for response to some "letters"—writings, on papers, the kind my Grandma Nettie, for all of her lack of formal education, piled into a life's enabling building blocks, and which (no matter their hearty existence in Asimov's book) are quickly being marginalized and left like shoreside litter by our onrushing currents of consciousness.

---

* Is a can of pop twelve ounces because our human thirst is standardly twelve ounces? Or has our thirst learned to be satisfied as sized to a can of pop?

3.

We drove out to the Indiana dunes in a 1951 Chevrolet that had the high-crowned, rounded smoothness of a Stetson hat—an altogether admirable design, as I look back on it now, although it must have been a model from the bottom of the line at the time. My father was a studious driver, of many fussy attentions to the road and his machine; and this, I guess, was part reaction to his first chaotic stint behind the wheel. The story goes that Uncle Morrie taught him to drive by taking them out in Morrie's car some dozen miles, stopping, switching places, and saying, "Okay, Irv, now you take us back." It must have been one hell of a bucking ride.

I would have been, oh, seventeen or so when Morrie suddenly died of a heart attack, a healthy man who went down like a great tree. While I don't remember the funeral or the week of *shiva,* I clearly recall *his* mother, an elderly stocky-bodied, Yiddish-speaking woman, dramatically planting herself in a doorway and moaning—staying there unbudgeably in that niche as if it became an official moaning station, and venting a grief that was larger than she was. Once, in her Old World, damaged English: "No! That the mother lives more than the son—*no!*"

She was right: it broke the normal narrative flow, and she became anachronistic, she became (unbearably so) another wrong time strapped to a wrist.

These days, when I think of the death of the printed page (or at least, the death of its primacy), I invoke her. I invoke her large-scale moan, since I ascribe it to the pell-mell rush-to-death of a fantasy creature I've invented. Listen . . .

. . . Proponents of change will always see (and will proselytize, in its imagistic terms) a shining horizon. That shine, or blaze, or steady clarifying gleam, is seen as the light of the phoenix, lifting from its ashes in transmogrified exultance. Print culture dies; *a flash;* the on-line paradise rises.

That's as valid a trope as any—as valid as mine. But I prefer mine, I prefer it more each day as my few lifetime choices polarize: either the omniwhambangbuzzbuzzinforama—or the quiet and maestroly guidance of a single book in a cone of watts; the storyless imagebarrage of MTVeese—or the serial, history-steeped accumulation of narrative language; the inter-rabble babblechat of the nownow everywhere colonymind—or one lone person's concentration on one invited exemplar of authorial ministration.

Out of the felt effects of a Gutenberg world that patterned the ethos of

. . . .

even trivial everyday *non*textual moments, my parents, who never graduated from high school, nonetheless structured a life for themselves and their children as solidly and yet modestly joindered together as paragraphs stitched to each other with sensible, supple transition statements. This is the world I care to honor; and this is the world that's disappearing, as *we're* disappearing, busy as we are, becoming other "WES."

Jerry Mander: "Technologies have organized themselves in relation to other technologies to create an interactive web, of which we're only one part. We feed it, and we serve it, and we interact with it, and we co-evolve with it, and we slowly become it. We're practicing a form of intra-species suicide."

Before the phoenix splendiferously rises, the phoenix's death is required. The resurrection may be, indeed, a glory hallelujah thing, I admit—but to the part that dies, the death itself is everything. And the fantasy creature I've thought up is the lemmix—because the lemming is the necessary first half of the tale of altering states. And to the lemming, the tale is never pretty.

The brightness *I* see is the glint of the sun on the water as the pell-mell rush tumbles over the rim of the cliff. Ten billion Chevrolets is one more way I see it, driving determinedly off the edge of the world, and changing into invisible, bodiless blips of data in midair. And then I hear, above this scene, the moan—the moan of Morrie's mother, become the ionosphere, an overarching elegy-moan. *Its* proper business isn't the life to come, but the life that's leaving.

4.

Not that I'm a proponent of some kind of cultural stay-in-place jellyfish float. Not that I'm a child of stasis.

If anything, the atomic go-go sparkle of the baby boom attended my birth in 1948, a year that also saw the patenting of the holograph and the transistor. In the glossary to the *Funk & Wagnalls 1948 Yearbook*, these new terms—as if still smoking with the press of creation—need to be defined: *aureomycin, chemosurgery, cosmotron, discophile, heliport, LP record, micronutrient, photocomposition, pollster, transistor, vitamin B-12*. Also on the list is *update*, "to bring up to date," already in its natal year a seemingly hopeless concept in an ever-vooming world. The continuous morphing of *that* into *this*, and of the humdrum into the ohwow, is my birthright.

I can see myself at thirteen, at the Hanukkah and Thanksgiving family get-togethers, absenting myself from the drone of dweeby adult conversation (psychologically, attitudinally, but not physically: I wouldn't have been allowed to leave the room) by plugging one ear into my pocket-sized AM transistor radio: yes, and I'd hum at the end of that pale plastic umbilicus, sweetly imbibing the hot Top 40 playlist, tunes that must have seemed to me then to be the anthems by which a fierce and fearless generation would enter the gates of Tomorrow. It may as well have been a "cosmotron," not a radio from the dime store, and its rock and roll may as well have been the music by which the spheres of the heavens revolve.

Then why *didn't* I turn out to be like Rhinoceros? A 1969 issue of *Harper's* profiled that (then-)next-to-hit-it-Big rock band. The author, Sara Davidson, visits its sleepy-eyed jam sessions at their dilapidated upstate New York mansion, natters comfortably with their groupies, travels along to various gigs, like one at "the Aerodrome, a warehouse converted into a seedy psychedelic nightclub." She says, "While all the members of Rhinoceros have agile minds, none of them reads anything at all. Four had extensive training in classical music. Michael taught piano at age twelve, and Alan was composing chamber music at Chicago Musical College when he quit to join the band. But they don't read. It's as if the print medium, with its even lines, is too confining and too laborious. Danny says, 'My mind is always going so fast I can't get into books or stories or anything.' "

That's twenty-six years gone. They *didn't* make it Big. What they did, I'd bet, those boy-men who don't read and their equally bookophobic groupie loves, is raise a generation of children, who, by now, are old enough themselves to vote, and sue, and screw, and raise their own Nintendo-trōpic broods with minds that are going so, so fast—too fast, in any case, for the turning of anything so outmoded as pages. These aren't fringe people I'm talking about—*these are* a valid version of the mainstream American dream as it's carried one quarter of a century in its swift sweep.

So it isn't surprising (although it's coincidental: this isn't a packaged-up "theme issue") that the same 1969 *Harper's*, in its cover story on *Time* magazine misfortunes, says in its final, list-centered paragraph that ". . . along with all the mundane, immediate problems, there's always McLuhan and his electric circuitry. Are print culture's hot linear days numbered? Will postindustrial, post-Chicago man be postliterate as well? Already television has put its cool whammy on *Life*. Who'll be next? In another ten years (five years!) will anyone want to read newsmagazines?

Or any other kind of magazine? Or newspapers? Or books? No one is quite sure."

Nor am I sure, in 1995, if the flinchless prophecy implied in those questions has so far turned out accurate, or is only a sample of hype-type: someone jacking-off his panic button for fun and profit. The magazine isn't dead (although it's visual at the expense of verbal, increasingly); specialty titles devoted to wine connoisseurship and lesbian outing and body piercing and angelology lushly rush over the racks like paper kudzu. Nor is the newspaper comic strip dead: a 1930s classic, *Terry and the Pirates,* has just been revived (although the average strip-of-the-moment uses two-thirds less in text than its earlier counterpart).

Nor is *Galaxy* dead, that far-out rocket-blazing science fiction magazine I read when I was thirteen and my eyes were alive with visions of sarong-wrapped vampish Venusians. No, not dead—but vanished, into its own predictions. It's available on-line, and on-line only. And then—? The text can be accompanied by animation sidebars. *Then?*—The animation wham!bam!zow! can be booted-up and accompanied by a token bar of text. And *then?*—And then we can all be barnacles cyberwired into the imagedream machine, while the lasercode of Nuevo Rhinoceros gets piped in through the chip implants, to the minds that are malls and the malls that are brainwave networks.

Is it divine? Or is it odium? I don't know, and it isn't my place to prescribe. But I *do* know that, when family convenings at Sally's and Morrie's dragged unbearably, I'd slip off to his back room, where he'd gadgeted a ham radio for his idle play (the only ham allowed in that kosher universe) and I'd twirl its dials a while, lost in gizmory.

For a while, I would. And then I'd find myself sneaking my cousins' comic books out from under their beds—I'd dive into them and stay submerged for an hour, and I'd return with the flicker of otherworldly experience in me. Now I can see how even reading *Buck Rogers* was, primarily, *reading*—communing not with the oomph of the zowie future, but with a sensibility that, as I was learning to love it, was already slipping into the past.

Or I'd really get ambitious, and try the books on Morrie's personal shelf, woolly reminiscences from African explorers, the life of the bee, the collected Twain. A favorite was *Animal Farm,* and I relished it so—that hand-size, drably olive green edition—that they made it a gift. I own it still, with their plate, *The Gilmans,* pasted into its front.

It would be many more years before I also read Orwell's prescient essay on the commercial and political degradations of language, but all of that was already here in *Animal Farm* as one by one the beasts of that book give up their freedoms—never having paid readerly attention to the words of their world.

5.

Last week I received a call from the marketing manager at one of my publishers. Simply: would I tape-record four minutes from out of my forthcoming book, so she could present it persuasively to her book reps? Yes I'd do it, I grumbled. But added, "God forbid anyone should just *read*." And then her long silence.

Look, I *don't want* to be Mr. Stuck-in-the-Mud, Sir Kvetch, some screed-impassioned crank with his mimeograph machine in the midst of the inter-global neighborhood. I don't care to bear placards and speechify. I *like* the contempo special effects in monster flicks, and caller ID on my wife's phone, and the tinny chipper voice that pipes up from some soda machines. Whatever passes for *credo* here, it doesn't attain the nobility of solar energy advocacy, or of William Morris's brilliantly backward-glancing attempts at medievalism.

But I know what I care to include in my days, to remain what I am, whatever that is; and I know what I need to refuse. I know this intuitively, the way we all know the quick of ourselves, the essentialness. And I'd like to be able to draw those lines of definition as hassle-free as the woman who says she's given up bourbon, the fellow who knows an adulterous liaison "isn't for me."

This essay is being written in the summer of 1995, by a Bic pen in a one-dollar spiral-bound notebook. I'm going to type it on my sturdy IBM Selectramatic (electric—no manual clunker for me). And then I'll have the crew at my local Kinko's duplicate six or seven copies on paper stock 2S. And although Tomorrow may be a compelling place, and all of Dickens may fit in a fiche that's smaller than a pepper grain, and be called to the fore by voice command, and come with a 3-D enhancement map of Dickens's gaslit London, and even if Dickens-simulation himself is pixel'ed-up to instruct me in whist . . . if it goes on a screen instead of a page, I'm sorry but the future stops *here*.

And *can* I, finally, predict that future with anything like assurance? No way. Some people's records are better than others. Wells foresaw the army tank. Twain had an inkling of television, as did a journalist, John E.

Watkins Jr., who in December 1900—with telephone only twenty-five years recent and radio nonexistent—wrote, of "the Next Hundred Years," that "persons and things of all kinds will be brought within focus of cameras connected electrically with screens at opposite ends of circuits, thousands of miles at a span. American audiences in their theatres will view upon huge curtains before them the coronations of kings in Europe or the progress of battles in the Orient. The instruments bringing these distant scenes to the very doors of people will be connected with a giant telephone apparatus transmitting each incidental sound into its appropriate place. Thus the guns of a distant battle will be heard to boom when seen to blaze, and thus the lips of a remote actor or singer will be heard to utter words or music when seen to move."

With the same astonishing accuracy, Watkins prophesied central heat and air-conditioning, subway tunnels, escalators, tractors, the phonograph, even our burst of physical-fitness awareness, warring submarines, "a university education . . . free to every man and woman," plus public-school free lunches for the poor, and fleets of refrigerated airplanes speeding "delicious fruits from the tropics" into Boston homes. Prognostication extraordinaire.

On the other hand (and more typically), the book *Here Comes Tomorrow!: Living and Working in the Year 2000* (1966) predicts with confidence that television (improving police surveillance) will mean a drastic decline in the number of urban crimes, and that "despite the trend to compactness and lower costs, it seems unlikely everyone will have his own computer any time soon." Also in 1966, the *Wall Street Journal* reported this laughable gaffe of an underestimate from RCA: "By the turn of the century, there will be 220,000 computers in the United States." In thirty years, the ascendancy of the microchip has made that assessment less viable than the Code of Hammurabi.

For the most part, our piddly attempts at science-fiction futurecast are much like 1950s envisionings of the Planet Patrol, its sleek-tipped rim-finned armadas of galaxycruisers, and a Space Command Center of frantically storming electrodes, all of it guided by a computer about the size of Wyoming, and then the day's statistics logged by hand in a plastic double-column entry ledger (the pen chained down so it won't float off in zero-grav)—nobody having even hazily seen the sons and daughters of silicon shrink the world and redefine its psychology.

For the most part we enter the future in bits and bytes so small, so disarmingly toe-at-a-time, we don't know it's happened until it's already a se-

. . . .

ries of foregone irreversible half-decisions. One day we're us; the next, we're Pac-Man us. And the rest, as they say, is history.

But I *do* allow myself one small but fantastical, loving forecast:

In the future, on some incredibly distant planet of parallel-evolution *homo sapiens* almost, *almost* just like us (except, of course, exquisitely advanced in matters both spiritual and techno), there are photoarcheologists whose calling is especially esteemed: for theirs is the labor of digging information (on a good day maybe, wisdom) out of light alone, the way *our* archeologists retrieve a splintered bone or a cusp of pottery from out of the earth and interpret it.

One day, these people unearth—or really "unlight"—a fragment of strange, oracular speech that, although it's vague in intent, is nonetheless so seemingly a verity, so manifestly summatory of everything that's promiseful and terrible at once, the single sentence and its speaker attain a legendary status: the words, the face, are stored in hundreds of millions of infolockets and magnobands around the throats of these extraterrestrial citizens.

There she is, the way I remember her. *I have seen,* she says, *a dark wonder.*

"The Fate of the Book"

. . . .

by

Sᴠᴇɴ Bɪʀᴋᴇʀᴛs

I would need the fingers of both hands to track how many times this past year I have been asked to give my thoughts on something called "the fate of the book." I have sat on symposia, perched on panels, opined on-line and rattled away on the radio—not once, it seems, addressing the fate of reading, or literacy, or imagination, but always that other thing: ᴛʜᴇ ꜰᴀᴛᴇ ᴏꜰ ᴛʜᴇ ʙᴏᴏᴋ. Which would be fine, really, except that the host or moderator never really wants to talk about the book—the artifact, the bundle of bound pages—or even much about the class of things to which it belongs. That class of things is of interest to people mainly insofar as it is bound up with innumerable cultural institutions and practices. In asking about the fate of the book, most askers really want to talk about the fate of a way of life. But no one ever just comes out and says so. This confirms my general intuition about Americans, even—or especially—American intellectuals. We want to talk about the big things but we just can't let ourselves admit it.

I begin with this observation because I am, paradoxically, always encountering intelligent people who argue that if we were to leave the book behind, replacing pages with screen displays, we would not be changing very much finally; that people would still read and write, only more efficiently; and that the outlook for education would be very likely improved. There are many people out there who don't make a strong connection between the book and the idea, or culture, of the book. I would say that this connection is everything.

My position in the matter is fairly simple. The fate of the book must be considered side by side with the fate of electronic chip and screen-based technologies. It is only by asking about both that we can see what is happening around us, and *to* us. Which is, I insist, a total redrawing of the map. Here are changes so fundamental as to force us to redraft our hitherto sacred articles of faith about public and private life.

We make a mistake if we view books and screen technologies as competing for popularity or acknowledged superiority. These are not two approaches to the same thing, but two different things. Books cannot—and should not have to—compete with chip-powered implements.

Nor is there a war going on. It is not as if we are waiting to see what the battlefield will look like once the musket smoke has blown off. No, screens and circuits are here to stay—their empery is growing daily—and the only real question is whether the book will remain, and in what form, and to what end? And: what will it mean when the functions of the book have been superseded, or rewritten as new functions that no longer require paged things, only databases and screen displays?

New functions. That is, in a way, what it all comes down to. The book will disappear, if it does, because the functions and habits for which it is ideally suited will themselves disappear. And what will the world be like then? How will people act toward one another?

Many questions—and here is another: is technology driving the change of functions and habits, or is it the other way around? Could it be that *we* are changing, evolving, and beckoning that future toward us? The lightbulb was invented, it has been said, when the world was clamoring, like the dying Goethe, for more light. Inventions don't just initiate change—they are themselves responses to changed needs and circumstances.

Maybe we are ready to embrace the pain of leaving the book behind; maybe we are shedding a skin; maybe the meaning and purpose of being human is itself undergoing metamorphosis. I fully accept that my grandchildren will hear me tell of people sitting in rooms quietly turning the pages of books with the same disbelief with which I listened to my grandfather tell of riding in carriages or pitching hay. These images trigger a deep nostalgia in many of us, and we will have a similar nostalgia for the idea of solitary reading and everything it represents.

But evolution is evolution, and no amount of nostalgia can temper its inexorability. We need to look past the accrued associations and longings and to see the book in a historical light, as a technology. A need was felt, and the ingenuity arose to meet the need. And so happy was the result that we have great difficulty in letting it go, in facing the fact that the new imperatives now dictate new solutions. These new imperatives do not yet define us, but they may come to. To understand what they are, we need to look closely at both the old technology and the new. For the technology takes the print of our needs and our desires.

How *do* books and screen technologies differ? Or—and—how will a dominantly electronic culture differ from the print-centered culture we have known these past few centuries? The basic oppositions, we will find, give lie to the claim that screen technologies are only modifications and improvements of the pre-existing.

I. CLOSURE VERSUS OPEN-ENDEDNESS. Whether scholarly or non-, the book has always represented the ideal of completion. The printed text has strived to be standardized, authorized, a summa. Indeed, we may notice that when new materials are added, requiring a "new" or "expanded" edition, the effect is often to compromise the original edition, suggesting retrospectively that its original appearance of authoritativeness was ill founded, its completion spurious, and making us wonder if all such appearances should not be considered skeptically. Similarly, an erratum is like a pimple on an otherwise creamy complexion. The fixity of the word imprinted on the page, and our awareness of the enormous editorial and institutional pressure behind that fixity, send the message that here is a formulation, an expression, that must be attended to. The array of bound volumes on the library shelves communicates that knowledge and understanding are themselves a kind of structure assembled from these parts. The societal imprimatur is manifest in the physical characteristics: the lettering on the spine, the publisher's colophon embossed on the title page. . . .

Screen technologies undo these cultural assumptions implicitly. Stripping the work of its proud material trappings, its solid three-dimensionality, they further subject it to fragmentation. That a work comes to us by way of a circuit means that we think of it as being open—available—in various ways, whether or not we avail ourselves of those ways. We can enter cleanly and strategically at any number of points; we can elide passages or chapters with an elastic ease that allows us to forget the surrounding textual tissue. With a book, the pages we thumb past are a palpable reproach. Whereas the new texts, or texts of the future, those that come via screen, already advertise (many of them) features that fly in the face of definitive closure. The medium not only allows—it all but cries out for—links, glosses, supplements, and the like.

Suddenly it appears that the deconstructionists were the hierophants of the new dispensation. Their questioning of closure, of authority, of the univocal nature of texts, heralded the arrival of a new kind of text—a text made possible by a technology that was only beginning to unfold its possibilities when the first deconstructionist writings were published. How odd, then, to see that the temper of the academy is turning against the theoreticians of the decentered, the polysemous, just as what was indirectly prophesied is coming to pass.

Already we find the idea of boundlessness encapsulated in the technically finite CD-ROM packages that are coming on the market. The structure—the referentiality—is such that one never reads or uses them with the totality in view. One uses them open-endedly, always with the awareness that the options have scarcely been exhausted. This would be true, in a sense, of a print encyclopedia—except, of course, that the material orientation is such that as a user, you never forget exactly where you have landed and where that situates you with reference to the whole body of text. Fittingly, encyclopedias and compendious reference works have been first in line for transfer onto CD-ROM.

II. HIERARCHY VERSUS THE LEVELING OF HIERARCHY. With finality, with closure, there follows ineluctably the idea of canonicity, that great bugbear of the deconstructionists. Where texts are deemed closed and where expressions are seen to strive for finality, it is unavoidable that vertical ranking systems will result. The push to finality, to closure, is also the push for the last word; which is another term for the struggle for vertical ascendancy. If intellectual culture is seen as the product, or benefit, of book learning, then it is the marketplace of ideas that decides which books will shape our thinking and our values. The battle of the books.

But now substitute circuit-driven screen textuality, put mutability and open-endedness in the place of definitiveness, and it's easy to see that notions of hierarchy will be very hard to sustain. In the theoretically infinite database, all work is present and available—and, in a way, equal. Where discourse is seen to be woven and, technologically speaking, collective, the idea of ranking dissipates. New systems of search and access will eventually render the notion of the enclosed work antiquated. Without a system of rigorously closed and definitive authored works the whole concept of hierarchy is useless.

III. HISTORICAL LAYERING VERSUS SIMULTANEITY. The system of print textuality has always promoted the idea of culture as a matter of tradition and succession, with printed works leading back into time like so many footprints. The library or special collections department gives this notion concrete embodiment. Tracking an idea, an influence, we literally go from newer to older physical texts. The scholar's finger brushes the actual molecules of bygone eras. And historical depth is one of our most powerful metaphors—for centuries it has been our way of figuring the idea of time, of past receding from recent to ancient.

Screen technologies, circuited to their truly mind-boggling databases, work implicitly against the sedimentary paradigm. To plunder the analogy, they are metamorphic: they have the power to transpose the layered recession of texts into a single, vast collection of cross-referenced materials; they change the standard diachronic approach to history to one that is—in the absence of the material markers that are books—synchronic. And in this they further promote the postmodern suspicion of the historical time line or the notion of narrative. The picture of history that data base and screen unscroll is of webs and "trees," a field of relations and connections that eluded earlier historical projections, and that submerges any notion of story (and recall that the etymological root of history is "storia," meaning story), submerges it in vast informational complexity.

But the impact of such a paradigm change is less upon scholars and historians, who certainly don't need to be reminded that historical time is a kind of depth; rather, it will be the generations of students who learn about the past from these connection-rich databases who will, over time, internalize a very different understanding of the past than was held by the many generations preceding them. Is this good, bad, or neither? I naturally incline to the view that while we can never really *know* the past, or grasp history except fleetingly in the comprehended detail, time past is a powerful Other, a mystery that we never stop trying to solve, one which is closely bound up with our somewhat poetic conception of depth.

IV. THE PRIVATE SPHERE VERSUS THE PUBLIC SPACE. Although the technology of the book originally evolved to preserve and transmit information outside the intimate space of the geographical community—a fact which can be understood as giving the word a much larger public—it is also true that book reading is essentially private in character. This is not only because of the need for self-possessed concentration on the part of the reader, but also because the medium itself—the book—is opaque. The word signifies against the dead-endedness of the paper it is printed on, and in the process of signifying it incessantly enforces the awareness that that word is a missive from an individual sensibility, that its inscription originated in a privacy. Whatever one reads, the act is understood to be a one-to-one communication: Henry David Thoreau or Roland Barthes to myself. In this, reading has always been the verso of writing; the two acts are more intimately bound than we usually imagine them to be.

Reading from a screen invokes, automatically, the circuit system that underwrites all screen transmissions. Again, on a subliminal level the traditional assumptions are modified, undone. The words on the screen, although very possibly the same as the words on the page, are not felt to dead-end in their transmitting element. Rather, they keep us actively aware of the quasi-public transparency out of which they emerge. These words are not *found* in the way that one can thumb forward in a printed text and locate the words one will be reading. No, they emerge; they are arriving, and from a place, moreover, that carries complex collective associations. To read from a screen—even if one *is* simply scrolling *Walden*—is to occupy a cognitive environment that is very different from that which you occupy when reading a book. On a small scale this does not amount to much. But when the majority of reading acts take place at the screen, then we might argue that a blow of some sort has been dealt to solitary subjectivity. Especially as the book has always been more than a carrier of information or entertainment—it has traditionally represented a redoubt against the pressures of public life, a retreat wherein one can regroup the scattered elements of the self.

The other obvious difference between printed and screen-delivered text derives from the fact that chip-driven systems not only allow but encourage collaborative and interactive operations. Texts programmed for CD-ROM are the obvious instance of this, but there is little doubt that we will see more and more of these applications, especially in classroom settings. Which suggests once again that the developments which may strike those of us who are children of the book as exotic will seem perfectly natural to the generation now carrying out its first exploratory mouse clicks. And who will doubt that when reading CD-ROM is normal, reading the linear, missionary-position way will seem just a little bit strange. Moreover, as more and more texts get written on the computer, we will probably see writers experimenting with the new presentation options that the medium accommodates. Though conservatively minded critics may question the aesthetic validity of collaborative hypertext ventures, these ventures will certainly flourish and further undercut the old paradigm of the lone reader turning the pages of some one author's book. Again, this is not just a change in reading modes; it is at the same time a major alteration of our cognitive environment. By degrees we will see much of our intellectual and artistic enterprise move away from strictly private exchange and in the direction of the collective. Maybe the day will come when most of our thought—and its expression—is carried out by teams. The lone creator or thinker will be a figure in our nostalgia banks, a memory preserved on commemorative postage stamps—although the odds are that postage stamps, too, will have vanished into that museum of images that will be the past.

We are moving, then, toward Roland Barthes's "Death of the Author," and toward his idea that texts are not bounded entities, but weavings ("textus" means weaving). The idea that the individual can be a carrier of some relevant vision or message will give way to a suspicion of the individual producer as atavistic romantic. Indeed, the "romantic," bound up as it is with notions about the symbolic agon of the solitary self, is already something of a category of derision. To call somebody a "romantic" nowadays is like calling them a "hippie"—a term that signifies as unambiguously in the cultural sphere as Edsel does in the automotive.

This may seem like a wild extrapolation—and I hope it is—but if one spends some time factoring tendencies, it's hard to get a significantly different outcome. The point is that subjective individualism is on the wane, and that, given the larger dynamics of a circuit-driven mass society, the tendency is more likely to intensify than to abate. Of course, the transition from book to screen that I've been speculating about is not the driving force behind the change—there is no one culprit to finger—but it is certainly part of the system of changes; it stands as yet another instance of what in the larger view has begun to assume an evolutionary character.

V. EXPRESSIVE VERSUS FUNCTIONAL USES OF LANGUAGE. Hand in hand with the shifts noted above—and abetting the move toward the collective/collaborative configuration of our intellectual culture—will be the redefinition of our expressive ideals. That is, our very usage of language will change—as it is already changing—and literary style will be the obvious casualty. This makes perfect sense. Style has always been predicated upon absence and distance. A writer refines a style in order to compensate for the fact that she has nothing but words on the page with which to transmit her thoughts and emotions. Style is, in a sense, the injection of personality into communication, the attempt to leap the gap of time and space using the wings of expressiveness. But as any habitué of the Internet or e-mail user will tell you, style is not of the essence in screen-to-screen communication. For the very premise of this communication is near immediacy. The more we are linked up, the more available we are to each other, the less we need to ponder what Flaubert called the "mot juste." We don't slave over our sentences when we are face-to-face—don't because we can use gesture and inflection, and because we are present to supplement or amend our point if we detect that our listener has not gotten it right. In this respect, screen communications are closer to conversation than to, say, letters, even though they use the written word as their means of delivery.

So long as we take the view that style is merely an adornment—a superfluous extra—this may not seem like a great loss. There is even a bias in certain quarters that style is some kind of corruption or affectation, that we should prefer Hemingway to Fitzgerald, or Orwell to Nabokov, because less is more and plain speaking is both a virtue and the high road to truth. But this is a narrow and reductive perspective. For not all truths can be sent through the telegraph, and not all insights find a home in the declarative sentence. To represent experience as a shaded spectrum, we need the subtle shading instruments of language—which is to say that we need the myriad refinements of verbal style. This is my fear: that if the screen becomes the dominant mode of communication, and if the effective use of that mode requires a banishing of whatever is not plain or direct, then we may condition ourselves into a kind of low-definition consciousness. There may result an atrophy, a gradual loss of expressions that are provisional, poetic, or subjectively nuanced. We should worry, then, not just about the "dumbing down" that is fast becoming the buzzword for this possibility, but also about the loss of subjective reach. If there is one line of defense against the coming of the herd mentality, it is the private intransigence of individuals, and that intransigence feeds on particularity as a plant feeds on sunlight.

If I am right about these tendencies, about the shift from page-centered to screen-centered communication, then we will be driven either to acquiesce in or to resist what amounts to a significant modification of our patterns of living. Those who assent will either do so passively, because it is easier to move with what appears to be the current of the times, or else they will forge on with zeal because they believe in the promise of the new. Resisters will have to take an active stance—to go against the current, you must use paddles. In both contingents, upstreamers and downstreamers, we will find a small number of people who recognize what is truly at stake, who understand that page and screen are really just an arena where a larger contest of forces is being played out.

. . . .

Though I class myself as one of the resisters, I think I can see how certain tendencies that I deplore might seem seductive to others. Is there anything intrinsically *wrong* with viewing the work of culture as fundamentally collaborative rather than as an individual-based enterprise? Have we not made too great a fetish of the book, and too large a cult of the author? Aren't we ready for a change, a new set of possibilities?

Mired as I am in the romance of subjective individualism, in the Emersonian mythos of self-reliance, I cannot concede it. I have my reasons.

Let me begin by appropriating Nicholas Negroponte's now familiar distinction between *atoms* and *bits*. A simple definition should suffice. Atoms, though invisible to the naked eye, exist in space; they are the foundation stones of the material order. Bits, by contrast, are digits; they are coded information—arrangements of zeros and ones—and while they pass through appliances made of atoms, they do not themselves have any materiality. They weigh literally nothing. Atoms are like bodies and bits are like the thoughts and impulses that instruct them in their motions. Indeed, we can assert that ideas and the language that expresses them are bits; books are atoms, the bodies that sustain them.

Mr. Negroponte and I agree that we are but in the first flushes of the much-ballyhooed Information Age, and that by the time the gathering momentum has expended itself—a decade or two hence—the world will look and feel and *be* utterly different from the more slowly evolving place we all grew up in. Atoms will, of course, still exist—after all, we are significantly atoms, and computers themselves are atoms. But the determining transactions in our lives will happen mainly by way of bits. Images, impulses, codes, and data. Screen events and exchanges that will, except for those who refuse—and some will—comprise an incessant agitation through one whole layer of the implicated self. For many this will bring a comforting sense of connectedness—they will be saying good-bye to the primal solitude that all but defined selfhood down through the millennia. The citizen of the not-so-distant future will always be, in a sense, on-line; she will live inside an envelope of impulses. And to be on-line thus is to no longer be alone. This will be less and less a world hospitable to old-style individualism; that will be seen to have been an evolutionary phase, not a human given.

The relevance of this admittedly grand projection to the fate of the book should be starting to come clear. The book as we know it now—the printed artifact that holds in its pages the writer's unique vision of the world, or some aspect of it—is the emblem par excellence of our threatened subjectivity. The book represents the efforts of the private self both at the point of origin, in the writer, and at the point of arrival, in the reader. That these are words on a page and not a screen has enormous symbolic significance. As I have suggested, the opaque silence of the page is the habitat, the nesting place, of the deeper self.

This is a bit abstract, and I will have to get more abstract still before coming around full circle. The book, you see, the tangible paper item, the very ink shapes of the words on the page—these are things. Atoms. But what the atoms are configured to convey—what gives value to the book— is the intangible element. The bit. In this way alone the book is a primitive computer, or an analogue to brain and mind. Visions and thoughts and their expression in language have never been atomic. They are *about* the atomic, the material, at least in very large part. Though they are without dimension or gravity, bits refer mainly to entities that have both.

Well, you might say, if this is true, then what is all the fuss about? What's the difference whether the content of these bits comes across on the page or on the screen? How can I argue that the digital future threatens anything that really matters?

I have two thoughts on this.

On a micro scale, I would propose that a significant, if highly elusive, part of the reading operation is marked by the transfer from atom to bit. The eye motion converts the former to the latter. The printed word becomes a figment in the mind much as water becomes vapor. There is a change of state, one that is a subthreshold part of the reading transaction. Words on a screen, already part of the order of bits, are not made to undergo this same fundamental translation. There is a difference in process. When we read from a screen, or write directly onto a screen (without printing out), we in fact never cross the border from atom to bit, or bit to atom. There is a slight, but somehow consequential, loss of gravity; the word is denied its landing place in the order of material things, and its impact on the reader is subtly lessened.

"Ridiculous!" you say. To which I can only reply that outwardly nothing about our fiscal processes changed when we went off the gold standard (nobody but tourists ever saw the vaults at Fort Knox), but that an untethered dollar feels different, spends differently, than one secured by its minim of bullion.

On a macro scale, I am also preoccupied with the shifting of the ground of value. By moving increasingly from A to B—from atom toward bit—we are severing the ancient connection between things and their value. Or if not that, then we are certainly tipping the sacred ontological scales. Bits are steadily supplanting atoms. Meaning what? Meaning that our living has gradually less to do with things, places, and human presence, and more to do with messages, mediated exchanges, ersatz environments, and virtual engagements of all descriptions. It is hard to catch hold of this by looking only at the present. But try a different focal adjustment. Think about life in America in the 1950s in terms of these fundamentals and then project forward to the millennium, now less than five years away. You cannot fail to note how that balance has shifted—from the thing to its representation, from presence to mediation. And if this is the case, then life, the age-old subject matter of all art, cannot be rendered in the same way anymore. The ground premises of literature—indeed of all written content—are altered, or need to be, for everything is altered. Instead of bits referring simply to atoms, we find more and more that bits refer to other bits. If the book is a mirror moving alongside our common reality, then the future of the book—and of writer and reader—is tied to that reality.

When we ask about the future—the fate—of the book, I interpret this to mean not just the artifact, but a whole kind of sensibility. Questions about that future are, really, larger questions about ourselves. How will we live? Who will we be? What will be the place of the private self in the emergent new scheme of things?

Myself, I see no shame in the label "romantic" and I will not accept that it is now unfashionable to be tilting at windmills. The idea that the book has a "fate" implies, in some way, the *fait accompli*. And while I believe that there is a strong evolutionary tendency underlying our moment-to-moment dealings and decisions, I don't believe that it is pointless to counter or protest that tendency. My instinct, signaling from some vestigial part of the psyche, tells me to avoid placing all my faith in the coming of the chip-driven future. It bids me to question the consequences of the myriad promised simplifications and streamlinings and to stall somehow the rush to interconnectivity, that comes—as all interconnectivity must—at the expense of the here and now. Certainly the survival of that archaic entity called the soul depends on resistance. And soul or not, our remaining individuals depends on our keeping the atom to bit ratio weighted, as it ever has been, toward the atom. Otherwise we are in danger of falling into a dream that is not ours or anybody else's, that spreads inexorably on the legs of its ones and zeroes.

Either / Or

for Kris and Anna

. . . .

by
THOMAS FRICK

> In the perusal of books men are able to lead artificial lives which
> are often truer than those circumstances have forced upon them.
> SOMERSET MAUGHAM

In the spring of 1994 my wife invited for dinner her former cinematogra-
phy teacher and his wife. He was a graduate of the famous Polish Film
Academy (with Roman Polanski), had written this country's best-selling
cinematography textbook (I had used it myself eighteen years before), and
was, along with his wife, well traveled, highly literate, and widely curious.
We were seated around a small table in the kitchen extension of our East
Hollywood apartment enjoying, with a second bottle of a decent Trader
Joe Médoc, the process of learning to converse as friends.

Our apartment, though not tiny, had bookshelves in every room, including the kitchen, the bathroom, and the walk-in closet. Many of these
were still of brick and board, although reduced in height since the January
quake that had nearly marked my skull with a flying cinder block as I
slept. The cinematographer's house, I saw on subsequent visits, was also
filled with books. It was intriguing to me to peruse Polish translations of
Musil, Proust, Hemingway, Joyce, Shakespeare, and Tolstoy alongside an
extensive literature originally in Polish, vibrating in its own language.

Between the bouillabaisse and the dessert we emptied the second bottle. At one pause the cinematographer, slowly swirling his glass and
watching the wine play around in it, threw a sidelong glance my way. I've
since wondered what in our conversation led to his query, or if he had sim-

•   •   •   •   •   •   •   •   •   •

ply been saving it up. In the mild gravity of his inimitable though frequently imitated accent he asked, "So, Tom. Why is no good literature
being produced anymore?" Without knowing what I was about to say,
simply aware that I was taking the question seriously and that some pronouncement was rolling along on the lubricated bearings of my tongue, I
stared at the air for a bit and then replied, "I think good literature is still
being produced. In fact, I think there are more good novels than ever. It's
just that they don't matter now." The cinematographer murmured an ac-
knowledgment and the topic was dropped.

I was surprised and perplexed by what I'd said with such seeming authority and that it was accepted with such ease. For months I continued to
wonder what I'd meant by it. The obvious things, of course. Writing programs have raised the ante. Literary skills and strategies abound. We have
a surfeit of well-crafted literature that somehow amounts to less than ever
before in this century. "Publication day" is now a virtual, not a real, event,
competing with *Entertainment Weekly* and *TV Guide.* Indeed, a book
may well be sold to Hollywood before it's sold to a publisher. The reigning
supply-side mentality presumes that because of abundance, everything is
well, although how would we know? We don't have time to pay sufficient
attention to even a minute fraction of what is so painstakingly produced.

Quiet reading, demanding at least an attunement of attention and the
modest will to pick one's way continually forward on the viny path
of words, has for a long time been losing ground to the competition.
Through a kind of Grisham's Law of Infotainment, books have been
moved to the margins of our collective sensorium by noisy visual narra-
tives that we receive in a largely passive, even distracted condition, or absorb from the environment without any intention at all. Part of the seduction of our visual glut is precisely the ease of "access"—one needn't shape
an inner image from one's own experience (which also means taking a
kind of responsibility, unholding one's end of a contract with the author).

For most visual exposition there is in no meaningful sense a single author with whom to contract. Nor is one able to govern the pace of one's reception of such material in accordance with pleasure, need, or understanding. This preimaged and relentless phantasmagoria is the product of
complex collaborative campaigns inflected by the twists of high finance.
The ceaseless inundation inflicts thought-boggling stresses on eyes, ears,
and cortex that pass unnoticed—this is the water we swim in. It doesn't
matter if we don't "watch" TV or "listen" to talk radio—their displacement of anything we might once have called authentic life colonizes our

consciousness anyway. The ad-driven concerns of televisual reality are re-iterated on billboards and buses, in newspapers and magazines, in daily conversation, in book reviews and even books. One knows the premises, characters, and plots of TV shows one's never seen. One is aware of bizarre controversies that palpate the nation, a giddy peristalsis of in-scrutable agendas. One even forms opinions about such wonders. The theme song of an old TV show about "identical cousins" pops into my head in the middle of lunch, although I never once watched it.

There's something occult about the process, as if we are mutating, under the guise of "normality," in order to absorb strange new data. And the assault is not merely steadily increasing; it's changing gears weekly. Our computer hookups to hypertext, e-mail, fax, the Internet—every movie has a home page—the unstoppable arrival of virtual reality (what-ever that will turn out to be, at least we have a name for it), all threaten to deliver the knockout punch to what was once, not very long ago, called "reading," a solitary, puzzling entrancement carried out for long stretches alone, in the privacy of one's room. Or perhaps less a KO than a swift, narcotic injection, rather like the spider's, paralyzing its web-bound prey for mummification and eventual ingestion. In truth our electronic, digi-tized web is ingesting the word and transforming it.

The first uses of the term "virtual," in the sense of what is so "in essence or effect, although not formally or actually," were religious. The earliest cita-tion in the OED refers to the "Virtual Church," an ecumenical council "acting in the name of the whole church." In 1659 the word is employed in a dispute over the efficacy of the host—taking Christ "by the mouth" as opposed to "virtually," by faith. Since "virtual" is drawn from the constel-lation surrounding "virtue," it contains a subtext concerned with power, or strength. In 1704 the term is "applied to the apparent focus or image re-sulting from the effect of reflection or refraction upon rays of light," a move in the direction of the visualized ulterior world we begin to outline in our concept of "virtual reality." In 1959 a computational sense is added: "not physically existing as such but made by software to appear to do so." The source of "virtual" in religious polity and disputation is fitting insofar as the urge to disembody ourselves and get on-line in every possible way, even beepers, while not without its umbilical, infantile aspect, is saturated with a messianic fervor having the capacity to spark mutual incomprehen-sion as only true belief and true doubt can do.

. . . .

A friend of mine, an entrepreneurial investment partner in high-tech start-ups—an extremely bright, engaging, and literate man with two large bookcases in his home office filled with poetry from which he is able to quote fluently—pictured this ingestion of the word to me in vivid terms late one evening in Tucson as a thing he is burning to bring about: "Within ten years you'll be able to hold in your hand a screen the size of a magazine. That will be your book, the only one you'll need. With it you can access millions of books, the contents of a huge library. Without moving from your seat by the fire. We'll still have our favorite physical books, of course. We like to feel them, smell them, the look of ink on paper. But our virtual libraries will be beyond the dreams of popes and princes."

None of this is news, of course. We've heard such things almost daily for much of our lives. Today for instance, in the *Los Angeles Times*: "This spring the Library of Congress joined with 14 other major research libraries to begin a national digital library. As a start they hope to have 5 million digital documents available to the public through the Internet and CD-ROM by decade's end." And Washington University has an up-and-running sixty-gigabyte virtual library "with several hundred thousand files of text, software, and images available instantaneously worldwide." Documents, files, text, software, images—do these bear any relation to what we once called reading? Although we're repeatedly coached in the marvels of our age, we've not yet begun to absorb their true import.

Indeed, how could we? Five hundred years after the earliest books printed by movable type (itself a primitive digitizing of composition), Marshall McLuhan published *The Gutenberg Galaxy,* swarming with belated insights into the changing mental and social habits initiated by print technology. The changes in the noosphere wrought by our current modal shifts will be far broader and deeper, but human time, the time of reading, say, is still donkeytrotting along. In the year 3000 will a new McLuhan look back and finally be able to descry our circumstances? Or will the "great day for the race—the human race" be so vividly hardwired to still further futures that no one will care to look backwards, or even know what backwards means? One easy guess is that, able to call up on our bookscreens any text on demand, able to change its appearance, to query it, to "interact" with it, we will derive a wholly different import from *War and Peace* or *The Voyage of the Beagle* than we would in the quiet corner of a library, slowly turning pages under a lamp. The uses we have for texts (and the concept of textual "utility" itself is part of the question), the way we comprehend them, indeed what we mean by comprehension, will certainly undergo great shifts, comparable to the sea change from orality to literacy (something the effects of which, again, have only been discerned in this century). What texts will prove more "virtually friendly" than others? Forster, say, over Henry James? Beckett over Pound? (The essentially typewritten nature of much of Pound's composition—pointed out by Hugh Kenner—may mean that its adaptation to the televisual raster is problematic.)

Bookstores have been around a long time, but nothing lasts forever. Modes of meaning can quickly change. Many things that *look* like books are clearly not. A stack, more like a sculpture, of 250 copies of *Blue Skies, No Candy* surrounding a mirrored, circular column in a Fifth Avenue bookstore would be as good an emblem as any of a mutation in that medium. Even so new an art form as cinema is in the throes of becoming something else. Films that thirty years ago staked out a large claim for themselves as an art as subtle and profound as any—let me name only *8½* and *Persona*—could not now find financing. Lest we accept this as a simple reflection of changing audience taste, we may read of a recent bungled CIA operation designed to undermine French resistance to Hollywood domination of distribution networks. That Fellini's last films were not distributed in the United States for years struck some observers as a fact not explicable solely by audience lassitude.

My mother, a former mayor and lifelong educator, has been upset recently to observe my brother's children encountering her favorite texts—those she'd read aloud to spellbound children for two generations, those they'd been overjoyed to read by themselves—through videos. Over the course of a quarter-century, she watched on the playground the mutation in children's imaginations from exterior elaboration of internal fantasy to repetitive imitation of televisual constructs.

I was pleased recently to discover an excellent and spacious used bookshop within walking distance of my mid–Los Angeles home. One afternoon, when I was exchanging a stack of review copies for a facsimile reprint of Erdmann's edition of Leibniz, a well-groomed eight-year-old boy came into the shop and silently scurried to the back. He was greeted as a familiar by the owners. As I sidled my way through the "literature in translation" and "history of ideas" sections, I looked over my shoulder to see what the funny noises were; the boy had logged onto the shop's computer and was playing game after game of Klondike, complete with tinny shuf-

. . . .

fling sounds, groans when he lost, and congratulations when he won. After twenty minutes, he got up and left without a word. And so we may find ourselves wandering in a world with lots of books but very little reading.

If the world spends less time with books, then undoubtedly we will, too. The subtle displeasures of the word scanned and screened will inflect themselves on our sense of choice. If books assume more and more the instrumentalist character of something to which we have "access," then they come to partake of the condition of technology that Heidegger calls the "standing reserve." On a recent list from Voyager, a company at the forefront of CD-ROM packaging, we find *Macbeth,* among whose "wealth of features" is "a Macbeth karaoke," right next to *Dazzeloids:* "In an absurd and eye-popping universe, the Dazzeloids save little Jeremy from turning to mush in front of the television."

What is reading, if it is not simply moving one's ocular susceptibilities over arrays of symbols? What is inherently the difference between reading Danielle Steel and *Daniel Deronda?* Or this page? What's the difference between reading a textbook and a checkbook? Qua reading, how does Marx's study of Hegel differ from the sophomore's struggle with *The Waves* in a literature class? The "mechanism," if we so stoop to call it, is clearly the same. Are there "levels" of reading? If so, are they ranked in accordance with some evaluation of the material itself? As children, we each had worlds open up to us through books we would not now press on anyone else or even read again ourselves. As an adult, I might find profundities in Doris Lessing that are invisible to you. If the import of reading is in its soul effects, are there to be no objective criteria for textual evaluation? What if you can't remember something you have read, and thus can't prove you have read it, even if you distinctly remember loving (or hating) it? Is whatever we might say about reading of no more import than the person who tells us he is dreaming, as in Wittgenstein: "Someone who, dreaming, says 'I am dreaming,' even if he speaks audibly in doing so, is no more right than if he said in his dream 'it is raining,' while it was in fact raining. Even if his dream were actually connected with the noise of the rain."

> I came away with a few books I had been wanting to read. I put these books on the shelf in the alcove above my bed alongside the other books I had recently acquired . . . I looked at their spines often. The colors of their spines, and the few words of their titles, naming other possible visions of the world, were always part of what I saw in the room, and I always liked

. . . .

to have these signs of other worlds near me, even if for months or years I did not open the books, even if there were many I never read but packed into boxes and unpacked again, over and over, taking them with me from one place to the next. Some, in fact, I still have on shelves here in this house, still unread.

LYDIA DAVIS, *The End of the Story*

Reading makes nothing happen. Even the driver's license manual or *French for Travelers* must be mysteriously translated by will from desire into action. Certainly one of the objections of my parents' generation to their children's excessive reading must have been that it constituted an invisible realm, inaccessible, anarchic, and beyond authority, productive of nothing in the world's terms. Who can say where we are when we read, what is being transacted or "accomplished" there?

But as integral text is ingested by simulacral technologies, a sensation of "interactive" power over such material begins to accrue. On the most basic level we can shunt phrases around like freight cars in a switchyard, although unimaginably faster and at the click of a button. We can change fonts in a whim's flicker, carefully design the look of the page we compose; and we can do the same with others' digitally imported texts. When it is routine to choose the typefaces one reads in, such choices will have subtle effects on our reception. These matters are only beginning to be investigated by the emerging textual materialists. This morning I learned from an essay by Kundera that Kafka's translators and editors have, to greater and lesser degrees, divided into paragraphs long stretches of unparagraphed prose, and have eliminated certain crucial repetitions of words and names. He has almost never received the extra-large typeface he requested. These infringements may well have significant bearing on our reading of him and on his reading of the power and authority of language.

More ominously and importantly, new forms of media are drastically altering the meaning of reading. When I can click on "right whale," for instance, or "Nantucket," or "Leviathan" in my interactive *Moby-Dick,* and call up pictures, sounds, and assorted addenda (with or without a provenance), I acquire a spurious feeling of accomplishment. I can demand things of this text. I don't submit to it in the same way as before, carefully constructing my own vision of it, what it means to me. I challenge it—"explain yourself; give me more." The subtle physical satisfactions of my interrogation—clicking, opening, accessing, a minute sort of video game—are not to be ignored. Yet paradoxically with such inter-

·   ·   ·   ·   ·   ·   ·   ·   ·

activity I am in a more passive position regarding the text. Although I can punch buttons to ramify and illustrate it, these enhancements don't deepen my involvement with, my responsibility to, or my own ideas about the text. Like a good consumer, I merely accept the repressive "choices" that are offered me.

This seductive entwining of power and passivity is undoubtedly the reason why a younger generation has less and less patience with bare text that's "just black and white and doesn't move," as an M.F.A. student re-marked to a teacher I know, explaining why he couldn't read books— "too slow"—indeed, hadn't read a single one in graduate school. Less and less time spent in reading can only hasten the day when a page of naked print seems as strange as a field plowed by oxen.

The Aristotelian logic—A / not A, either / or, yes / no—that we've battled so mightily to put behind us has now returned with a vengeance, inhabiting not only the decision-making processes of our computers but infecting our very representations of reality. Thomas Pynchon has inscribed this digital dissolution and its dire spiritual import into a text with the indelible mas-tery of Dickens, when in *Bleak House* old Krook chalks the name JARNDYCE (the case that dissolves everything in its path), one letter at a time, on the wall of his rag-and-bone shop, rubbing each one out before writing the next ("I have a turn for copying from memory, you see, miss, though I can neither read nor write") or of Kafka, when the penal colony's Harrow carves the disobeyed commandment deeper and deeper into the malefactor's flesh, a script difficult to decipher "with one's eyes; but our man deciphers it with his wounds." In Pynchon's *Vineland* Frenesi Gates, on the lam, trying unsuccessfully to cash a check at a quickie mart, has a vi-sion: "If patterns of ones and zeros were 'like' patterns of human lives and deaths, if everything about an individual could be represented in a com-puter record by a long string of ones and zeros, then what kind of creature would be represented by a long string of lives and deaths? It would have to be up one level at least—an angel, a minor god, something in a UFO. It would take eight human lives and deaths just to form one character in this being's name—its complete dossier might take up a considerable piece of the history of the world. We are lights in God's computer, she not so much thought as hummed to herself to a sort of standard gospel tune, And the only thing we're good for, to be dead or to be living, is the only thing He sees. What we cry, what we contend for, in our world of toil and blood, it all lies beneath the notice of the hacker we call God."

Does the logic of yes / no, on / off, either / or on the circuit level engender a climate of replaceability on the level of things and people? Does the "virtual" destroy the credence of "reality?" Does the disintegration of the image through digital simulation fuel our increasing indifference to the idea of an original, our mistrust of the concept of authority itself? Does software make us impatient with hardware?

There certainly seems reason enough to speculate on the computerized environment's involvement with postmodernism—deconstruction, the death of the author, appropriation, the simulacral. The consequent upending of received interpretive verities has been liberating, and the resulting freedom heady. But underneath our deconstructive frenzy, can we discern a kind of desperation—the feeling that if we don't allow for all possible readings, something crucial (a privileged reading, an authoritative one, the "correct" one) may escape us? Although, of course, we are bereft of any means of recognizing it.

It's not possible to look around the once-privileged "real" without acknowledging an increasingly pervasive shoddiness. It's now common in our household that "durable goods"—clocks, scales, answering machines, tape recorders, and the like—will be quickly returned or thrown away in disgust, or just become persistent irritants because of defects or design flaws. The manifest destiny of the virtual imperative can only aggravate this tendency, as we less and less frequently choose responsibility to the physical world for objects in our care. The lessons about the spiritual that we learn through attention to the physical will not be learnt, and nothing will be well made—including, necessarily, the hardware on which the virtual depends.

Our immersion in the welter of new forms of communication and representation has resulted in, among other confusions, great imprecision in the use of the word "media." The distinctions are subtle and complex, their effects on meaning still all but unknown. Touch-Tone phones are different from rotary. (I recall from childhood the special gravity of the time required for the 9 and 0 to whir back into place when I dialed them.) LCD screens are different—in both visual and health terms—from VDT. Videotape is a different experience from television, and both are profoundly removed from the film that often serves as their source. (Videotaped movies could be thought of as translations from the language of film, useful for access but not the real thing.) A world with Post-its and with e-mail suggests new modes of interaction that shape communicative

. . . .

content. Writing a letter with a ballpoint confers a different rhythm than writing one with a fountain pen. A large-screen color TV with a remote control and cable services is an experience quite apart from the small black-and-white idiot box of my childhood. A one-newspaper city is a differently ramified information conduit than the now rare two- or three-paper one. And so on.

Compact satellite delivery systems will soon render the local video store obsolete, I was told by a man who had just sold his. Film directors now watch their films being shot on video monitors, and edit them that way as well. Can anything now be thought of as a "pure" medium or mode of symbolic exchange? (If a T-shirt is involved, one can harbor doubts.) There was a time when film and photography, among the mechanical media, seemed to preserve allegiance to analog representation, an indexical transcription of the world whose unit was a whole image. But as a result of our inexorably quantized view of the physical universe, even this is seen to be a fiction. Like the orderly, Newtonian, billiard-ball cosmos, it serves only approximately. The reception of film is digitized in time, and any single photographic image is simply an assemblage of tiny, discrete clumps of silver and dyes. In a profound and fateful way, through the investigations of science, we are now living in a postholistic universe.

During the summer of 1995 my wife and I were taking care of a house in Silver Lake with two neurotic though friendly dogs, a wise, aged cat, and a ninety-eight channel, wide-screen TV. As we were both working very hard, it was easy to spend two or three hours in the evenings channel surfing. In part it was sheer novelty. We're not TV watchers. The set we've had for years is an old clunker, color permanently washed out, primitively connected by a tangle of wires to broken rabbit ears and VCR, with two noisy knobs for changing channels, and a Swiss Army knife somehow involved in improving reception; it's a rudimentary tool my wife had used to prepare her film lectures.

Something essential about TV is revealed by the behavior we immediately adopted in a strange bed with a remote and many channels on tap. Hardly anything is ever good enough (or bizarrely bad enough) to watch for more than a few minutes. And yet, the essential badness of any single viewing option is mitigated by the beneficence of a huge supply—a standing reserve—of more badness. At the same time that it makes you impatient with any one thing, such televisual access gives you the illusion that there's something else. By the time you've cycled through ninety-eight channels, enough is "different" that you can justify starting again.

Muting, channel hopping—behaviors that purportedly give the viewer more "control"—these have not in any essential way affected the nature of TV as an advertising medium. We may not "pay attention" to the ads; it doesn't matter. The televisual world is a seamless one composed of endlessly teeming, noisy, phantasmagorical shards that magnetize our attention, whether we pay it or not. This "whole" is not "composed" of separate entities called "ads" and "programs"; it is a total *mode* of viewing, a structural fiction of difference that is a kind of generalized looking-as-such, rather than at any particular thing.

What is implied by this about our changing habits of attention is important to grasp. Heidegger's essay "The Age of the World View" bears on the issue: "World view, properly understood . . . means, not a view of the world, but the world understood as view. The existent as a whole is now so understood that it is existent when and only when . . . it is held at bay by the person who represents and establishes it . . . But wherever the existent is *not* conceived of in this sense, the world cannot change into a view. . . ." I can't remember a single thing we watched.

Perhaps this month of televisual overload had its result later in a small epiphany. I had once again watched little TV for a while. In a motel on I-10 near Las Cruces after a long day's drive, I lay back and switched on the tube. *American Gladiators* gave rise to some exhausted bemusement at the dissolute nature of pure spectacle; here no type of contest stayed the same long enough to acquire any depth of field, any accreted meaning. McLuhan's massive, perturbing insight as to the irrelevance of televisual content loomed large. It's truly not about "what's on." As a billboard in Los Angeles advertising three new CBS fall 1995 shows proclaimed: "You're on."

Quite suddenly the plastic box seemed to collapse before my eyes, the way the picture once did when the set was turned off. It was no longer fully occupying perceptual space, but blithering madly in a tiny corner of it. And I saw with complete calm and clarity the obvious thing that is usually invisible: the insane and dangerous deviance of TV's seamlessly constructed counterworld, its darkly hermetic consistency, its manic paucity of human feeling and response. In this moment it appeared truly remarkable that we willingly installed such agents of insidious madness in our living rooms and bedrooms. We might as well be agreeing to neural implants by aliens.

. . . .

The televisual real clearly infects everything, convincing us—the genius of it!—that its deeply disturbed simulacrum—a HAL gone round the bend in every home!—is the norm, our home world, the reference point for all our thoughts and activities. But apparently there is nothing we can do. We've allowed it to destroy our politics, our neighborhoods, and our common sense by sucking our attention up into its ubiquitous reification of the world *as view*, not of any particular thing but *as such*. And it is a destiny, like the automobile and the telephone. We can't go back. TV has replaced too many things we can no longer regain after its systematic transformation of attention, perception, exposition, logic, boundaries of interior and exterior, symbolization, story. We are undoubtedly in the midst of a change as profound as the Homeric entrance into literacy, although it is happening with incredibly greater speed. One tries to imagine looking backward from a Homeric distance in the future and wondering what happened to all that came before. Will it have disappeared completely?

In a prescient essay from 1972 called "After the Book," George Steiner wrote of the ambiguous democracy of the paperback revolution: "Mickey Spillane and Plato share the same book rack in the airport lounge or drug store." He penned that sentence at the last possible moment for which it could still have been true, at least in this country. The great Anglo-American paperback experiment of the '50s and '60s is long over. For us, looking back less than twenty-five years later, Steiner's juxtaposition seems like a golden age, not a cautionary emblem.

My teens were spent in proximity to no bookstore worthy of the name. A Christian trinket shop in town for a while called itself a bookstore; it failed. The bookshop at the small college offered pennants, sweatshirts, textbooks. But all through those years I found numerous interesting things in the spinning wire rack in the front of Parks Drug Store on the main street of town, where I stopped with my pals after school for hand-mixed nickel Cokes: attractively packaged editions of essays by De Quincey (Signet), William Golding (Pocket), Thoreau (Bantam). I bought a lot of science fiction as well from that rack, but the jobber who stocked it filled it with a wide range of goods.

A little bibliographical research reveals that for fifteen or twenty years an unprecedented range of serious books became available to the mass market in rack-size editions from such imprints as Mentor, Anchor, Meridian, Grove, Capricorn, and New Directions. Often even university press titles were packaged and distributed in this way. (Classics of fiction are, of course, still widely available in inexpensive format. Serious non-fiction, however, has vanished from mass-market editions, which once gave substance to the idea of the self-educated person.)

What kinds of books am I talking about? In a cursory glance at my shelves, I spot Stock's *Life of Ezra Pound*, Toynbee's *Greek Historical Thought*, Bowra's *Primitive Song*, Marrou's 600-page *History of Education in Antiquity*, Tawney's *Religion and the Rise of Capitalism*, and the notebooks of Leonardo. Henry Adams's *John Randolph*. Glob's classic *The Bog People*. *Dialogues with Alfred North Whitehead*. Jung on flying saucers. All of these were once available as mass market paperbacks, which could, and often did, turn up on wire racks in the oddest corners. These are now almost entirely out of print or are short-discount titles found only in university-area shops if they happen to be used in courses.

Books do go in and out of print, but my point here is a different one: the massive migration of books from highly diffused and accessible formats and distribution arrangements to less accessible ones. We may be told that the great experiment was a failure because the books ultimately didn't sell; that Toulmin and Goodfield's *The Discovery of Time*, Gillespie's *Genesis and Geology*, Mâle's *The Gothic Image*, Origen's *On First Principles*, Momigliano's *Studies in Historiography*, or *Hegel on Tragedy* just were not "popular enough" to be trade paperbacks that any bookstore might choose to carry. But who makes that claim, and what is "popular enough"? Such arguments today are usually another version of corporate insistence on maximal profit and absolve the publisher of any moral responsibility for what is published. Of course, maybe the books sold at first and then didn't, the dimming and dumbing of our culture happening that quickly — phhhht! — before our eyes, televisual amusement invading our brains, converting our complex thought chambers into simple sensoriums. But a notion once more current than now is that cultural custodians have a provident obligation; why else would one enter publishing, except for the various pleasures attendant on that privileged duty?

> "Is there anything quite as old, as little changed, as modern literature?"
> GORE VIDAL

During that same summer I edited an exhibition catalog for the first Fauve show to visit Australia. Perhaps musing on Thomas Keneally's description of Australia as a "foreign planet" for early settlers, or perhaps thinking of his elaboration in *The Playmaker* of the first play performed at the antipodes, I imagined, squinting through my loupe at the highly colored work of Derain, Matisse, Valtat, Manguin, Braque, van Dongen, and Vlaminck, that I was seeing them when they were new, in the first decade of the century. I *was* seeing them for the first time, in the sense that I had never looked at the group with such concentration. Of course, in a more fundamental sense I wasn't seeing them at all; I was merely looking at transparencies whose flattened color, one hoped, was fairly accurate. The seduction of their scenery—sweet life for these peripatetic beachmongers before the First World War!—to some degree prevents us (as do our own savaged sensibilities) from seeing the profound and startling way in which these works from early in the century presented the world anew, changing (and potentially still doing so) our way of seeing it.

Freeing color from its referent was a profound move whose meaning hasn't yet been fathomed, has grown almost impossible even to appreciate in our throes of digital effects and visual supersaturation. (Trakl and others would follow up these cues in the textures of poetry.) One thing these artists opened was the possibility of seeing the meaning of color in relation to time, the spiritual meaning of the color of time, the way that time has different colors and many of these are lost to us.

These reflections slowly led me to my beginning, the question posed by the cinematographer a year and a half before. Perhaps the sense of "not mattering" that now suffuses our current artistic productions lingers poignantly, in part, because we have not yet come to terms with the great works of modernism. We refuse to let them stand as unsurpassed monuments. Instead we seem concerned to bury or unravel them. Photography, another destiny, suddenly gobbling up painting's mimetic function, unwittingly gave birth to abstraction, impressionism and expressionism, hyperrealism, and appropriation, as well as conceptual and environmental art forms. Literature, however, has hardly responded to narrative usurpation by visual media, except by lamely attempting to mimic visual descriptive and expository logic. Words are, more and more, merely the means to "get us there," rather than to place us here.

The current vitality of the visual arts, while theory-driven, comes from their refusal to capitulate, from their playful, violent, obsessive attempts to absorb the commodified televisual onslaught, to beat it, for better or worse, at its own game. The result may constitute an endgame, but it is fundamentally a generous, if desperate, impulse—an attempt through simulation, appropriation, and reframing to re*real*ize and focus our attention on the demolished real of our media landscape. Literature, on the other hand, has simply retreated from its brave modernist beachheads.

Perhaps in that retreat we'll eventually find a new direction; perhaps a
new source of strength—and not simply febrility—will emerge. But there
are no signs of it yet.

The French have supplied us with many military metaphors. The term
"avant-garde" in its familiar connotation was first employed by scientific
socialist Saint-Simon (1760–1825), a man who proposed a canal linking
the Atlantic and Pacific, and whose valet was instructed to wake him
every morning with the words "Remember monsieur le comte, that you
have great things to do." In his 1825 *Opinions littéraires, philosophiques,
et industrielles,* an artist, in conversation with a scientist, says, "It is we,
the artists, who will serve you as avant-garde . . ." And so they did for a
while. Now it's the other way around. As art's embattlement has immured
it in strategies of recycling and repetition, it's high time to lay to rest this
vaulting metaphor, a historical curiosity no longer of any use. Today instead we have *faits divers,* which—if we can rescue from it true diversity—
will be a good thing. But in our rapid, shallow time we have no protocols
or gauges for meaning or distinction. All interpretations are allowed, none
privileged. With no rational criteria for judging authoritatively, we run the
risk of rhetoric spilling insensibly into propaganda and authoritarianism,
precisely because we no longer acknowledge authority.

But what is meaning? What do words do when they mean? Why do we
have so many of them? All dictionaries are language-to-language operations—they don't get us any closer to that goal. One can't mean meaning,
one can only mean.

From a letter to my writer friend, Quendrith: "I think you may be over-
interpreting 'muckamoo, baba, gup,' or rather *under*interpreting it. This
phrase may indeed accompany your child's desire for 'milk in a bottle or a
cup,' but surely it means much more than that, simply because it has not
yet been forced into the bloody glove of syntax. You as a writer and
mother should recognize these inchoate, truly mysterious motivations and
experiences that nonetheless blackmail us into creating verbal smoke
screens and hedgerows that conceal as much as embody what we set out
to say. This letter is no exception . . . Times like these shake the dictionary
and vulnerable words fall out. Pray we don't lose words like 'kindness.'
Once the word is gone, and we have no means of politely addressing the
thing, it grows wary and goes into hiding. Things exist, Narcissus-like, for

. . . .

the sake of their referents; they glow more brightly in the light of rich language, fade when fine words are few. . . ."

If, as George Steiner once proposed, "lexical resistance is the armature of meaning," then our departure from the endless interpretations of reading, from our bookish struggles, portends a great decline in meaning. Certainly we cannot know what any of this, what we, will mean to those who come after, those who attempt to look back and divine us.

"For each small group of three or four written words, there were around it a hundred others which could not be written . . . and a thousand others would not have sufficed to unveil what was *behind* these words. . . ."
HENRI MICHAUX

Dreadful Excitements:
Pensées and Proverbs for the Converted

for Liam

.   .   .   .

by
ASKOLD MELNYCZUK

The essence of the 20th century is the triumph of science, and religion's efforts to escape from the clutches of science have not yet been successful.
CZESLAW MILOSZ

Better the drunken gods of Greece
Than a life ordained by computers.
JAMES LAUGHLIN

Now his wars on God begin;
At stroke of midnight God shall win.
W. B. YEATS

THE CLASS STRUGGLE: ENGLISH VERSUS MATH

My senior year of high school, a quarter of a century ago, I took a computer math class. It was designed for educables on whom the assymetrical beauties of calculus would be wasted. There were eight of us: six men and two women. Working at terminals that resembled teletypes, we learned a new language with which we charmed the machines into performing for us. Every Tuesday, we hooked up to the mainframe in Pittsburgh, dedicated that day to servicing the handful of "on-line" high schools in New Jersey, and watched how the programs we'd written ran.

At the same time we were also studying what humans had already said about each other over several thousand years of Western civilization.

. . . .

That year, in English class, with the energetic help of Mrs. Buettner, we read Homer, Shakespeare, Austen, Solzhenitsyn.

Everyone in that math class, except myself, is now either working with computers directly, or in a related field. The guys with the slide rules have sold the world their vision of things. Maybe that's because they had something to sell in the first place. English class merely tried teaching values and a vocabulary for understanding the shadowier regions of the psyche. It occurs to me that these values might even be summarized in a few words: Man is more than the sum of his parts. The mathematicians and engineers, meanwhile, had a product with an ever-widening range of applications. They were dutiful—if unwitting—descendants of Jacob Bigelow, Harvard's first Rumford professor "for the application of science to the art of living" who, in 1829, coined the word *technology.*

I'd like to believe there's a reason one discipline prospered while another declined, although I fear there may not be. Some things take, others wither. But there are days when I deny the role of natural selection in the evolution of societies and instead indulge conspiracy theories: the bilderbergers, masters of the world, meet in a cave in Nepal to discuss the future of the planet. Up with science, they cry. Down with humanities. Humanity.

There's comfort in imagining policymakers and social engineers asking themselves: should we support English teachers or computers? Naturally, the technocrats vote for the machines. It's economics: you can have only so many people teaching *King Lear,* whereas you always need machines helping to make more machines. Especially when they can be used to keep the poor in their place.

In one scenario, the history of the twentieth century is acted out in terms of the class struggle.

IN THE CAVE

I imagine myself arguing with my phantom masters. English profs do more than promote proper punctuation, I insist. My voice is clipped; I'm nervous. A lot rides on this. I go on: they also help to decode those texts society has decided carry its fundamental tribal memories. Who are you, stranger-neighbor-father-wife, and what was your world like? What was it like *for an individual* living through the Civil Rights movement, the Great Depression, the wars? Created by a solitary consciousness, literature stands alone in its capacity for articulating an uncompromised vision of how life feels from the inside. A book is the fingerprint of conscience.

Helen Vendler's description of one of the "true tasks" of poetry would serve as well for prose: "to clone, in words, the uniqueness of a single person." No corporate or communal venture can replicate this. (I have nothing against corporate or communal enterprises per se, but I desire a society where individuals matter.) Imagine Solzhenitsyn's project of documenting the Gulag in a world without books.

The bilderbergers turn away. They reject my plea. They do not care to make any more Solzhenitsyns.

CCCCRITICS

Thank God, chime the literary critics. They too dislike Solzhenitsyn.

Yet Solzhenitsyn—or Joyce, or Mansfield, or Walcott—are nothing more than the temporary names of Gulliver, of the human soul fighting to stay free. Of what? Of the myriad shackles thrown over us each day. In *Provincialism The Enemy*, Ezra Pound observed: "I think the work of the subtlest thinkers for the last thirty years has been a tentative exploration for the means to prevent slavery to a 'state' or a 'democracy' or some such corporation. . . ."

Odd that agents of freedom, such as Pound and Solzhenitsyn, should be so similarly stupid in their political sympathies.

THE PAST AS SOUVENIR

According to a recent newspaper article, the most popular tourist site in Boston is no longer Paul Revere's house, or the Tea Party ship, or the Freedom Trail, but the bronze statue of Bugs Bunny in Fanueil Hall.

As Cornel West observes in *Race Matters,* our market-driven society is built around the idea of pleasure, which for our purposes appears to depend on "comfort, convenience, and sexual stimulation." This, perhaps, is how our age has interpreted that "pursuit of happiness" guaranteed us by our constitution. Our period has little interest in the deeper past and, as West further notes, "views the future as no more than a repetition of an hedonistically driven present." History is a bore. Entertainment rules.

KVETCH KVETCH KVETCH

What I hate most about technology is its regular and shameless insistence that I think about it. Have I ever felt similarly compelled by a pencil or

. . . .

even a Smith Corona *electric?* No. Their purpose was clear. Neither pencil nor typewriter distracted us with choices we never knew we needed: do I boldface, italicize, move? Afterwards, do I play a computer game, go online for news, zines, the stock market? Not really. I'd rather write this essay and then have a typist or typesetter take care of the other stuff. Yet, despite my pretty good intentions, curiosity wins. For the next hour, I sniff and poke at the tool on my table. Once, form suited function. A pencil resembled the poem of MacLeish's description and was happily "mute as a globed fruit." Now the computer talks back to you. Soon we will be the ones taking dictation.

FOLLOWING THE MONEY

Let me see if I can establish a chronology of the essential stuff that's sat on my various desks over the last twenty-five years:

1970: My first typewriter, a full-size Olivetti, heavy-duty office model—purchased in a lot of two at a government surplus auction in Newark (both for about $30).

1972: A Smith-Corona portable, bought just before I left for college, from an old friend ($40).

1981: A Smith-Corona electric (I went through three or four of these in the next years; all bought used, they seemed ill-suited to my kind of prose—cost, between $30 and $50 each).

1985: A Smith-Corona electric with memory, automatic erase, etc. (a passable machine, with a changeable font wheel, which would break down on average once every three months—price, $300; repairs, $150 a year).

1989: A Tandy computer, with a printer ($800—I enter the computer revolution: a bitch of a learning curve, as I remember).

1991: A Panasonic, faster, with a deeper memory ($300—bought used from a colleague).

1994: Mac 165c Powerbook ($1,700, + $600 for various programs and peripherals; + $300 for an HP Deskjet; + $150 for a service contract; + whatever I pay for America Online each month; + $400 to replace the motherboard, which blew a fuse earlier this year = $3,100+ and climbing . . .).

POSITIVELY TOLSTOY

The year after finishing *War and Peace,* Tolstoy wrote in a letter to his friend, the poet Fet: "I do not take in a single magazine or newspaper this year, and I consider it very useful not to."

Newsmakers, you might say, don't have time to read the news.

Who among us hasn't suffered such an itch—to disconnect, unplug, go, as they say, "off the grid" awhile and (to quote Pasternak) *"just live"*?

I tried it once. Some years ago, temporarily retired from love, I left Cambridge behind and camped for six weeks in Vermont's Northeast Kingdom. My site consisted of three tents: one for visitors, a small one for myself, and a screen house in which I did my work. What did I do that summer, without city distractions, without family, with no resources beyond books, a manual typewriter, a battery-powered old radio on which some nights I listened to country-western songs?

I walked: down hills crosshatched with light, past pink, loose lady's slippers and bracken, through pine forests and apple orchards and pastures, along Bailey Hazen Road to Harvey's Lake, with Mount Blue reflected on its northern side. In the country, in unmediated nature, my soul dilates—currents of energy course through me. Entering a man-made environment, I contract, grow smaller, tighter. Not everyone responds this way, of course.

I read twenty books, rewrote a novel for the sixth time, and rarely mourned the absence of the conveniences with which I console myself in the city. I missed friends but seldom wished for a phone. I wondered why people left farms for the city—although I remembered quickly enough all I'd read about the tough life of the farmer, and so on. I wasn't dependent on the land for a living. I hope one day to test that way of life again.

While it's tempting to retreat, the greater challenge is to stay. Today, the true *via* is not the *negativa* of the eremite but rather of his opposite. We've got to become spiritual philanderers, assuming new selves lightly, as though we were doffing caps turned backward. The only road, as Liam Rector writes, is "through it."

THE HORSEMEN

Milosz is right when he notes that "science and technology transform man from within, changing his imagination." What can be more important than chronicling this transformation? But am I not one of the infected ones?

. . . .

THE MASTERS OF THE WORLD

"Let us snow the masses with ersatz life," says one lone figure standing before the fire—no electricity here, no bugging devices.

We are back in Nepal, where the monstrous masters smirk like cartoon villains.

"Give them access to the images of the material things they crave, let them rub elbows with Roseanne, Cher, and Oprah on TV, and most will feel as glutted as if they'd sampled the pleasures and personalities first hand. Just watch: the poor will rejoice in their poverty; the powerless will think themselves pimps and kings."

How can I hear this and do nothing?

Don DeLillo plays with this idea in *White Noise* where he describes a drug, Dylar, which causes the user to confuse a word for the thing the word denotes. Somebody says "shoot": the person on Dylar thinks he's been shot, and drops to the ground. Surely that's a metaphor suggesting the way our vaguely sedated population, glued to the Tube, attaches its emotions to images on the screen.

TRASHING TELEVISION

A book can, and often does, incite readers to moral action. While I could adduce hundreds of instances of such influence—from *Oliver Twist*'s effect on child labor laws in England, to the birth of the environmental movement prompted partly by Rachel Carson's exposure of the dangers of DDT in *Silent Spring*, surely the power of language is still best demonstrated by the Bible's undiminished sway over readers. Books aim to influence. They admit it.

Television, on the other hand, pretends to objectivity, and its advocates persist in issuing disclaimers about its power to incite, say, children to violence. We could certainly build a case for its ineffectuality: how many people have been led to faith by Charlton Heston or Cecil B. DeMille? Could a culture preserve and recreate itself from a movie?

TV is a peculiarly procrustean vehicle, reducing where it should concentrate. It can't feed the imagination—it is itself a generator of images. Watching it leaves the viewer vaguely spent, feeling like he's actually done something: participated in the war on drugs, been to Bali, seen the symphony.

The so-called interactive technologies will further refine television's illusions—designed, my masters tell me, to keep a population passive—but the changes they promise will be ones of degree, not kind. Even as you welcome a holograph of Ted Koppel into your living room, you will no more believe he's "live" than when you see him, small and flat, on your twenty-one-inch screen.

And television helped stop the war in Vietnam. How dare I knock it? "Remember the Playboy Channel," mutters the master mason.

TECHNOLOGY THE BEAUTIFUL

I've passed thousands of hours, maybe hundreds of days, in darkness drawn by those intricate shadow plays known as movies. I love films. Technology is addicting: the habit is hard to break. Like heroin, it feeds on our wish to escape the limits of time and space; and it consumes us.

CORPORATE CHALLENGES

Literature—"the news that stays news," as Pound defined it—aims to return us to reality fortified by a deeper understanding of life. It doesn't seek merely to distract, but also to instruct. Techniques for making the didactic elements palatable have been refined over millennia, and I won't deny that by the year 3000 technology may offer us comparably supple media—if our toys don't waste us first.

What troubles me, however, isn't that television can't preach or teach as subtly as books, but that it will always remain heavily regulated by the government and the markets. The medium's so overmedicated that its progeny are inevitably stillborn.

THE ARGUMENT IN BRIEF

The books I care about are secret agents of conscience. No technological toy can claim this, yet the devices themselves seem eager to steal me away from these vaults of immortal spirit. I hear their siren song even now. Someone, tie me to the mast!

MORE URINE SAMPLES

"Mass culture" might be understood as folk culture + popular culture + electronics + money. Ballads, folk songs, blues, protest music, vaudeville—

these, and other modes of representation, were transformed by electronics and quickly yoked to the business of selling. The *re-presentation* of experience as it's perceived by a single consciousness became something different as soon as it was packaged. And it's impossible to separate the growth of mass culture from the economic engine driving it.

The union between electronics, art, and commerce has led to a seductive yet ultimately tedious creation, heavily inclined toward tracing the hijinks of bodies in motion—by this I mean nearly everything you see recorded by cameras and digital tools, on television, film, and computers. The flickerings are almost as interesting as the braiding flames in a fireplace—although they're far less real.

And yet the Rodney King video proved sufficiently incendiary.

TRANSLATORESE

While electronic media usurp some of the devices of the literary arts—narrative, drama, dialogue, for instance—these devices lose *everything* in the translation. Or, rather, they become something else entirely.

To speak about visual effects as though they were the same as verbal ones is to blur essential outlines. By relying on analogies between techniques in different media, as a way of easing the transition between vastly disparate experiences, we blur crucial distinctions. Because we sometimes refer to the narrative elements of a novel and a film, we think the two are related. And I suppose they are—in the way that a pig is related to a sausage. One is the source of the other's existence. The word narrative, however, derives from the Latin *gnoscere*, meaning *to know.* But the kind of knowledge required to tell a story in prose is essentially different from what you need to know to make a film or a piece of television, because the means of discourse are so dissimilar.

In moving from introspection mediated by books addressed to one's imagination to the self-reflection encouraged by electronically generated images speaking to some other areas of the brain and nervous system, we enter a world whose phenomenologies have yet to be written. Or should that be *filmed?*

Art alone, almost by definition, approximates the intensity of a "live" experience. Meanwhile, the culture cares so little about teaching its citizens how to respond to it that the decimation of the National Endowment for the Arts received little or no notice in the national press—not even among the obits.

WHO ARE WE?

The nature of the self has changed. Now that the violation of persons by electronic means is fully established, the boundaries between self and other have been redrawn, if not eroded. Think of it: strangers phone you freely, soliciting money, political support, selling you things. You can have sex by phone. Physical presence is subordinated to the forces of desire that society keeps stoked through the endless duplication of sexually aggressive images and words.

MONEY: MORE IS ENOUGH

Surely one reason this technology is spreading so quickly is its economic potential. Blessed by Al Gore, the Information Superhighway (already a quaint-sounding term) found construction in full swing almost overnight.

As many travelers have discovered, however, it's a toll road, and you'd be foolish to ask what portion of the earnings will return to benefit the community.

Moreover, the distance between the plugged-in nations and those countries wanting or needing our technologies grows. How will our development affect the balance of power between nations? Who benefits when we drive down this highway? Are we going where we need to go? Could we get there faster by other means? Who or what we're keeping up with is irrelevant. Whether we're getting anything more done with the equipment we're buying is irrelevant—whether we needed to get more done is even less important. Only the leisure class has time for such idle questions, anyway. (Have these labor-saving devices saved you any time, reader?).

Technology is class war by other means.

THE HELL WITH CARS, TOO

Kipling declared that transportation was civilization, but I believe that cars wrecked everything. Who remembers a world without them, when the word *distance* meant something? Today it holds a fixed meaning only for people too poor to surmount it. Geography—physical space—has become a function of economics.

Before that, it was trains and time: we first formalized our treatment of

. . . .

time, establishing uniform time zones, so that we could tell people in Kansas City when to arrive at the station to meet their visitors from New York.

To be poor in today's world is to be more insignificant than ever. Money moves across continents faster than you can cross the street.

STROBES SET THE TEMPO TO WHICH WE DANCE, IF WE DANCE

In reinforcing our ability to separate ourselves from our fellows, technology encourages traits that grow out of interactions with machines rather than with humans.

Once cars altered our relation to place, it wasn't long before other ties to the physical world were similarly transformed. Might the higher incidence of divorce and casual violence signal the weakening of our commitment to bodies? We're increasingly abstract to each other—we can bomb a city, yet grieve no more over the ensuing deaths than over the flattening of a kick boxer in a video game. The war in Iraq some years ago was so unreal to most people that I've never met three who could agree on how many Iraqi civilians actually died there. Yet we, collectively, sanctioned the killing of anywhere from 10,000 to 200,000 beings. Once it was over, the war had as little weight for most people as any other televised event.

While matter has shown its submissiveness to the penetrating mind, its relationship to soul hasn't altered one bit. Can I prove this? Certainly not. But let us go into it a bit further.

ELEMENTARY, YOU FOOLS

"Man has become the fifth element."

This remark of Czeslaw Milosz's struck me with great force: in seeking to dominate the elements—fire, air, earth, and water—humankind has become one of them. With the invention of the bomb, it's transformed itself into a force of nature. Along the way, we've turned our backs on another course once open to us: humankind formerly tried to escape nature's processes through spiritual development. By struggling with nature, by taking it on in the physical arena, humankind has more fully rooted itself in it.

We haven't humanized the world. Instead, we've assumed something of the natural world's harshness and implacability.

TIMOR MORTIS CONTURBAT ME

Our modern conveniences are intended to make our physical existence easier; but microwaves and cellular phones are excrescences of a far wilder dream. Lying deeper even than the economic motive is our hope that we can defeat death. Man is born to die but wants to live: he wants physical immortality. Technology's ultimate mission is to discover a way to sustain physical being. This fantasy is the unstated organizing principle determining the decisions made by the burghers in Nepal.

In striving to secure our grip on material existence, we've rallied unparalleled destructive forces. Fade-out car and television. Cut to an image of the luminous mushroom. The average citizen (me) knows little about the weapons he's helped pay for—and increasingly, he forgets they're even there. However, their presence has subtly yet fundamentally altered our sense of ourselves. We are either diminished or enlarged by them, depending on whether we imagine ourselves as likely victims or probable victors. Throughout the '70s and part of the '80s, we were actively trying to come to terms with our macabre power through marches, rallies, and movies like *The Day After,* a made-for-TV film that scared people almost as much as Orson Welles's radio play about a Martian invasion.

TOLSTOY AGAIN

Tolstoy didn't exactly turn his back on society when he holed up. He had his own country to consider. I don't mean Russia so much as his estate, the two-thousand-plus acre Yasnaya Polyana, whose scores of servants and hundreds of serfs made it larger than many a small New England town. The Russian writer became obsessed with trying to improve the lives of the peasants who depended on him. Might he not have been pleased by our new visionary technology, which cuts worlds of information into chips smaller than sand grains, and makes it possible to erect pyramids with relatively little elbow grease? I suspect he would have approved of the way technology eases the physical strain of making a living from the earth.

But was physical labor that bad?

Paradoxically (and this whole question incites double-mindedness and paradox: on the one hand, and the other), Tolstoy believed physical labor was redemptive. He claimed that some of his happiest moments were those he spent mowing grass with a scythe—which he kept on the wall of

. . . .

his study. The clarity of manual labor can be satisfying when you don't have to do it. Even the largest lawn has boundaries. The body in mindful motion may find itself in sync, and experience a blissful fullness of being. Intellectual labor has no clear beginning, no inevitable end: mental flight can appear a one-way journey without a discernible destination. How satisfying to get away from it now and again.

While Tolstoy found solace in swinging a scythe, the peasantry hated it. As soon as they could, they quit the fields and flocked to the cities, to factory life, pollution, squalor, and alienation—all of which must have seemed sweeter to them than the tedium of farm rituals.

It's possible that those peasants were not only tired, and angry, and strong, and godly, and godless, but also foolish.

Tolstoy sought to prevent war between the classes. He'd be appalled at the increasingly unequal distribution of wealth our complex society fosters, as well as by the speed of the changes we're told, directly and implicitly, we should enjoy undergoing. But Tolstoy's battle is temporarily over: the poor have been soundly defeated.

THE WHY

Note to myself: remember the needs and desires underlying our deconstruction of nature. First: the longing for safety and refuge. Having achieved essential protection against nature's whims, the next desire (not exactly a need) was for comfort, a wish to bring the mechanics of body care more fully under the individual's control.

98.6; 72 degrees; 0 humidity; supine or maybe on water skis. Isn't this the formula for comfort, the state we anxiously seek?

PAUSE FOR A PC ANNOUNCEMENT

One of the immortal bilderbergers, cigar in hand, buttonholes me:

"If you are a South African, or a Slav, if you are a woman, if you are an African American," he begins, "would you really like to return to the glorious nineteenth century? Can we unbraid our age to claim one strand of progress while ignoring how it's interwoven with all the others? Isn't technology developing so that it might one day do away with inequity in the labor force, isn't it there precisely because we don't wish to return to systems of slavery, serfdom, indentured labor?"

. . . .

LET US NOT FORGET THE MILITARY

Many of the technologies gushing out into the marketplace, such as the
Internet, were originally developed as part of a sham scramble for the security afforded by military supremacy. Does the invention of firearms and nuclear weapons really belong in a history of progress? So many of the terms
by which we measure and evaluate our experience beg for redefinition.

THE MYSTERY DEEPENS

As a consequence of technological development, the world's even more
mysterious to me than when I was a child. I've no idea how the instrument
(a Mac PB 165c) on which I am writing this works. My ignorance has its
virtues. Retaining a sense of awe before all that lies outside our own skin
is crucial if we're to continue approaching life with fresh curiosity.

And the people who provide me with these new tools, my former class-
mates: are they similarly surrounded by the unfathomable? Do they know
or care about the mysteries that hold me in deeper thrall than even their
inventions? I mean the novels of Cees Nooteboom, the stories of Alasdair
Gray, my garden with its great hibiscus, whose flowers are larger than dinner plates?

HEAVEN'S WILL

Time now to define a key term in this meditation.

The soul, in my conception, is an immortal entity linked for the course
of our lives to our temporary, earthbound identity. Sometimes I imagine it
as an invisible sheath surrounding our physical body, through which
everything we perceive, the sensual data, passes: it's like the thinnest mist
above a river. It constitutes, as it were, a second self. Because all have one,
it is the basis for our interspecies sense of kinship. However else we may
differ, we have the soul in common: in that one way, we are created equal.

It's the soul that knows and tries to teach us moral law. The physical self
is a unique bundle of appetites and inchoate longings, conditioned by history, family, geography, and other accidents of birth. While it's possible to
be in sync with one's soul, it's equally easy to fall out of tune with it. The
two—the physical self and the soul—are in constant negotiation. The
physical body is always changing (in response to the elements, the passage
of time, or because of new inventions designed to alter the way material entities interact—i.e., all technological developments); the soul remains the

same from birth to death and maybe beyond. The healthy body* chases after the new products science offers, eager to put them to use. The soul approaches them with friendly skepticism, asking: how will this affect me? When soul and body move in harmony, we experience bliss. We feel spiritual pain when they oppose each other. The soul is, in Yeats's account, "self-sufficient, self-delighting, self-affrighting," and "its own sweet will is heaven's will."

In short, I am a dualist. Moreover, I believe every soul has its own mission—and a good part of our work on earth lies in discovering just what that is. Maybe the most important service art offers is in helping us to find our purpose. In other words, art gives meaning to what would otherwise be mere undifferentiated sensation, and it differs from many religions in that it generally celebrates the sensual world.

Because the world of physical entities, of matter, is always changing, the soul is constantly called on to adapt itself to new surroundings. To my mind, the role of the writer who hopes for art is to discover that language capable of addressing both soul and body with equal force. "To bring the soul of man to God," as Yeats (again) put it, is the artist's highest goal. Nor will that change.

WHAT WE GONNA DO

The soul *is* under seige: it is being devoured by its own curiosity, its own craving, and openness. Having discovered just how much authority mind can have over material reality, soul is not about to tell it to stop exploring this territory. If, indeed, it even has that power.

Let us respond to our situation creatively.

Let's begin by fulfilling our duties as scribes of the tribe.

The history of our time will not be written in our time. We don't know who the twenty-first century will recognize as the heroes of our waning day. I propose that we—the contributors to this anthology, for starters— begin a new project: let's create a book in which are inscribed the names and brief biographies of those friends of humankind who, as the late Stephen Spender put it, "in their lives fought for life." A people's history— along the lines of the work done by Howard Zinn and others. Walter Benjamin proposed something along these lines more than half a century ago when he wrote: "Only that historian will have the gift of fanning the spark

---

* I take mind to be, as it is defined in some Buddhist texts, as no more and no less than one of the senses, and hence a function of body.

of hope in the past who is firmly convinced that *even the dead* will not be safe from the enemy (the ruling class) if he wins. And this enemy has not ceased to be victorious."

Time will consign the pseudofigures, whose names and faces appear in the newspapers and journals they themselves own, to the dustbin. It will elevate, as it always has, despite the official histories composed by hacks at the behest of emperors, the people of conscience who stood by their fellows against the onslaught of the greedy and the briefly powerful. Let us compile a list of such names and quietly circulate it among ourselves. Because future generations will need some reliable sources.

THE FUTURE, OUR T(R)OY

For his eightieth birthday, Tolstoy received a present from a pragmatic American admirer. Thomas Alva Edison sent the Russian a Dictaphone. How grateful Leo's long-suffering wife Sonya might have been had the gift arrived before the composition of her husband's big books—it was Sonya who copied *War and Peace* over seven times, after all.

Tolstoy never made much use of the gift, however. Not because he opposed it on moral grounds. Hardly. He was, in fact, so enthusiastic about another present, recently received from the new world, that he dubbed his study "The Remington Room" in honor of the typewriter he enshrined there.

No, Tolstoy eschewed the Dictaphone because he found it to be "too dreadfully exciting" and so a distraction to him as he tried to compose. He didn't reject the invention, nor did he fume about the contradictions inherent in the idea of progress.

FATHERS AND SONS

My father, at seventy-three, has recently gone on-line. Home from his volunteer work at the credit union, he logs on and downloads the day's stock market quotations. Sometimes he surfs a bit, though he's not nearly as distractable as I am. Half of our phone conversations now center on browsers, bulletin boards, and of course the inevitable glitches—those mechanical failures that do more than anything else to humanize technology. When I ask leading questions about times past, hoping for some damning detail that will confirm my doubts about our tools and toys, he laughs and says flatly: "They weren't so hot, the old days. This *is* better."

Humanity's Humanity in the Digital Twenty-First

.   .   .   .

by

RALPH LOMBREGLIA

Here at millennium's end, as the descendants of Hieronymus Bosch set up their digital cameras and paint programs and media workstations to capture the big windup or wind-down of a spectacularly exalted and depraved one thousand years, the question has been sounded from various quarters: in our willy-nilly plunge into electronic information processing and global, networked communications, are we unintentionally and irrevocably losing something essential to our history and identity as human beings?

After seeing the morning paper, with its profusion of car bombs and mail bombs and baby-carriage bombs, civil and tribal and gangster war, and unrelenting "conservative" assaults upon health care, social programs, and the arts, I'm inclined to answer, "Let's hope so. Let's hope we lose something essential to our history and identity. Soon. And let's hope it's the right something." And since many a true thing is said in jest, and I'm not even jesting, let me join the critics in considering that grand idea — that the proliferation of a technology might bring about profound species transformation.

It seems a lot to ask, even of something as big as electronic digital computing. The critics are concerned, of course, that what's happening is bad — that by consorting with these machines we are losing something precious. But what if it were the other way around? Could the undeniably radical transition from analog to digital information processing — historically great and philosophically momentous as it surely is — leave humanity not only changed utterly but changed utterly *for the better?* Is it possible that in the process of achieving a vastly improved and connected *organization* of our collective mentality and creativity, we might manage to effect a great planetary draining of our bathwater while somehow hanging onto the baby? And what exactly is the baby anyway?

Hold that thought.

I may look like a scientific humanist to the naked eye, but actually I'm a Poet (in the old-fashioned sense of "imaginative writer"), and thus I believe that life has a "spiritual" dimension and that something about reality is "divine." When I search myself on the question of "God," I find that I can still respect a belief in the divine entity represented by that word, as long as "God" is not defined as a large man with a white beard who lives in the sky, and as long as belief in God does not entitle believers to kill other people. There's the God who has been "dead" for decades for the scientific humanists, and there's the vividly alive and vengeful God of the various fundamentalists, and—for me—neither can possibly be the real God.

This may seem a funny thing to be talking about when I'm supposed to be discussing computers, but remember that I'm really discussing the possibility that humanity might finally agree on what's really "important" about itself, and then prevent that importance from going down the drain.

Plato wouldn't have poets in his republic, but he's still welcome in most poets' homes. Most artists are some species of Platonist, meaning that our concept of "reality" includes a metaphysical dimension not directly perceivable by the physical senses, and that we feel called upon to create physical things that testify to the existence of this dimension, that suggest its nature analogously and might even convey a "foretaste" (to borrow from Nabokov) of that invisible realm of reality. It may be that this "invisible realm" is the very fact of consciousness, and that art is one way that consciousness attempts to manifest and perceive itself. That would be more than sufficiently mysterious for me. At any rate, when I use the word "spiritual," that's what I'm referring to—the ordinarily invisible sector of "reality" where Plato located his Ideal Forms, and which is, until I find out otherwise, identical to the "divine."

Many people will ridicule the very idea that "reality" has any "invisible" aspects at all. Paradoxically, among this camp you will find people who think of themselves as "deeply religious," as well as people who call themselves poets. We're at the end of a millennium, and you have to expect this kind of thing.

It's not controversial to say that we must "conserve" the important elements of our past as we move into the next millennium. Everyone agrees on that. We just don't agree on what's important. And we certainly don't agree that the people going around calling themselves "conservatives" have any monopoly on the truth about what's important. You can't be a "conservative" without an unshakable sense not only of "tradition"—something you can count on hearing about in reverential and sanctimonious tones if you encounter a conservative—but of "reality" itself. I've said that the "spiritual" is essential to my own understanding of art. So are "tradition" and "reality," properly defined, and they're all essential to my understanding of humanity's humanity in the digital twenty-first century.

It annoys conservatives to see the word "reality" in quotes. They consider that to be a coy parlor game, a weak, sickly embrace of relativity. We know perfectly well what reality is, they say, and then they kick you in the shin, as Samuel Johnson reportedly did, and they say, "There's reality for you!" And yet these same masters of reality cannot tell us what's on the radio right now. Why not? Because the radio is not turned on, and the radio has to be on for human beings to perceive radio waves, those perfectly ordinary, noncontroversial (but invisible) elements of "reality."

Is it not possible that other human-created devices, other technological "extensions of the senses" may enable us to perceive and work with other presently unknown elements of "reality"—phenomena that are very small, very fast or slow, very far away? Of course it's possible, and no one can say for certain what "reality" is. It's the function of poets and artists to remind us that there is more to life than meets the eye, and to provide us with small glimpses or tastes of it. And to do this by entertaining us.

Consciousness, although clearly arising from physical phenomena and processes, is not itself "physical" in any ordinary sense, and yet I assume we can agree that consciousness is part of "reality." Or can we?

Not knowing what "reality" is makes it difficult to be a doctrinaire conservative. As to that venerable thing, "tradition," I have noticed that both in politics and the arts the word is most often used to mean "conventional." And yet the terms are anything but interchangeable. Conventions are the seed casings of tradition, forms and gestures that were originally— like everything—alive and vital, but are now empty and dead. In art, conventions are jerks of the knee, husks of emotion and meaning, and their unironic use betrays thoughtlessness and usually leads to the poetic defects of sentimentality and melodrama, the failure to experience something freshly and authentically and to express it originally. Tradition, by contrast, is the germinal thing that was inside the husk when the husk was alive, but that the dead husk cannot now convey.

T. S. Eliot (a more complex conservative than our current champions of "family values") loved Milton and Virgil and the metaphysical poets, and he certainly felt that in his own poetry he was "carrying on" that literary tradition. But you are not likely to mistake "The Love Song of J. Alfred Prufrock" or *The Waste Land* for anything by Milton. Eliot felt, sanely enough, that artists should find a way to manifest their "individual talent" inside a tradition, thus extending and expanding that tradition, and obviously this did not entail the mere repetition of existing conventions.

Is something being irretrievably lost as we move into the future? Absolutely. But when, in recorded history, has *something* not been lost as civilized life developed? We *have* a recorded history, for one thing, unlike the golden retrievers and the tropical fish. We are not unreflective animals eternally imbedded in some static "natural" state. It's not "romantic" but childish to believe that human circumstances will not or should not change, or that the inevitable changes won't come at a price. But we can certainly make the effort to conserve the genuinely traditional, and let go of the merely conventional.

Not long ago, we got rid of leaded gasoline. That was a good idea. Now we should get rid of gasoline-powered cars altogether. Such cars should have been a transitional phenomenon; they have hung around entirely too long as it is, because short-term interests blocked the natural evolution of human design in this area. But unless the vested interests use weapons and prisons, they cannot permanently stifle human creativity and the evolution of human intelligence. Gasoline cars, being unintelligent, will begin to vanish. Many people will feel sentimental about gasoline cars, and the news media will "reach" those people with stories pitched to that sentimentality, supported by advertising bought by those with a financial stake in that sentimentality.

Sentimentality and nostalgia are not manifestations of the eternally human, intelligent, and spiritual. Sentimentality (I'm using the term in the decidedly pejorative, twentieth-century sense) is false emotion, self-deception. It clouds vision. You can't separate the baby from the bathwater sentimentally. Traditionally, we have learned the perils of sentimentality in the study of literature, where we have also learned to read poetic texts (like the Bible) symbolically or emblematically, and not to construe literary or spiritual expression in a simplistic, literal way. These are important matters. Without an understanding of them, people conclude that Adam and Eve were real people because they're in a story in the Bible, and everything in the Bible is "true."

In our rush into technocratic prosperity since World War II, we have progressively lost our appreciation of a humanities education. Today, for

. . . .

example, "being an English major" is commonly thought to be a waste of time and money, and—in a related development—our newly empowered conservative "leadership" in the United States has decided, in its infinite wisdom, that art in general is bad. This "leadership" has withdrawn official public support for artists and writers by destroying the National Endowment for the Arts, and begun an organized propaganda campaign to suggest that artists are somehow a threat to our national "morality."

How exactly are we supposed to move intelligently into the next millennium when we are systematically disparaging and marginalizing the very people who have "traditionally" been the voices of long-term big thinking and vision?

The shortsighted careerist bureaucrats and politicians—people who produce nothing but want to "manage" everything—are the true "technologists with no soul," and they are far different from the visionaries whose work has driven the historically important developments in "virtual" technologies. For those technobureaucrats in business and government, there is no invisible "poetic" dimension of reality. There is nothing more than meets the eye, and there is nothing important that they don't already know. They are as literal-minded as creationists.

There can be a great difference between the "actual" and the "true," and it's the difference between life and art. Without poets and artists, without the complex veneration of "reality" that one finds in art as well as in true science, we develop an arrogant and simplistic view of "the truth." But try telling that to a technobureaucrat.

If you want to embrace change while preserving what's eternally human and genuinely important, you have to know where the baby ends and the bathwater begins. In the case of cars, it's simple to see that mobility is the baby and petroleum fuel is the bathwater. But it's not always so easy. Things can get pretty tricky deep down there at that baby-bathwater interface.

And we're systematically throwing the poets out of our republics.

■ ■ ■

For part of my childhood, my father was an electrician, and I grew up with plugs and switches and sockets in my toy box alongside the "real" toys. I built my own stereo with a soldering iron when I was thirteen, and I've played with electric guitars and amplifiers all my life. When I was in college majoring in literature, I probably had more friends in the electrical engineering and music departments than I did in the English department. I liked it like that.

I've never believed in the inevitability of a widening gap between the "two cultures"—the culture of arts and humanities set against the culture of science and technology—and although we're clearly seeing the bad effects of such a disjunction today, at the same time there has never been a better opportunity to unite these halves of ourselves, to resist and deny soulless materialism, than that offered by the present-day revolution in global digital communication.

We have inspiring examples of the "two cultures" gloriously united in certain broad-spirited individuals. R. Buckminster Fuller, the architect, inventor, and philosopher of technology, believed that the evolution of design involved the increasing presence of mentality alongside the presence of matter. His metaphysics could be seen operating in the physical world. (He was the nephew of Margaret Fuller, the nineteenth-century feminist writer and transcendentalist friend of Emerson and Thoreau.) Fuller noted that one overarching tendency of human evolution is that we learn to do more with less. The Sphinx of antiquity persists through the ages by virtue of its mass, the brute weight of its stones. The airy lattice of the Eiffel Tower persists as much by virtue of mentality (design science) as of mere material. Fuller called this phenomenon "ephemeralization," and in architecture his own famous "geodesic" structures epitomize it.

Buckminster Fuller devoted his life to finding simple, elegant solutions to practical problems facing all people on earth, solutions involving minimum motion and material. He cared deeply about the future of humanity, and tried to put his technological gifts in the service of our common welfare on this planet. He founded the World Game to help understand the "synergy" (he invented the word) of global forces, and he traveled the world to tell people that, among other things, the solution to world hunger was easily within our grasp if only we wanted the solution and were willing to cooperate to get it. We were not, and we still are not, willing.

As a designer, Fuller would have appreciated the nearly poetic value that good computer programmers place upon elegant, efficient, "optimized" code, and his attitude toward knowledge was essentially the "hacker ethic"—all information freely available to all people. He felt not only that all inventions and engineering and technology should eventually enter a kind of public domain, but that all human thought itself was rightly the common property of humanity.

.   .   .   .

A French Jesuit priest and world-renowned paleontologist, Pierre Teilhard de Chardin, writing in the 1920s, felt not only that all human thought *should* be humanity's property, but that it literally *was,* and that it was permanently accessible as one of the "spheres" surrounding the planet Earth, like the biosphere or atmosphere. Teilhard believed that the conscious communication of human beings persisted apart from its recorded forms or manifestations, and formed a web of thought inside the biosphere, a web or mesh he called the "noosphere."

Teilhard rejoiced in all evidence that the inanimate dust of the earth had somehow evolved into life that could think about itself. He would have seen a global electronic network like the Internet not as a threat to the spiritual life of human beings but as crowning evidence of that spiritual life. Further, he might well have seen it as a facilitator of ongoing spiritual evolution. Human consciousness "rises," Teilhard said, and "all that rises must converge." The contemporary architect Paolo Soleri, much influenced by Teilhard, wrote a book whose title captures, for me, the essence of both the "noosphere" and Fuller's "ephemeralization": *The Bridge Between Matter and Spirit Is Matter Becoming Spirit.*

Buckminster Fuller and Teilhard de Chardin wrote about these ideas long before electronic data processing and global computer networks became commonplace, but the mushrooming manifestations of digital information make both men seem prescient. Those two thinkers represent, in their very different ways, a confluence of scientific intelligence and metaphysics we don't often associate with contemporary American letters (Thomas Pynchon being one obvious exception), but we should remember that real artists pay attention to everything, and they don't separate reality into little boxes. One of the most influential (and truly traditional) fiction writers of our time, Flannery O'Connor, read Teilhard in connection with her profound Catholicism, and titled one of her short story collections *Everything that Rises Must Converge.*

■ ■ ■

Will we win the world (digitize all information, computerize everything, network all the world's computers together into one vast, global "virtual machine") only to lose our souls (cease to have any inner lives)?

Losing one's soul is a process, and we've been embarked on it for a long time. In the late 1970s, the Russian writer and Nobel laureate Aleksandr Solzhenitsyn delivered a now-famous commencement address at Harvard

University that discomfited many members of his audience. Although the Cold War was still on, the Soviet Union was in obvious trouble, and that familiar mood of self-congratulation was upon our land. And Solzhenitsyn stood up to tell people something startling. He said, essentially, that far from being mythical archenemies, earthly embodiments of good and evil, the United States and the Soviet Union were functionally identical in the only way that really mattered: both nations had pursued materialism without restraint or balance, and now neither had any spiritual life.

Nearly twenty years later, the Soviet Union is defunct, yet the song remains the same.

I used to access the Internet via a service that could randomly choose a small textual "fortune cookie" for you whenever you logged on. One of my favorites (I stole it and used it in a short story) said, *Never attribute to malice that which is adequately explained by stupidity.* To this I would like to add a corollary, *Never attribute to technology that which is adequately explained by people.*

Technology is value-neutral. Any disappointments we have with technology (e.g., the atomic bomb) are disappointments we should rightly have with ourselves. This point has been made now for decades in all the classic works on the subject, yet does not often figure in the mass media treatment of technology. You sell more magazines if you personify machines and make them seem to be embodiments of good or evil.

But doesn't a specific technology imply a specific activity and thus lead us in one or another specific historical direction? It's certainly true that guns lead people to shoot guns, but guns have nothing to do with what people shoot *at*. I happen to think guns should be controlled much more strictly than they are, but that's necessary mostly because we have allowed the unrestrained pursuit of short-term self-interest to mold societies that provoke and intensify the most fearful and aggressive human impulses.

Like all technology, digital computing will reflect everything about the people who use it. And so we should be much more concerned about who we are and what we're doing to ourselves than about what "computers will do to us." Our insatiable desire for complete passivity has allowed the marvel of broadcast television to be misused to the point of perversion. Happily, interactive global networks will not lend themselves to that particular excess, but they will soon be commandeered to some extent by commerce.

By commerce.

It should not amaze me (and yet it does) that decades after the shame of McCarthyism in American politics, and with our alleged nemesis the So-

. . . .

viet Union dead, it is still forbidden in most spheres of American life to say anything critical of capitalism. One critical word can provoke the idea that you are not one of us, that you don't believe in our God, that you are an enemy. The tribal clannishness of it is startling. The most that is acceptable to say to the rank and file, once a year, is that "Christmas has gotten too commercial," and this is possible only because on that one occasion every year, the occasion of the "sacred holidays," we throw ourselves into a materialist orgy—a feeding frenzy on plastic, shrink-wrapped, glittery trash—so grotesque that even the most unreflective man in the street knows something's wrong and says, "Christmas has gotten too commercial," and we all nod our heads piously and say it's a shame.

And then we throw ourselves on the glittery heap and gorge some more.

We tell ourselves that we do this to express love for friends and family by buying gifts, and there could scarcely be a better example of the social function of sentimentality. The occasion of this essay is the worry, among some of our better brains, that "the machines are winning" (to borrow film director Sidney Lumet's phrase) and that we will soon live to serve global information networks. In fact we have been, for a long time, the servants of a much more insidious "virtual machine"—our so-called "free market" economy, a system that will crash, apparently, if not goosed at least quarterly by consumer spending reports and short-term corporate earnings reports good enough to keep "investors" from taking their capital away from one horse and betting it on a different horse that can make them a faster buck.

The free market giveth and the free market taketh away.

I happen to love the entrepreneurial spirit. I come from a hard-working small-business family, and I'm an entrepreneur myself, like any freelancer. I'm not a big-time operator, but I'm out there greasing the wheels of the system with my bone marrow, same as everybody else. I'm out there doing the beneficial, people-scale capitalism that most humanities-loving types have no trouble including in their map of reality. Capitalism with a human face. Alas, it's not the only kind.

■ ■ ■

If we should manage, despite ourselves, to leave enough planet Earth behind to sustain the lives of our great-grandchildren, their greatest curse upon us should be reserved for the phony lip service we pay to "education" while building social and economic systems that not only tolerate but require a benighted citizenry. We call the United States, with maximum sentimentality, a "democracy." But here at millennium's end in the greatest country in recorded history, we can't even get half the adult population to vote for a president.

We act out our real priorities in the most blatant and excessive manner, while publicly insisting on our spiritual, moral, and humanitarian "values." We couldn't fool anybody, except ourselves. Mesmerized by our own public relations campaign, broadcast nonstop at ourselves on TV, we never look at the drama we're actually playing out. In our country (and we're certainly not alone), twenty-five-year-old stockbrokers routinely "earn" Christmas bonuses that are four to five times the annual salary of the highest-paid public school teacher. And we wonder why Johnny not only can't read but is packing a gun and doesn't think killing people is really all that bad. If public school teachers were among the best-paid professionals in our society, we could count on beneficial change.

But they're not, and we can't point to any technology as the source of our collective "shallowness." The Tube is not the "source" of it. The source of our collective shallowness is us. We may worry that living in a thoroughly digital, networked world will slowly warp our consciousness until we no longer value "traditional" experiences such as, say, reading serious literature. But who is "we" and what is "our" consciousness? As far as I know, serious literature has never been of any interest to most citizens of my country. Herman Melville, who may have been the greatest fiction writer in the history of the United States, died a forgotten pauper in 1891. He'd had great commercial success early in his career when he wrote diverting nautical adventures of limited literary ambition. But when he began to produce serious, demanding works of art, things didn't go well for Melville in the marketplace. At his death, his best late work was never published or even known to exist. If Melville had had his own World Wide Web site on the Internet, at least he could have put *Billy Budd* out there in front of the world.

As long as we continue to allow our children's future to be squandered on obscenities like the militarization of outer space (among countless other examples of governmental waste, fraud, and mismanagement), we have no right to lament that those children will not spend enough time reading, or that their reading won't be done in the familiar bound books of our past.

. . . .

Some people feel that reading text on a screen is utterly unlike reading text on paper, to which they have a nearly mystical attachment. But there are many mysticisms. I'm acquainted with people who feel an equally transcendental connection to text presented to them electronically on the Internet. In my experience, text on a screen is not *utterly* unlike text on paper; it's quite similar in many respects. And where it is indeed inferior to the oft-invoked convenience or "sensory experience" of reading print on paper, it will soon improve. Although it makes me feel a bit like the voice-over track at the World of Tomorrow pavilion to say it, the flat, light-weight computer screens of the near future will provide a reading experience strikingly close to that of a printed page. Many common concerns about the failings of digital technology are criticisms of a massive process still in its infancy. For certain edifications we'll all just have to use our imaginations and wait.

Some people are suspicious of education involving computers because everything electronic seems "compelling," regardless of content. It's true that electronic presentations contain, by their nature, an energy—literally, physically—greater than their nonelectronic counterparts. One of my friends likes to go to a "sports bar" for lunch. I can never remember what he and I talked about at these lunches, because a dozen TVs are mounted all over the walls, tuned to different athletic events I have no interest in but keep looking at. I've been in plenty of quaint taverns with shelves of books all over their walls, and I had no trouble concentrating on my lunchmate. All other things being equal, electronic productions will make greater demands and a stronger impact on the sensorium.

But all other things aren't equal. Our citizenry sits mesmerized in front of the Tube not because it's a box of brighter lights and louder sounds than the lights and sounds of "natural" objects like books. They're not watching the weather channel or a test pattern or using bright TV snow to provoke a meditative state. Sad to say, they're glued to the Tube to be entertained and to have stories told to them. *And this was the job of the poets and dramatists.* They're frozen in front of their sets because they're lazy, and because we've made it very easy for them, and because we've failed to inculcate the taste and discernment that might make them yearn for something better than the cheap fix they can get from TV. Long before desktop computers, we dropped the ball badly in this culture by allowing the perennial human need for story and drama to be fulfilled largely by a broadcast medium controlled entirely by large corporations, and to which the general public had no access as producers, as storytellers.

Simplistic popular discussion of most issues shackles us with reductive false dichotomies. It is simply not true that there are two mutually exclusive positions on the "digital future," for and against, and that everyone must adopt one of those positions. As to books, no one is saying that they will or should cease to exist altogether. Traditional, physical publishing will persist for texts that merit that kind of production, and for which there is a paying audience—an audience that will include me, in many instances. Far from spelling the end of our intimacy with the written word, global computer networks—which handle text extremely well, better than they handle graphics and audio/video—might just become the salvation of the written word on a planet so overpopulated and deforested and polluted that voluminous, thoughtless, business-as-usual paper publishing must cease in any event. The eventual electronic dissemination of newspapers, reference works, and most writing from the "professions" does not represent a spiritual slide for humanity; it's plain good news for researchers and the ecosphere alike. One can only hope, for the sake of the trees and our breathable air, that the demise of paper-based potboiler novels is equally assured.

■ ■ ■

I never could write—compose prose, create good sentences—on a typewriter. The grossly mechanical apparatus was an ever-present hostility. The loud racket of metal type slamming paper-covered platen obliterated the shapes and rhythms of the language formulating itself in my head. The machine was damaging my ability to think, because a writer's thoughts scarcely exist independent of those milky phrasings struggling to be born. And then one was always dimly aware that one's piece of paper would come to an end, although one didn't know precisely when; many times, engrossed in a passage, I typed one, two, three precious lines of prose onto a senseless rubber spindle before perceiving that page bottom had come and gone.

Long before personal computers, I complained about all this to my many writer friends who composed on typewriters. They didn't understand my problem. And unlike our present-day controversies about computers (which usually require that one join a kind of religion), it didn't matter that they didn't understand it. Artists do whatever works, and we are famously fickle; we use whatever combination of locale, stimuli, and devices it takes to make our art happen. So I wrote on legal pads with pencils and typed it up later, and whatever virtues or failings my work may have had relative to that of my typewriting friends, none of us would have thought to credit or blame our tools.

Today, even the clackiest personal computer keyboard is vastly quieter than a mechanical typewriter; and on a computer, a writer's workspace is not chopped into small physical chunks that must be rolled in and out of a machine. Those differences were more than enough for me; I could make prose on one of those wonderful gizmos, and I started to. But I don't do so always, even today. In fact, at least half the words in any piece of mine—the phrases as well as their arrangement in the larger structure—are done with a pencil or pen on paper. I'm doing it right this minute.

The point is simply this: to make my own literary work, I use a blend of old and new methods that gives me everything I want. Human beings are organisms, after all (though I wonder if this is so obvious to everyone), and we weary of any single, undifferentiated experience after a while. The desire for variety is not a character flaw. When I grow tired of the keyboard and the screen, I can go to my pen and paper. And then I can go back. I enjoy the mix. I feel refreshed by it. Organisms like to be refreshed.

Now, since countless other writers doubtless use word processing in the very same way, why am I bothering to stress this simple-minded point? Because this common-as-dirt use of computers for writing—moving smoothly into the future without tossing out the baby with the bathwater—seems to represent a sane, commonsensical balance, a moderate openness that might profitably characterize our attitude toward, and popular discussion of, digital technology in general, and its effects on people and society.

As opposed to terror and holy war.

I've written fiction with a computer for almost fifteen years, and I've been logging onto electronic networks for half that time. I must have been one of the first "literary" fiction writers in America to "publish on-line" (for the *Atlantic Monthly*), and to this day I'm the only fiction writer I know who maintains writerly notebooks in a personal computer database—something I undertook not to be "first" but because it made sense; I still can't understand why most other writers think of their computers as only electronic typewriters.

I've been at the front, but recently I ventured well into the combat zone. Just before writing this essay, I spent a year and a half coproducing (with my wife, Kate Bernhardt) a commercial CD-ROM, cofunded and distributed by a major book publisher. I did this partly to fulfill a long-standing interest of mine, and partly to make a living. It was as deep an immersion in the digital world as anybody could be expected to make—deeper, indeed, than I had bargained for. (The project, about Jack Kerouac, was conceived by our client, not by me, and its subject was chosen for the necessary blend of literary interest and market potential.) As producers we were asked to "set the standard for literary multimedia," circa 1995, and I think we did that, or at least we came close.

But it was tough. Electronic multimedia production is in an embryonic state, and projects of large ambition are extremely difficult—technically difficult, legally difficult. It took more time and energy than I'd expected, and forced a longer lull in my fiction-writing life than I would have wished. Still, when people ask if I'd do it again, I say, "What have you got in mind?" If I did it again, I'd need a bigger budget and staff, better timetable, and fewer contact hours with lawyers, but in theory there's no reason why working with digital media need be any more harmful to an artist's vocation or consciousness than any other day job—including the insurance jobs held by Wallace Stevens and Charles Ives, or T. S. Eliot's banking job, or the teaching jobs that most publishing literary writers hold in the United States.

I freely admit that the "distractions" of modern life, particularly the electronic ones, can be a danger to the artist, but they are part of the signature of contemporary experience, and it won't do (or it won't do for me) to pretend that they don't exist, or that I live in some other century.

After much hard experience, I can testify that Hemingway was right: the telephone is the single greatest impediment to a writer's getting anything done. It's much worse than any computer, even a computer with a CD-ROM drive and several e-mail accounts. But in 1938, for the introduction to a collection of his first forty-nine short stories, Hemingway was also right about the balance between living in the world and writing about living in the world:

> In going where you have to go, and doing what you have to do, and seeing what you have to see, you dull and blunt the instrument you write with. But I would rather have it bent and dull and know I had to put it on the grindstone again and hammer it into shape and put a whetstone to it, and know that I had something to write about, than to have it bright and shining and nothing to say, or smooth and well-oiled in the closet, but unused.

No one can envision the specific applications of digital technology that will occur even in the five years remaining in this millennium (I'm writing this in 1995). The recent explosion of the World Wide Web—which simply puts a graphical, mouse-clickable interface on the same old Internet we've had for decades—illustrates this perfectly. The vast majority of professionals in the computer industry were blindsided by the World Wide Web. It seemed too simple and (this is important) nonproprietary to be of any real value to them. It came out of educational institutions, not from software giants or glamorous, heavily funded start-ups, and thus the industry could not take it seriously. The professionals had had at least ten years to realize the most important things about computers for the public: easy-to-use graphical interfaces and intuitive access to linked information—precisely what the Web affords. But the professionals—even Bill Gates of Microsoft, who once really did see the future, however self-servingly—did not flock to develop this extraordinary new forum. Then, six months after public access to the World Wide Web became available, it was commonly viewed as one of the most important developments in the whole history of computers and networks, and all the big players wanted to play. The screenwriter William Goldman's well-known comment about Hollywood applies to Silicon Valley and Microsoft's Redmond, Washington: "Nobody knows anything."

The wonderful thing about public digital networks is that they're not monopolized by anybody. Because users of such systems have unprecedented control over how they navigate and view content, and because that control is an essential part of the appeal and promise of this technology, digital networks are in no danger of becoming the Gobi Desert of passivity that commercial television has been for decades. Short of instituting a virtual military state in which electronic signals are censored at the household wall outlet, neither the government nor any consortium of companies will ever control public telecommunication. The technology is too well distributed and too widely understood to allow for that. Indeed, the Internet's World Wide Web is fast becoming the only democratic global mass medium in history.

Although we can see only the general outlines of what's in store, I predict that the most hardened skeptics will soon be hard-pressed to conceal their delight and their desire to work with the wonderful tools that are coming. If we genuinely care about our connection to the past, we should welcome the ability to represent information digitally. It means that we will have more copious and intelligent access to historical materials than would ever have been possible otherwise. If we really want to be fully human, computer technology offers us extraordinary power to get work done and share our work with humanity. It offers unprecedented ability to collaborate with the other people of the planet, rather than fight with them.

Few critics of digital technology have criticized it in the right spirit or for the right reasons. Where they say that "information" is not enough, no matter how much of it there is, they are quite correct. We need poetry—all our traditional poetries of text and image and music, and new poetries, too, heretofore unexpected creations made possible by new tools and new occasions. There will be, eventually, a "new media" Fellini. There will be a digital Kafka.

The bad news is that computer-based tools and information systems—like feather quills, three-by-five cards, and typewriters before them—cannot, in and of themselves, give us poetry. The good news is . . . well, it's the same as the bad news. Machines can't take the poetry away. Only we can do that.

In the end, it all comes down to your attitude, your mentality—those invisible, monumental things. You choose how to look at it, what aspects of your consciousness to project into electronic technology. Some people fear that it will kill life's poetry—the manifestations of spirit, of God. For me, it *is* poetry, it is one of the manifestations. Sven Birkerts closes *The Gutenberg Elegies* by saying of digital computing, "Refuse it." I say, "Use it," but I close with the observation that he and I are friends regardless.

And that's the spirit.

Baudy Bandwidth

.   .   .   .

by
HARVEY BLUME

> The more I observed phone sex, the more I realized I was observing
> very practical applications of data compression.
> SANDY STONE

The mainstreaming of S and M: for a while I thought Robert Mapplethorpe had done it; or the gay community, some of whose more specialized sexual practices Mapplethorpe transformed into art; or Madonna,
who danced it, wore it, performed it onstage; or MTV, which broadcast it
and helped turn it into fashion; or even, for a certain crowd more or less
inured to other sources, Michel Foucault, for whom, as James Miller
shows in his biography, S and M was a thread stitching thought and action
together in a single philosophical and erotic life. It is true there are now
graduate seminars (at Cornell, for one) in S and M, legitimized and intel-
lectually underwritten, at least in part, by Michel Foucault. And there are
those who, unmoved by Madonna, are nevertheless defenseless against
Foucault when he writes (as taken from Miller):

> S / M is . . . the real creation of new possibilities of pleasure, which
> people had no idea about previously.
>   . . . *the* real pleasure would be so deep, so intense, so overwhelming that
> I couldn't survive it.
>   This is something 'unnameable,' useless, outside of all the programs of
> desire: It is the body made totally plastic by pleasure.
>   Man needs what is most evil in him for what is best in him.

Strong stuff—seductive, esoteric, French, with an oh so French promise of
initiation into secret societies of the sexual illuminati.

247

So I thought Mapplethorpe, Madonna, Michel Foucault were the fore-runners. Defining an entire spectrum of culture, from pop to high, they lured a furtive, bashful sexuality out of the closet and gave it glamour. Now I think their roles were subsidiary, at best. Had they not spoken, written, danced, taken pictures, others would have. They were puppets of a much more monumental force that, as Borges said of God, you can't see because it is everywhere.

The real forebear was Thomas Edison, the real agent electricity, the real avatar electronic media, which in its multiplication of bandwidths scours even the most recessed aspect of our psyches, extracting personae from fleeting desires and endowing those personae with voice—not to mention graphics, text, video, and the rest. The lightbulb, the dynamo, the phonograph, the radio, telephone, television, and computer: all the rest is permutation and combination. Edison mixed perspiration and inspiration in just the right amount to blow up taboo.

■ ■ ■

I was listening, at a salon, to a friend read computer-generated poetry, which he had then edited, humanizing it to some degree, warming it, re-ducing its strangeness, and even, in some measure, sentimentalizing it. And all of a sudden I understood John Ashbery. I remembered how Ash-bery's poetry had burst upon the scene some thirty years ago. It seemed without the usual human clues or residues, as if the product, although I don't recall anyone saying so at the time, of an alien intelligence, the kind of thing the dogs in *The Terminator* were trained to howl at and identify as a killer machine masquerading in flesh and blood.

Ashbery's poems were without anything we could recognize as emo-tional or narrative logic. The connections between thoughts and impres-sions were hairpin and oblique; you couldn't track them back to origins in a human mind. And yet, if you resisted your resistance, you found they were fascinating, hypnotizing. The lines of poetry appeared on the screen of human consciousness in a random pattern of blips that put you under their spell.

No one in the 1960s associated the huge but somehow sadly brain-dead machines we knew as computers with the possibility of poetry, even computer poetry. But I now know John Ashbery had been writing and editing computer poetry all along, in a technique that today would be far less difficult to pinpoint. Ashbery's poems were products of a cyborgian

. . . .

intelligence, part man and part machine, before the machine had really come to be. I'm not saying his poetry couldn't have been written had computers not yet been invented—there was little connection, in any case, between a mainframe and an Ashbery poem. I'm saying his poems couldn't have been written had not poetry-generating software existed some twenty years down the line.

And I'm saying this peculiar concordance between art and machine happens all the time in this century without the line of influence ever being adequately defined. Examples dot the arts. E. L. Doctorow, for example, inveighs against television for spelling the death of literacy—and in the next breath credits the Tube with suggesting editing techniques used in his novels. The structure of *The Book of Daniel,* he explained, was inspired by *Laugh-In,* and *Loon Lake,* too, was "powered by discontinuity, switches in scene, tense, voice, the mystery of who's talking." Why was he sure such literary techniques would be comprehensible? Because readers, like novelists, had been brought up on mass media: "Anyone who's ever watched a news broadcast on television knows all about discontinuity."

The lines of force operate in either direction. In his marvelous essay "False Documents," Doctorow notes, "Weather reports are constructed on television with exact attention to conflict (high pressure areas clashing with lows), suspense (the climax of tomorrow's weather prediction coming after the commercial), and other basic elements of narrative." Doctorow worries that the narrative methods honed by fiction will be exhausted by their distribution throughout the media.

Walter Benjamin seems to have his finger on the acupuncture point of the problem when he writes (in "The Work of Art in an Age of Mechanical Reproduction"): "Much futile thought had been devoted to the question or whether photography is an art. The primary question—whether the very invention of photography had not transformed the entire nature of art—was not raised." But even he, Walter Benjamin, proposed too simple a model when he added, "The history of every art form shows critical epochs in which a certain art form aspires to effects which could be fully obtained only with a changed technical standard. . . ."

The artist expresses a wish and the genie of technology delivers on the hardware. But it doesn't really seem to work that way. The rhythms of Steve Reich's minimalist music shift in and out of phase with each other in a way that defies intuition and suggests programmability; it's the kind of music the computer was made for. For Reich, the computers required are not a premonition, as for John Ashbery, but a fact, albeit one which does not prevent him from continuing to compose computer music (at least partly) by hand.

Maybe the process is exactly opposite to the one Benjamin describes; maybe the technology exists—or will come into being a few decades later, which seems, the normal temporal constraints notwithstanding, to be just as good—and the artist aspires to fully realize *its* potential. Rudolf Serkin, when asked who he performed for, himself, the audience, or the dead composer, answered, none of them, he performed solely for the piano.

And maybe the lines of influence between art and technology run toward convergence. The artist fulfills the potential of the machine just as much as the machine fulfills the potential of the art. In the end, their aims are indivisible.

■ ■ ■

I am looking at footnotes, thinking of books and articles it would be interesting to get and read, when all of a sudden I'm thinking of Web sites and hot links to other Web sites, and I realize it's the same notion. The footnote is a slowpoke hot link, the hot link a warp-speed footnote.

■ ■ ■

On the relationship of art to technology, McLuhan, one shouldn't be too surprised, has several things to say (in *Through the Vanishing Point: Space in Poetry and Painting*): "Artists tend to have this power to probe and explore new environments even when most people are unhappy and uneasy about them. Theirs is not so much the power to foresee as the readiness to recognize that which is immediately present." For McLuhan, the structure of *The Waste Land* and the structure of the newspaper, fragmentary and discontinuous from column to column and, indeed, story to story, are congruent.

The negative side of discontinuity: we can't hold ourselves together. The integral self has been traumatized, pulverized, blown to smithereens, the result of child abuse, war, genocide, and, not to put too fine a point on it, a very nasty century.

Not so for McLuhan, champion of the discontinuous. For him, breaks in continuity are a call to the imagination. "Paradoxically," he writes, "connected spaces and situations exclude participation whereas discontinuity affords room for involvement."

. . . .

Another odd convergence: what the theoreticians of trauma—Judith Herman, Alice Miller, and others—put high on their bill of damages, their list of the symptoms suffered by survivors of abuse (disassociation, discontinuity, fragmentation) are the very things the celebrants of new media value most. So far as Marshall McLuhan or, say, Brian Eno are concerned, disassociation, discontinuity, and fragmentation are not the bugs but the breakthroughs.

They are certainly, and increasingly, distinguishing features of twentieth-century art. Why? Did electronic media do it? Did trauma do it? Or is there a sense in which electronic media is itself traumatic, at least to a received form of consciousness whose disassembly is of infinite value to the artist?

Jerzy Kosinski, both the most media-savvy of writers and the most traumatized (if, as a child, he suffered even a fraction of the abuses recounted in *The Painted Bird*), saw the insistence on continuity as a form of tyranny carried over from the Middle Ages. He wrote that insistence on a plot, in life as in fiction, ruled out "choices which we could and should make from day to day, from moment to moment." And, he added, "Accept the notion of a 'central plot' in our lives, and we might as well believe in astrology." Having survived Hitler and Stalin, although perhaps not the American media blitz, Kosinski was quick to recognize tryanny in its many forms. Or was he, in the end, too traumatized for us to believe?

■ ■ ■

We tend to cast Marshall McLuhan solely as the advocate of electronic media as it subverts the printed page and the imprinted consciousness. But McLuhan also wrote that the "rewards," of literacy "are very rich," and a keening of regret for a form of life being left behind can be heard in many of his words. While a number of his books break out of graphical and typographical conventions—they were "sprung" books, as multimedia as he could make them, Web sites before their time—McLuhan also wrote some of the more indefatigably literate analyses of postliteracy. Or perhaps a certain order of hyperliteracy is not so different from postliteracy, into which it dovetails; this could explain the near unintelligibility of several "unsprung," McLuhan classics. (Has anyone read *The Gutenberg Galaxy*, progenitor of a certain type of postmodern criticism, from cover to cover lately?)

We tend to misread Walter Benjamin even more seriously, seeing only regret in his analysis of the disappearing aura of the work of art, when in fact he prefaces his great essay, "The Work of Art in an Age of Mechanical Reproduction," with a quote from Valéry: "We must expect great innovations to transform the entire technique of the arts . . . perhaps even bringing about an amazing change in our very notion of art." This announces both authors' unwillingness to dismiss the changes just around the technological bend.

In a time of complexity, there is a certain comfort in cultivating polar oppositions.

In a time of sea change, even the rocks we hold onto are made of water.

■ ■ ■

McLuhan did for media what Freud for sex; he talked about it, and with similar results. Before him, nobody was talking about it; then, everyone was. Now you can hardly pick up a journal without having to wade through a discussion on whether the digital future is heaven or hell.

But there's a problem with the analytic project, whether McLuhan's or Freud's, a difficulty inherent in consciousness-toggling. As Gregory Bateson asked, if consciousness is in finite supply, what happens when what was previously unconscious enters into conscious mind? Where, then, do the contents of consciousness go? The only answer, it would seem, is that they slink downstairs into soggy, dusty basement storage, where they take up the role of the new unconscious (and no doubt scheme to return with a vengeance).

We are exquisitely aware of the many births of hydra-headed new media. We might even say we are transfixed, obsessed. Certainly no media births have been in and of themselves such ongoing media events, if only because never before has so much media been trained so unceasingly upon itself.

What then, in recompense, are we forgetting?

If Freud is the McLuhan of sex, and McLuhan the Freud of media, now that we have attained a sex- and media-oriented consciousness, what crucial material is being evicted from awareness and sent downstairs?

■ ■ ■

It's Chicago, 1893, and we are at the World's Fair, the greatest of a century that planned its fairs the way other eras planned their wars. From city

. . . .

planning to interfaith religious councils to technological development to sheer entertainment, Chicago was the main event. With no mass media, there was nothing to distract from the national centrality of the fair.

Onstage, a man is electrocuting himself. Nikola Tesla, Serbian immigrant, Edison's foe, is running a million volts of alternating current though his body. His clothes spark and smoke a bit. He gives the impression that he merely has to look at a lightbulb for it to flicker on. While the crowd waits for him to sizzle and crisp, he discourses instead on the nature of electricity and on the resources of infinite power available to man. Pioneer of the AC motor and of radio waves, Tesla is also an unrivaled performer, the Paganini of the electrode.

Another performer, impressionable, gifted, not yet out of his teens, is working the fair, and may well have been in that audience. Eric Weiss, aka Harry Houdini, watches Tesla burn in electric fire without being consumed.

Three years earlier, the country had been equally absorbed by a more macabre kind of electric show, when Edison, who controlled the production and distribution of direct current, made sure that the electric chair that killed William Kemmler, the first condemned man so executed, was powered by alternating current. AC was, or so Edison wanted the public to believe, unmanageable and murderous, the dark side of the force.

One of Harry Houdini's prize possessions—he occasionally lent it to other magicians—was an electric chair, quite probably the one in which William Kemmler died at Sing Sing in 1890.

■ ■ ■

Tesla and Edison didn't really know what electricity was or exactly what they were tampering with—the electron had not yet been discovered— and they strove against each other in the public eye as much like magicians as scientists.

Electricity was first seen as an elevated version of the life force, a distillate of animal magnetism. Early applications were medicinal. Electrodes were standard in the late nineteenth-century doctor's office, where it was assumed that a little voltage went a long way toward replenishing élan vital. There was electric tea, advertised as "good for the nerves," and battery-powered electric hats, good for headaches and a cure for baldness. Tumors were routinely shocked into remission, and in the 1880s there was even a room in the basement of the Capitol Building, where

· · · · · · · · · ·

worn-out congressmen could repair to "take" their electricity. (See Carolyn Marvin's *When Old Technologies Were New*).

After medicine came aesthetics. Henry Adams gaped at the show of electricity made at the St. Louis Fair of 1904: "The world had never witnessed so marvelous a phantasm," he gushed, extolling the "long lines of white palaces, exquisitely lighted by thousands of electric candles; soft, rich, shadowy, palpable in their sensuous depths . . .[a] vast, white, monumental solitude, bathed in the pure light of the setting suns." Being Henry Adams, he wanted the spectacle for himself: "Had there been no exhibits at all, and no visitors, one would have enjoyed it only the more." Then, as if repenting his moment of surrender to the hallucinatory powers of electric light, Adams sailed to France and the less guilty pleasures of the cathedrals at Chartres, Rouen, and Amiens.

Maxim Gorky reacted much like Adams when he first laid eyes on Coney Island in the early years of the twentieth century. He saw "shapely towers of miraculous castles, palaces and temples," and sang that "fabulous beyond conceiving, ineffably beautiful, is this fiery scintillation." Later, he too recanted. As if coming to his senses after absinthe or LSD, he denounced the bright lights of the amusement park as yet another illusion foisted on the working masses. Electricity had enthusiastic boosters and harsh critics, often lodged in the same person.

Finally, the use of electricity became rationalized. You ceased to notice. Electricity just made everything work; it was most conspicuous by its absence (blackouts). The electron was just another subatomic particle, all mystery gone. Or was it? How much quantum mechanics does it take before you admit that "electron" may be a word, thereby conferring the same feeling of solidity as "chair" or "tomato" but that it hardly points to a comparable thing. "Electron" is a verbal wrapping for a mathematical perplex, a linguistic fig leaf for quantum nakedness. McLuhan's main contribution may have been to notice how completely contemporary civilization was shuddering in current, and to yell, Look up, readers, the whole damn enterprise is being run on magic while you blithely turn the page!

It would be fitting if the electric chair employed at Sing Sing and stored thereafter in Houdini's basement wound up somehow in Marshall McLuhan's library.

■ ■ ■

McLuhan wrote, "Any medium, by dilating sense to fill the whole field, creates the necessary conditions of hypnosis in that area." By that standard, language is media. (It might be useful for the stauncher opponents of new media to imagine our hominid ancestors in the African savanna regarding each other in dismay as the young'uns began to experiment with words—whole traditions of highly nuanced growling and grooming forgotten with each new vocalization, meaningful grunting and gnashing of teeth soon a lost art.)

Language qualifies as media, if for no other reason than that it is magical, like all media, and possesses the primordial power to reconstitute the whole in any number of its parts. "In the beginning was the . . ." The Word creates, summons, evokes a cosmos. Electronic media is no different in that regard except for how quickly it mutates and hybridizes, the sheer quantity and combinatory variety of the bandwidths it proffers. How many different slices of self can there be, each one sufficient unto the totality?

Consider phone sex, for example, and its ability to trigger carnal pleasure by means only of voice tethered to imagination. And that's not even taking into account computer chat lines on which men become women, women become men, black becomes white and vice versa, old becomes young, and dominance turns inside out into submission. You get to be the part of yourself you never had the language, the daring, the occasion—or the media—to be. Media sucks it out of you. The media magnet lifts it to the surface.

Steven Marcus, in his book *The Other Victorians,* defines the ideal setting for pornography, the place from which all considerations extraneous to sex have been deleted, as "pornotopia." We now know pornotopia to be an island floating just offshore in cyberspace. It is only a modem away.

■ ■ ■

"'They'll never get me up in one of those,' says the caterpillar to the butterfly," wrote Timothy Leary.

Leary understood way ahead of most of us that psychedelic and virtual reality share a crucial condition—identity weightlessness. His rapid transition from drugs to computers, slowed down only by several trips to jail, was not opportunistic, as I once supposed, but visionary.

■ ■ ■

I can list three movies made in the last few years—there may be more—that are variations on the same theme, namely, that a portion of the mind, of experience itself, can be ported intact from one individual to another. In *Johnny Mnemonic,* the listless adaptation of William Gibson's story, the portion of the mind in question contains industrial secrets worth killing for. In *The City of Lost Children* it consists of dreams, transfused like blood from children to a tyrant incapable of dreaming on his own. In *Strange Days* it is, like an extension of the movies themselves, the gut-wrenching recall of significant events.

You could say this is yet another misuse of a model of mind taken from cybernetics; that it supposes human memory is no different than computer storage, which in turn presupposes that what is stored can always in principle be retrieved and transferred. But in fact, the assumption that we can partake of another's experience is far older than the computer. It was the driving force, for example, of the novel in its heyday when the novelist's function was to amplify experience and make it communicable. And the novel is only one mode of an intensifying modern desire to crack open the shell guarding experience and get at the thing itself: think of the interview, for example, and its prevalence in our culture.

From interviews with vampires, to interviews with bystanders during the Holocaust (*Shoah* consists entirely of these), to Q & A with artists, scientists, and celebs on radio, on television, and in print, interviews are the way we tell the story, interviews are the way we probe and connect. We are insatiable for otherness; experience, like the dollar bill, is our contemporary currency. Electronic media cannot be credited with creating that currency, only with devising new ways of circulating it.

Or it can be argued that experience is now considered so readily transferable because there is so much less to exchange. We no longer talk about conformism because we have lost the ability to recognize how well we have already conformed. "The more the data banks record about us," wrote McLuhan in one of his less sanguine moods, "the less we exist."

This is the theory of the hive. We will glean what we know about each other by electronic means, as social insects rapidly sum each other up by means of olfaction, and forget there was ever an aspect of our existence that defied quick conversion into electronic currency. As Sven Birkerts has put it, "Individualism and circuited interconnection are, at primary level, inimical notions." Connectivity gives you width, but only in a fateful trade-off for depth. The devil connects but collects the soul.

The forecast of the future as a digital hive has to be taken seriously. I

. . . .

think of Emile Cioran's searing vision of a "scattered human herd [that] will be united under the guardianship of one pitiless shepherd, a kind of planetary monster before whom the nations will prostrate themselves in an alarm bordering on ecstasy" and I imagine, should that monster arise, he will launch himself at us from cyberspace. But the vision of the hive breaks down under pressure. For one thing, it lacks sufficient ambivalence. Walter Benjamin looked both ways as he crossed from the auratic work of art to the world of film. Plato objected to the advent of writing in terms hauntingly familiar—it would confuse knowledge with information, cripple memory, replace real wisdom with ersatz—but made sure to express his opinions by means of the written word. Ambivalence, paradox, and double vision may be indispensable elements in an age undergoing profound media change.

The image of the hive is the nightmare version of an irrepressible and recurrent dream. As Robert Pinsky put it in "Poem About People":

All dream it, the dark wind crossing
The wide spaces between us.

In that dream, we enter into, we partake of each other, cognitively and erotically. Gnosis and Eros, two forms of the old dream of union.

So far as human beings go, olfaction won't do it. Our brains are too big, our senses too varied. It would be nice, of course, if aroma were enough. Have you never wondered what privileged information a dog extracts about your mood, the last time you ate, the last time you made love, and maybe even with whom, from nothing more than a single sniff? It's a good thing that as of now, at least, a hound has no way of marketing this information.

Some forms of bacteria pass on critical data even more directly, by means of protoplasmic extensions called plasmids, through which they pump elements of DNA. To see pictures of these plasmids is to marvel at communication at its most elemental. Cells even manage to connect on an interspecies basis. There is currently fear that an innocuous microbe immune to every known antibiotic may pass on the secret of the genetic reshuffling that confers immunity to the more dangerous staphylococcus bacillus, thereby wreaking havoc on our health and our health care system.

But humans require more complex media, starting with language. And once you boot up the Word, it's only a matter of millennia until you get to the World Wide Web—and beyond. Eros, Gnosis won't be denied, although it is hard to know whether the multiplication of electronic means brings about a great closeness or a more complex disunity.

■ ■ ■

I picture an installation.

A photograph, many photographs of me, some of them turned upside down, others turned toward the wall, as if they were inane, private, or obscene.

I picture a wall phone, ringing now and then. Nothing stops you from picking it up.

I picture myself on video and in an animated cartoon. I am the outgoing message on an answering machine.

There is a death mask of my face, and something I have written curling like a Möbius strip down from the ceiling. There are many samples of text, excerpts from a love letter, a juicy portion of my journal.

I would like one wall to be dedicated entirely to a colorized diagram of my DNA. Close by, I want to hang a scroll of code, preferably in C, which—cryptic and lowercase—looks from a distance a lot like a poem by William Carlos Williams.

Of course I will have a Web page, and of course you will be able to access it, and of course it will contain digitalized versions of all of the above, which will load slowly and occasionally crash.

I would like to see an arm, like the holographic arms in Cocteau's *Beauty and the Beast,* protrude from a wall with, say, a mouse, a modem, and a remote in its hand.

For sound, I would have a hiss, bell, and roar of a satisfied modem, a modem making contact, amplified many times. I want the whistle of the information wind. Modems in cahoots. A gathering herd of horned cybersomethings.

This is the room of myself, the meeting place, the command center, from which I send the elements of my self out into the world to seek other beings on their bandwidth. Perhaps I am, if I am, only their filling station. I fill them with ego and libido.

I want to call the exhibit "Homecoming" or "Send-Off," I'm not sure which.

. . . .

SVEN BIRKERTS is the author of four books of essays, most recently *The Gutenberg Elegies: The Fate of Reading in an Electronic Age*. He is a member of the core faculty of the low-residency M.F.A. writing program at Bennington College. He publishes essays in the *Atlantic Monthly*, *Harper's*, the *New York Times Book Review*, and other periodicals. He lives with his wife and two children in Arlington, Massachusetts.

HARVEY BLUME is coauthor of *Ota Benga: Pygmy in the Zoo*. He lives in Cambridge, Massachusetts and is a contributing editor to the *Boston Book Review*.

DANIEL MARK EPSTEIN has published six books of poetry, most recently, *The Boy in the Well*. He has, in addition, published essays, stories, and a biography; several of his plays have been produced. Winner of a Guggenheim Fellowship and a Prix de Rome, he lives in Baltimore.

JONATHAN FRANZEN is the author of two novels, *The Twenty-Seventh City* and *Strong Motion*, and the recipient of a Whiting Award. His fiction and nonfiction have appeared in the *New Yorker*, *Harper's*, *Details*, *Grand Street*, and *Fiction International*. He lives in New York City.

THOMAS FRICK is an editor at the Los Angeles County Museum of Art. In collaboration with his wife, the choreographer and filmmaker Janice Margolis, he has written numerous texts for dance performances and for a film, *First Lady of the Reich*. He contributes frequently to the *Los Angeles Book Review*, *Art in America*, and many other publications.

ALICE FULTON's books are *Sensual Math*, *Powers of Congress*, *Palladium*, and *Dance Script with Electric Ballerina*. She has received fellowships from the John D. and Catherine T. MacArthur Foundation, the Ingram Merrill Foundation, and the Guggenheim Foundation. She is a professor of English at the University of Michigan, Ann Arbor.

ALBERT GOLDBARTH lives in Wichita, Kansas. His collection of poems, *Heaven and Earth*, received the National Book Critics Circle Award, and has been followed by *The Gods, Across the Layers*, and *Marriage and Other Science Fiction*. His most recent collection of essays is *Great Topics of the World*.

CAROLYN GUYER is a hypertext fiction writer and also a visual artist in Raku, papermaking, and quilts. She is also the founder of HiPitched Voices, a women's hypertext collective. She lives on the Hudson River amid the Catskill Mountains in New Hamburg, New York.

GERALD HOWARD works as an editor in the trade department of W. W. Norton & Co. He has published his essays on literary matters in the *Nation*, the *New York Times Book Review*, the *American Scholar*, and the *Hungry Mind Review*. He has edited an anthology titled *The Sixties*.

WENDY LESSER edits the *Threepenny Review*, which she founded in 1980. Her books include *The Life below the Ground*, *His Other Half*, and, most recently, *Pictures at an Execution*. She is currently at work on a book about the English theater director Stephen Daldry.

RALPH LOMBREGLIA is the author of two story collections, *Men Under Water* and *Make Me Work*. He contributes stories regularly to the *New Yorker*, and the *Atlantic*. With his wife, Kate Bernhardt, he recently produced and directed *A Jack Kerouac ROMnibus*, a work of literary multimedia on CD-ROM.

CAROLE MASO's four novels – *Ghost Dance*, *The Art Lover*, *Ava*, and *The American Woman in the Chinese Hat* – were all released in paperback last year. She recently became the director of the creative writing program at Brown University.

ASKOLD MELNYCZUK's first novel, *What Is Told*, was a *New York Times* Notable Book for 1994. He has published poetry, fiction, and essays in *Grand Street*, the *Nation*, the *Boston Globe*, the *New York Times Book Review*, the *Southwest Review*, and other journals. In 1972 he founded *AGNI*, which he currently edits at Boston University while also teaching the Bennington Writing Seminars.

ROBERT PINSKY's *The Figured Wheel: New and Collected Poems 1965–1995* was published this year. His previous books include *An Explanation of America* and his translation, *The Inferno of Dante*, which last year was awarded the *Los Angeles Times Book Award* in poetry. He is also author of the 1985 interactive narrative *Mindwheel*, marketed at the time by Brøderbund Software as an "Electronic Novel."

WULF REHDER has lived in Germany, Italy, Japan, and currently makes his home in Mountain View, California, where he works with Hewlett-Packard. He has published essays and reviews in the *San Francisco Review of Books*, the *Hungry Mind Review*, the *Boston Book Review*, and the *Bloomsbury Review*, where he is a contributing editor.

LYNNE SHARON SCHWARTZ's most recent book is *Ruined by Reading: A Life in Books*. Her earlier books include the novels, *The Fatigue Artist*, *Disturbances in the Field*, *Rough Strife* (nominated for a National Book Award), *Leaving Brooklyn*, and *Balancing Acts*, and two story collections, *The Melting Pot and Other Subversive Stories* and *Acquainted with the Night*.

TOM SLEIGH is the author of *After One*, *Waking*, and most recently *The Chain*. He teaches at Dartmouth College and has received grants from the NEA, the Guggenheim Foundation, and the Lila Wallace–Reader's Digest Fund. He has also written reviews and essays for the *New York Times Book Review*, the *Boston Review*, and other journals.

MARK SLOUKA, author of *War of the Worlds: Cyberspace and the Hi-Tech Assault on Reality*, teaches literature and culture at the University of California, San Diego. He is currently working on a new book about community relations in a global age.

PAUL WEST has published some fifteen novels, most recently *Love's Mansion*, which won the 1993 Lannan Fiction Prize, and *The Tent of Orange Mist*, which was nominated for the National Book Critics Circle Award in Fiction. His most recent nonfiction books are *A Stroke of Genius* and *My Mother's Music*. The government of France has recently made him a Chevalier of the Order of Arts and Letters.

This book was designed by Will Powers. It is set in Sabon and Helvetica type by Stanton Publication Services, Inc. and manufactured by Edwards Brothers on acid-free paper.